Misunderstanding in Social Life

LANGUAGE IN SOCIAL LIFE SERIES

Series Editor: Professor Christopher N Candlin

Senior Research Professor

Department of Linguistics

Division of Linguistics & Psychology

Macquarie University

Sydney

For a complete list of books in this series see pages *v* and *vi*

Misunderstanding in Social Life

Discourse approaches to problematic talk

Edited by

Juliane House, Gabriele Kasper and Steven Ross

An imprint of **Pearson Education**

London · New York · Toronto · Sydney · Tokyo · Singapore · Hong Kong · Cape Town
Madrid · Paris · Amsterdam · Munich · Milan

Pearson Education Limited
Edinburgh Gate
Harlow
Essex CM20 2JE
England

and Associated Companies throughout the world

Visit us on the World Wide Web at:
www.pearsoneduc.com

First published in Great Britain in 2003

© Pearson Education Limited 2003

The right of Juliane House, Gabriele Kasper and Steven Ross to be identified as Authors of this Work has been asserted by them in accordance with the Copyright, Designs and Patents Act 1988.

ISBN 0-582-38222 X

British Library Cataloguing in Publication Data

A CIP catalogue record for this book can be obtained from the British Library

Library of Congress Cataloging-in-Publication Data

A catalog record for this book is available from the Library of Congress

10   9   8   7   6   5   4   3   2   1

Typeset in 10/12pt Janson by Graphicraft Limited, Hong Kong
Printed and bound in Malaysia

The Publishers' policy is to use paper manufactured from sustainable forests.

LANGUAGE IN SOCIAL LIFE SERIES

Series Editor: Professor Christopher N Candlin
Senior Research Professor
Department of Linguistics
Division of Linguistics & Psychology
Macquarie University
Sydney

Contents

1

Misunderstanding talk

Juliane House
Hamburg University

Gabriele Kasper
University of Hawai'i at Manoa

and

Steven Ross
Kwansei Gakuin University at Sanda

Introduction

As indicated by the large professional literature on misunderstanding, miscommunication, communicative (conversational, pragmatic) failure and
similarly labelled objects of inquiry (Dascal, 1999; Tzanne, 2000, pp. 33ff.),
social scientists occupied with language use and, specifically, with language use
in interaction recognise a so-designated research object and share a lively
interest in it. Misunderstandings have been addressed from the vantage points
of various disciplines in the social sciences and the humanities and a wide range
of theoretical and analytical perspectives, resulting in diverse proposals of
definition, types, sources, significance, consequences and remediation of
misunderstanding. While this diversity of perspectives is to be expected
in any cross- and interdisciplinary venture and will be in strong evidence
in this book, it is perhaps surprising that assessments diverge even about
the relationship between misunderstanding and talk in which the parties
appear to 'understand' each other. Schegloff (1987) surmises that 'talk
in interaction is built for understanding, and on the whole effortless
understanding' (p. 202) when members of the same speech community
are involved. By contrast, apparently also in reference to interaction among
co-members of a speech community, Coupland *et al.* (1991b) note that 'language use and communication are . . . pervasively and even intrinsically flawed,

partial, and problematic', adding that by implication 'communication is itself miscommunication' (p. 3).

Arguments for either position can easily be made, but evidence may be harder to produce than it seems at first blush. In fact, some such 'evidence' may itself be claimed as support of either position. An intriguing case in point is repair, a universal and fundamental interactional resource special-ised for handling problems in speech production, perception and compre-hension. It could be argued that the pervasiveness of repair in interaction is in itself evidence of the inherent problematicity of language use, thus supporting the stance of Coupland *et al.* But it could also be pointed out that the structure of interaction comprises repair as an inbuilt design feature that enables understanding when it is temporarily threatened. Repair can thus be taken as evidence of both the fragility and the robustness of verbal interaction.

In a similar vein, Coupland *et al.*'s dictum of communication as in itself miscommunicative can be turned on its head – miscommunication is in itself communicative, and not only in the general and now perhaps trivial sense of Watzlawick *et al.*'s (1967) famous pragmatic axiom 'one cannot not commu-nicate'. Insofar as non- or misunderstandings reveal divergence and deficits in knowledge states, they serve as vehicles for acquiring, modifying, expand-ing, differentiating and coordinating knowledge in and through social interaction. For novices in the process of socialisation, students in formal educational settings, or language learners acquiring a primary or non-primary language, misunderstandings provide occasions for learning. With respect to children's induction into the linguistic and cultural practices of their community, Ochs (1991) notes that misunderstandings serve a constructive function in primary socialisation, for they introduce children to the cultural and situative contexts of their social environment and familiarise them with alternative options for social action and accompanying cultural evaluations. First and second language acquisition researchers recognise that misunder-standings (as well as misproductions) play multiple acquisitional roles, such as displaying the learner's current state of linguistic development and inviting feedback (e.g. Lieven, 1994; Long, 1996; Schachter, 1991). Irrespective of the structure of the material to be learnt, the characteristics of the learner and the sociocultural environment in which learning is going on, non- and misunderstanding appear as one – though not the only – driving force in all learning processes.

From a developmental perspective then, the (re)productive, 'prosocial' function of misunderstanding is widely acknowledged. In the precursor to this volume, Coupland *et al.*'s *'Miscommunication' and Problematic Talk* (1991a), the editors emphasise the dialectic of misunderstanding as a prob-lem and resource. However, when discourse analysts of varying theor-etical and methodological persuasions examine misunderstandings with a view to their emergence in interaction, their antecedents, treatment and consequences during and beyond the current encounter, more often than not they focus on the potentially or actually disruptive, non-affiliative, or otherwise troublesome aspects of misunderstanding. The concern with misunderstanding as 'problematic' talk is apparent in taxonomies of mis-understanding as they have been proposed by scholars grappling with this ubiquitous phenomenon of discursive action. As extensional definitions of the classified domain, taxonomies illustrate how misunderstandings have been conceptualised.

Some taxonomies of misunderstanding

Participant-based accounts

Reflecting then current models of communication, earlier proposals tended to locate the '*site*' of misunderstandings in individual discourse participants. We will begin our (necessarily selective) discussion with a paper by Dua (1990) which is not well known but illustrates rather succinctly some important features of earlier approaches to problematic talk. Dua made an initial dis-tinction between speaker-based and hearer-based misunderstandings. Speaker-based problems refer to 'the processes involved in the formation and expression of intentions which may be considered as internal to the speaker' (p. 115):

1. The speaker is not able to cognise or conceive of his intentions precisely.
2. The speaker is able to cognise or conceive of his intentions precisely but he is not able to express them properly.
3. The speaker is able, both in terms of cognition and expression, but he does not express his intentions either because he does not want to or because the rules of politeness, face-work, interaction, etc. force him not to.

In order to account for hearer-based misunderstandings, Dua (1990, p. 119) expanded Grimshaw's (1980) taxonomy to arrive at a classification that systematically distinguishes between more or less successful types of percep-tion and comprehension:

1	2	3	4
non-hearing	partial hearing	mishearing	hearing
non-understanding	partial understanding	misunderstanding	understanding

Figure 1.1 Classification of types of perception and comprehension
Source: Dua (1990, p. 119)

Dua offers two separate taxonomies for each participant role rather than a unified classification, a choice that iconically suggests a view of speaker and hearer as autonomous processors of messages rather than interdependent inter-actants in a speech event. The 'speaker-internal' processes involving 'intention, cognition and coding' (Dua, p. 114) are predicated on intentions pre-existing their linguistic expression, an assumption which commonly underlies psycholinguistic models of speech production (Levelt, 1989). Intention, volition and ability to cognise and encode, then, are essential components of speaker-based miscommunication. Mis*understanding* would be an obvious misnomer of problematic talk conceived as unilaterally speaker produced. The hearer-based taxonomy of misunderstandings, too, betrays its psycholinguistic origin. Here, two modes of input processing are distinguished: the decoding of sensory input (perception), which, in the processing of incoming speech, includes phonological analysis at the segmental and suprasegmental level, and comprehension, usually divided into sentence comprehension (parsing) and discourse comprehension. Dua characterises all forms of unsuccessful comprehension, including an added category of 'misinterpretation', as 'a failure of cognitive achievement' (p. 122). He emphasises that hearing is necessarily selective and usefully points out that selective speech processing constitutes a pervasive liability for successful listening, while redundancy in the composition of utterances compensates for partial hearing. The same is true, of course, of the entire process of listening comprehension. The robustness built into utterances thanks to linguistic and other semiotic redundancies has its correlate at the level of discourse in the remedial activities described by Goffman (1981) and repair work as detailed in conversation analysis (Schegloff *et al.*, 1977). By engaging different microsociological perspectives, the analysis shifts from con- sidering misunderstandings as *intrapersonally* anchored to an *interactional* view. Less than successful speaking and listening are thus no longer understood as falling into clearly demarcated speaker and listener domains but are seen as trouble in establishing intersubjectivity which cannot unambiguously be attributed to either discourse participant (Dua, 1990; Grimshaw, 1980).

Despite rather compelling challenges to the view of misunderstanding as an exclusively intrapersonal cognitive event, located in autonomous speakers and hearers and essentially involving unsuccessful mappings of intention and linguistic form, the intra-individual cognitive tack persists in more recent approaches to misunderstanding. Thus Tzanne (2000, p. 39) credits Humphrey-Jones (1986, p. 1) with proposing '(o)ne of the most successful definitions of 'misunderstanding', according to which:

A misunderstanding occurs when a communication attempt is unsuccessful because what the speaker intends to express differs from what the hearer believes to have been expressed.

Ironically, Tzanne adds the footnote:

> Detecting and attributing with precision a certain communicative intent to the speaker is in many cases very difficult, if not impossible.

and goes on to specify the sensible analytical policy that:

> (t)he issue of speaker's intention in this work will be raised only in cases when there is sufficient linguistic evidence to support my claims.

In related attempts to get a conceptual handle on misunderstandings, individual discourse participants' cognitive states and processes figure even more prominently. Weigand's (1999) project to determine 'the standard case of misunderstanding' explicitly excludes from the category misunderstandings planned or intended by the speaker (p. 764). She goes on to specify the 'constitutive features' of 'standard' misunderstandings:

- Misunderstanding is a form of understanding which is *partially or totally deviant* from what the speaker intended to communicate.
- As a form of understanding, it refers to the reverse side of meaning or to the reverse side of the utterance, and represents a *cognitive* phenomenon belonging to the interlocutor.
- The interlocutor who misunderstands is *not aware* of it (p. 769, italics in original).

Aside from the fact that regarding speech production and comprehension as 'reverse' processes has long been discredited in cognitive theories of sentence and discourse processing, it is noteworthy that misunderstanding is seen here as the hearer's unilateral cognitive 'possession', a particularly evocative metaphor. Lack of speaker's intent to produce misunderstanding is matched by the listener's unawareness that she is misunderstanding – in other words, a detected misunderstanding falls outside the scope of the 'standard case'. Even within the epistemological constraints of the model, this last criterion limits the scope of misunderstanding rather narrowly to detections of hearer's misunderstanding by the trouble-source speaker (as in third position repair, Schegloff, 1992) or another party to the interaction. It thereby excludes such listener-identified comprehension problems as addressed in other-initiated repair (Schegloff et al., 1977), which seems an unfortunate division of misunderstandings and their treatments by discourse participants.

From such perspectives as speech act theory, Gricean pragmatics and relevance theory, it is common to conceptualise misunderstandings as intra-individual events even when they happen in interaction. Later in this introduction, we will turn to discourse approaches that abstain from cognitive explanations altogether. At this point, we want to introduce a (partial) taxonomy that still maintains individual speakers and hearers as sites for communication problems but also recognises that misunderstanding may be constructed through the interaction itself. Bazzanella and Damiano (1999, p. 821) propose four categories of 'triggers of misunderstanding'. In addition to structural triggers, they distinguish three types of participant trigger:

Triggers relating to the speaker
(1) 'Local' factors, such as speaker's slips of the tongue, misconceptions, use of ambiguous forms.
(2) 'Global' factors concerning the structuring of information both on the pragmatic and on the syntactic level.
Triggers related to the interlocutor
(1) Knowledge problems, such as false beliefs, lexical incompetence, gaps in encyclopedic knowledge.
(2) Cognitive processes, such as wrong inferences, and the cognitive load and its effects on the interlocutor's production.
Triggers related to the interaction between the participants
(1) Non-shared knowledge
(2) Topic organisation
(3) Focusing problems

The first and third participant triggers refer to cognitive states and processes, yet no longer those of individual participants. Rather, problems emerging in the coordination of knowledge and attentional focus are located in inter-individual, joint cognition. Such views of misunderstanding are compatible with interactional theories of knowledge construction and coordination, such as ethnomethodology in sociology and collaborative theory (Wilkes-Gibbs, 1997) in cognitive psychology.

Sources of misunderstanding

Much effort has been invested in identifying the sources of misunderstanding. Tzanne (2000) reviews the pertinent literature in detail and Dascal (1999) provides a useful summary. Suffice it therefore to cite one suggestion that specifies the sources of misunderstandings according to the domain of language structure or usage in which they occur. Bazzanella and Damiano (1999, p. 819) distinguish different linguistic 'levels' of misunderstanding as follows:

1. Phonetic
2. Syntactic
3. Lexical

4. Semantic
   4.1 Propositional content
   4.2 Reference expressions
      4.2.1 'external'
      4.2.2 addressee
5. Pragmatic
   5.1 Illocutionary force and indirect speech acts
   5.2 Non-literal uses: implicatures, irony, metaphor, etc.
   5.3 Relevance
   5.4 Topic
   5.5 Plans

A similar taxonomy of sources, comprising types of linguistic ambiguities and non-literal language usage, was proposed by Vendler (1994, p. 19). The catch in Vendler's taxonomy is that ambiguities and non-literal language use regularly occur in natural discourse without resulting in displays of misunderstanding in the interaction. Therefore, it remains for theories of misunderstanding to specify when and how ambiguity and non-literal ways of speaking are implicated in actual (rather than potential) misunderstanding. Bazzanella and Damiano (1999) offer a descriptive grid that helps locate misunderstandings at a particular linguistic level but makes no pretence at explaining them.

The 'levels' of misunderstanding represent *discourse-internal* problem sources. But as has been widely acknowledged, the social context in which interactions unfold can equally be implicated in the production of misunderstanding. Discussing *discourse-external* sources, Tzanne (2000, pp. 85ff.) distinguishes such components as

- discourse roles associated with participant structure, e.g. (following Goffman) hearers as auditors, bystanders and audience
- social roles, categorised into societal, professional, activity and personal roles
- situational frames
- physical properties and settings.

How divergent frame orientations produce misalignments among discourse participants has been a recurrent theme in interactional-sociolinguistic studies of miscommunication, from John Gumperz's pioneering work (1982, 1992) to more recent studies on problematic encounters, often in intercultural gatekeeping events (Bremer *et al.*, 1996; Tyler, 1995). Just how to theorise and empirically investigate the relationship between discourse-external context and the ongoing interaction has been a longstanding theoretical problem with immediate methodological implications for data collection and analysis. The issue has been addressed from a number of social science perspectives in Duranti and Goodwin's influential collection *Rethinking Context* (1992). The contributions to this volume offer a range of different solutions to the 'text-context' or 'figure-ground' problem in the study of misunderstanding.

Coupland *et al.*'s integrative model

Of the phenomenologies of misunderstanding we have reviewed both 'text-internally' (i.e. as made public for the reader of this Introduction) and 'text-externally' (i.e. during our reading in preparation for this chapter), the most comprehensive classification is Coupland *et al.*'s 'integrative model of levels of analysis of "miscommunication"' (1991b, pp. 11ff.). Synthesising social-psychological and discourse-analytical perspectives, the model comprises six levels:

Level 1: Misunderstanding is viewed as 'pervasive, inherently constituted in the nature of symbolic meaning-exchange . . . The intrinsic imperfection of communicative interchange and the inherent ambiguity and incompleteness of messages . . . will not typically be construed as problems, and so repair is not a relevant concern' (p. 12).

Level 2: 'The primary goals of interactants are not the creation of perfect performances, but rather performing so as to avoid undue clarity, unpleasantness, threat, and confrontation. Equivocations, disqualifications . . . small deceptions, minor misunderstandings, interrupted turns at talk, and slips of the tongue are not at all uncommon. The "let it pass" rule . . . is observed as often as not' (p. 13).

Level 3: 'Miscommunication takes on implications of personal inadequacy and therefore, perhaps, blame. Whether poor communication skills, unwillingness to communicate, bad temper, personality problems, or some other individual difference is assumed, these attributes typically lead to downgraded evaluations of misperforming participants. The behavior itself is seen as non-normal according to some implicit standard of adequacy or as behavior that easily leads to misperceptions of content and/or intent by interlocutors' (p. 13ff.).

Level 4: Analyses at this level 'reveal the strategic value of commonplace activities thought to be miscommunicative at previous levels and frequently relate to goal management in everyday interaction'. Premised on the view that 'interaction is designed around multiple simultaneous goals . . . miscommunication at this level will reflect negotiation of conversational and relational control (relational goals), the maintenance of preferred personas and their modification (identity goals), and the achievement of specific task-related outcomes (instrumental goals)' (p. 14ff.).

Level 5:   'Miscommunication resides in group and cultural phenomena, and may be accountable in terms of code-based or other cultural differences in behaviors, beliefs, or construals. Culture is seen as having communicative consequences for participants. The salient dimensions of context in which interaction becomes miscommunicative are assumed to be status, one's (and one's group's) relationship to a power base or structure, and affiliation . . . identity is defined in social rather than personal terms. . . . Social group membership may be defined as ingroup/outgroup membership, giving rise to observable communication difficulties based on lack of understanding of differences, suspicion or fear of the outgroup, or threatened social identity. But from this cultural perspective, miscommunication can also be considered to offer a dimension for the positive socialisation and acculturation of speakers, be they children . . . linguistic minorities . . . immigrants . . . or conversationalists reaching new depths of understanding' (p. 15).

Level 6:   ' "Miscommunication" is an ideological analysis. Here interaction is seen as reinforcing or even constituting a societal value system and its associated social identities . . . What defines interaction sequences as "miscommunication" communicatively and sociolinguistically is that they implicitly or explicitly disadvantage people or, more likely, groups, while proposing themselves as normal, desirable, and even morally correct' (p. 15).

As Coupland *et al.* note, the model does not suggest that particular occurrences of misunderstandings can neatly be slotted into any single level. The same interactionally problematic event can be analysed at several levels, reflecting the analyst's perspectives – and at least occasionally those of the discourse participants. Precisely because the model shies away from an essentialist categorisation of what misunderstandings 'are', but offers a multilayered perspective of constructing them as increasingly complex and contextualised objects of study, we found that it helped our understanding of the commonalties and distinctiveness of the analyses offered in this volume. Therefore, despite unavoidable 'interstitial' and multiple-level categorisation, our introduction of the chapters in this book will refer to Coupland *et al.*'s model, even if only as one perspective among others.

This book

More than a decade has passed since Coupland *et al.*'s (1991a) edited volume appeared. Their work inspired the present collection and, as the first book publication on the topic, it remains a milestone in discourse studies of misunderstanding. Meanwhile, the literature on problematic talk has become too voluminous even for the dedicated misunderstanding specialist to keep track. In conceptualising this volume, we therefore had to establish a guiding principle to select and organise contributions. Whereas the chapters in Coupland *et al.*'s book offer comprehensive overviews of research on misunderstanding in a range of social domains, we were interested in exploring how misunderstandings in specific social activities and interactions can be analysed and understood from a range of different discourse-analytical perspectives.

In Chapter 2, Juliane House provides a broad overview of six different research strands which she deems relevant for a transdisciplinary approach to the analysis of misunderstanding sequences: social views, intercultural misunderstanding, pragmatic theory, philosophical views of the 'self-orientedness' of communication, psychopathological theories and information processing theory. In a second step, House proposes a framework which integrates these different approaches and which serves as a discourse comprehension and production model for the analysis and explanation of misunderstanding. In a way, this proposal supplements Coupland *et al.*'s model by adding a cognitive-linguistic perspective on misunderstanding, thus extending Coupland *et al.*'s predominantly social psychological perspective.

In order to demonstrate the operation of this model, House analyses three discourse extracts: two excerpts of intercultural institutional discourse in a German university setting and, by way of contrast, an interpersonal dinner table conversation between an American and a German student. The different role relationships in the institutional encounters (between a student and a university professor and between a student and a member of the university support staff) and the interpersonal interaction are indexed by a greater licence on the part of the institutional representatives to interrupt at transitionally irrelevant points in the discourse or to reject certain speech acts as inappropriate. But House also finds certain commonalities. These are explained with reference to previously noted differences in communicative conventions and preferences between German and Anglophone speakers (e.g. Byrnes, 1986; House, 1996; Kotthoff, 1993; Watts, 1989).

Consistent with her integrative transdisciplinary model, House offers the most comprehensive analysis of misunderstanding in this book. The remaining chapters adopt more exclusive analytical perspectives, varying in the extent to which they rely on one specific approach or combining several to a broader theoretical framework. By way of contrast with House's broadly discourse analytical approach, Chapters 3 and 4 deploy conversation analysis to misunderstandings in different types of interaction.

Above, we distinguished intra-individual vs. inter-individual and discourse-internal vs. discourse-external conceptualisations of misunderstanding. More unambiguously than most other approaches to misunderstanding in spoken discourse, conversation analysis is firmly committed to examining misunderstandings, as well as any other interactional event, as inter-individual and discourse-internal occurrences. While the conversation-analytic research strategy in general focuses analysts' attention on the understandings that participants display to each other through the sequential, temporal, prosodic, linguistic and non-verbal details of their interactional conduct, Schegloff (1987) specifically explicates and demonstrates how misunderstandings in discourse can be analysed without any recourse to discourse-external context. Following microsociological research practice, he limits the analysis to misunderstandings in interaction between participants sharing co-membership in (some) social categories, such as ethnolinguistic background. Co-member encounters compel the analyst to eliminate intercategory differences – Coupland *et al.*'s Level 5 – as a 'cause' of misunderstanding. But as Schegloff also notes, even misunderstandings between participants from different cultural and linguistic groups need not be grounded in social category differences. The possibility of 'mistaking one action for another' (p. 203) is a liability of interaction, regardless of participants' relative member status, although non-membership *may* 'induce' such problems. In either case, conversation analysts working with data from participants with diverse backgrounds adopt the same ascetic analytic tack as investigators of co-members' interactions. The two conversation-analytic chapters in this book examine misunderstandings occurring between co-members and participants from different ethnolinguistic backgrounds.

In order to frame different kinds of misunderstandings that 'live off' the expectations of interlocutors, in Chapter 3, Volker Hinnenkamp introduces seven exemplars of misunderstanding in three general categories – overt, covert and latent forms. He demonstrates how overt types of misunderstanding are in the main excised so as to return to the state immediately prior to the identified point of misunderstanding, presumably in the best interest of the transactional goals. Covert misunderstandings, in contrast, do not emerge in the immediate sequential ordering of the interaction. Rather, they become apparent to the participants when signs of discourse incoherence emerge. Compared to overt misunderstandings, the covert variety often cannot be repaired in time for the participants to return the point prior to the inception of a wrong inference. Covert misunderstandings are thus parasitic in the sense that their existence in the body of the discourse eventually results in a mutation of its form.

Hinnenkamp's latent misunderstanding occurs without all of the participants recognising that it has happened. Here, the evidence of a misunderstanding is a sense that a state of satisfactory communication was not reached. Since the source of the putative misunderstanding might not be identified, no recourse to negotiation is typically taken. Hinnenkamp's analyses demonstrate that in contrast to idealised notions of misunderstanding emerging as an unintended aberration from normative expectations of 'clean' communication, some forms of misunderstanding exist without interlocutors' awareness.

Others are purposely engineered in order to achieve the goals of one of the participants, for instance, a wily misunderstander intent on a comical interpretation.

To exemplify purposeful misunderstanding, Hinnenkamp also introduces parasitic misunderstandings as goal-oriented 'language games' that capitalise on, for instance, a double entendre. Here, a topic of talk may split into two levels of interpretation – the 'clean' one with propositional content intended by the speaker, and the parasitic level which, for the comical aim of the strategic misunderstander, subverts the message.

Hinnenkamp's examples of different forms of parasitic misunderstandings suggest some limits of host–parasite symbiosis. When transactional goals are apparent, the onus is on the interlocutors to identify and immediately repair errors of interpretation – thus saving the message – and, for instance, getting the pilots to land on the right runway. Interpersonal discourse, in contrast, may be open to side-sequencing, benign mishearing and the occasional strategic double entendre. Here, apparently parasitic misunderstandings may coexist innocuously within their host.

Moving from Hinnenkamp's collection of misunderstandings in ordinary conversation and institutional interactions to a distinct intercultural gate-keeping encounter, in Chapter 4 Gabriele Kasper and Steven Ross examine how participants misunderstand the interactional roles of repetition in 25 oral proficiency interviews. In particular, they consider from a polyfunctional perspective the actions interviewers carry out by repeating candidates' utterances. Kasper and Ross note that repetitions are often ambiguous in that they may serve as receipt tokens, to request clarification, show epistemic positioning of the listener vis-à-vis what has been said, can merely serve to induce continued talk on topic or signal that elaboration is needed. How repetition functions in the context of interview interaction is examined conversation-analytically by scrutinising candidates' reactions to interviewer repetition.

Kasper and Ross's analysis suggests that the functional role of the repetition varies depending on how the interlocutor fields the repeated element and responds to it. They show that differential prosodic features index actions on the part of the interviewer that are not met by candidates' uptake on the repetition token. In a single interview, more than half of the repeat tokens were misunderstood by the interview candidate as indicators of actions different from their sequential trajectory. Such variation in the interpretability of repetitions leads to a fundamental question about the sources of misunderstood repetition. The functional meaning of repetition may be encoded in its prosodic envelope. Here, the candidate's task is to decipher the form–function relationship and to project the repetition onto a pragmatic map in order to identify what kind of rejoinder matches the repeated element. Kasper and Ross also note that interlanguage pragmatic transfer may come into play. Under-elaborated rejoinders to repetitions projected as requests for clarification, for instance, may betoken candidate reticence in the asymmetric power relations that language proficiency interviews engender.

The misunderstandings discussed by Hinnenkamp and Kasper and Ross can be analysed as Coupland *et al.*'s Levels 1 and 2, with an extension to Level 3 towards the end of both chapters. Unlike the two conversation-analytic studies, the common denominator of the next six chapters is their effort to situate misunderstandings in their wider context, from the activity types in which they occur to their institutional settings and the ideological, political and sociocultural stances taken by participants to the examined encounters. But the studies also differ from each other in the range of the discourse-external contexts they represent and their theoretical and analytical approaches to misunderstandings. They show how the examined misunderstandings not only occur 'in' their social, cultural or institutional contexts, but are also brought into being and derive their specific forms through participants' differential orientations to those contexts. Likewise, the examined misunderstandings are not seen as objects already 'out there', waiting to be dug up and separated from layers of context so that their finer structure might become visible. Rather, the adopted theoretical perspectives privilege different aspects of context and thereby arrive at different but compatible conceptualisations of misunderstandings.

In Chapter 5, Shoshana Blum-Kulka and Elda Weizman examine misunderstandings in political news interviews broadcast on Israeli television against the backdrop of misunderstanding in ordinary conversation. Their comparative perspective echoes the analytical strategy to institutional discourse adopted by conversation analysts, according to which 'the practices underlying the management of ordinary conversation are treated as primary and as collectively constituting a fundamental matrix through which social interaction is organized' (Heritage and Greatbatch, 1991, p. 94). But the theoretical stance adopted by Blum-Kulka and Weizman contrasts strongly with that of the conversation-analytic chapters. Building on Grice (1968) and Dascal (1983), they propose a discourse-pragmatic theory of misunderstanding, grounded on a fundamental distinction between 'what is said' and 'what is meant'. While the potential for pragmatic ambivalence is inherent to ordinary conversation, it becomes a prime resource in political discourse, where intentional violations of the Gricean maxims fall squarely within the range of expected discourse strategies. Unlike in ordinary discourse, where metapragmatic acts, repairs and reformulations regularly indicate and redress misunderstandings, the same activities are deployed by journalists and politicians as rhetorical devices in conflictual interaction. In no small measure, these two transformations of misunderstandings and their discoursal treatment reflect the participation structure typical of broadcast media discourse, where the interlocutors perform for the benefit of an anonymous, diverse and displaced audience. 'Double articulation', a form of Goffman's (1974) keying, is thus a crucial strategy for managing political interviews as encounters between interviewers and politicians as immediate interlocutors and as spatially, sometimes also temporally, displaced interaction with the viewers. Blum-Kulka and Weizman's analysis meshes well with Level 4 in Coupland *et al.*'s model.

Chapter 6 by Claire Kramsch continues the theme of transformation and its relationship to misunderstanding in interaction. But whereas Blum-Kulka and Weizman examine the activity-type specific transformations of discourse practices, the transformations scrutinised by Kramsch operate primarily at the semantic and pragmatic level. She brings a multidimensional model to bear on her case study of a trilingual, tricultural seminar for language teachers. Adopting the social-constructionist accounts of identity, role and voice proposed by Berger and Luckmann (1966) and Shotter (1993a, 1993b), she analyses these constructs along four contextual dimensions – cultural, epistemic, self and interactional. The participants' efforts at mutual understanding are mediated by tropological discourse processes such as metaphorical, metonymic, synecdochic and ironic substitutions (White, 1978). Through these semantic and pragmatic discourse-level transformations, actors restructure one experiential domain in terms of another and thereby integrate otherwise disparate cognitive objects. On Kramsch's analysis, participants in the examined seminar collaboratively managed the demanding task of negotiating choices between three different languages, institutional identities and epistemic stances to a conflictual topic through tropological transformations that enabled them to take another look, as it were – trying to see things through the eyes of others. Insofar as the seminar participants developed their subject positions towards the topic through recourse to different institutional identities and ideologies in response to each other's contributions, their interaction can be understood as a Level 5 type of conflict talk according to Coupland *et al.*'s (1991a) model. But importantly, Kramsch also demonstrates how the participants collaboratively arrive at a 'third place' that affords an ironic stance and critical distance to institutional discourse *tout court*.

Applying tropological analysis to a different sort of academic speech event, in Chapter 7 Joan Turner and Masako Hiraga examine interactions in creative and performing art tutorials between British tutors and their British and Japanese students. In this study, their main concern is not the unequal power structure generated by the tutor's and tutee's institutional roles, nor the moment-by-moment unfolding of the tutorial discourse, but the culturally mediated educational ideologies that underlie participants' interactions in this speech event. In the Japanese context, educational ideologies crystallised in proverbs and metaphors conceptualise teaching and learning as a journey or path on which the student deferentially and loyally follows the teacher's lead. In contrast, the British tutors emphasised the students' responsibility for their own development as artists and fostered students' ability to self-evaluate their work and articulate its future directions. The tutor's role in this process was that of a facilitator 'drawing students out' rather than providing direct guidance and evaluation. Authentic tutorial data as well as questionnaire responses provided by Japanese and British students indicated that the British students provided elaborated responses to tutors' questions about their work, whereas the Japanese students tended to supply minimal affirmative or negative answers, often pretending to know less than they actually did.

The lack of elaboration documented in this chapter as well as Hiraga and Turner's earlier work parallels Kasper and Ross's observation of the same discourse practice in oral proficiency interviews, supporting Turner and Hiraga's proposal that, in the Japanese context, modesty and restraint in verbal expression index an educational ideology whose validity extends across activity types. In the fine arts tutorials, however, the different role expectations for teacher and student take on an activity-type specific shape. In the British tutorials, the interaction centres around the student's work, making it the tutor's job to push students forward in the direction chosen by them. In Japanese traditional arts, students are expected to learn from the master as their model through observation, imitation and repetition. These contrasting epistemologies also underpin the different emphasis placed on verbal expression during the tutorials. According to British practice, the students have to describe, explain and evaluate their work and where they are going with it. Turner and Hiraga link the prominence of linguistic expression to the logocentredness cultivated in western philosophical tradition, opposing it to the greater value placed on model learning without explicit instruction and scepticism towards linguistic communication in East Asian philosophy and educational practice. Turner and Hiraga demonstrate that misunderstandings conceptualised as pragmatic failure at one level of analysis can be reanalysed more insightfully against the backdrop of the educational ideologies that inform different pragmatic practices in tutorial interaction and other contexts of learning and teaching. Although Turner and Hiraga's focus on educational ideologies might suggest that their analysis is most compatible with Coupland et al.'s Level 6, a defining element of misunderstandings at that level is sociostructural imbalance between interacting groups. This, however, is not the focus of the analysis. Together with Kramsch's study, Turner and Hiraga's chapter therefore illustrates a Level 5 analysis.

Misunderstandings grounded in cross-culturally different discourse practices interrelating with societal inequality is the dominant theme of the final three chapters. In Chapter 8, Janet Holmes examines spontaneous narratives produced in conversations among friends in the Maori and Pakeha (white) communities in New Zealand. Analysis of these stories according to Labov's (1972) framework of narrative organisation revealed a number of differences between the Maori and Pakeha stories. In many instances, Maori narrators did not provide explicit evaluations of the reported action, ended their stories without an overt resolution or coda and used fewer quotatives to identify different speakers. Maori listeners preferred attentive silence to overt verbal feedback and asked few questions to promote further development of the story. In contrast, the Pakeha women (but less so the men) asked questions during the ongoing story and upon its completion as displays of positive politeness. Holmes emphasises that the observed differences were by no means categorical but that storytellers and listeners displayed many similarities across communities as well as variation within each ethnic group. However, in inter-ethnic encounters, the more implicit style preferred by Maori speakers and the more overt, explicit style favoured by Pakeha participants may turn into a source of misunderstanding. Holmes's examples illustrate this to be the case. As she notes, to the extent that miscommunication between Maori and Pakeha co-participants can be traced to differences in ethnic style – in particular, differential emphasis on 'listener responsibility' and 'speaker responsibility' – it can be understood as a Level 5 type of miscommunication in Coupland *et al.*'s model. But her analysis does more than provide yet another piece of evidence for the well-attested fact that divergent discourse-pragmatic practices *can* – though by no means must – result in misunderstanding. Further examination of her narrative material points to yet a deeper level of analysis, Level 6 in the Coupland *et al.* model, where:

> interaction is seen as reinforcing or even constituting a societal value system and its associated social identities ... What defines interaction sequences as 'miscommunication' communicatively and sociolinguistically is that they implicitly or explicitly disadvantage people or, more likely, groups, while proposing themselves as normal, desirable, and even morally correct.

> (1991b, p. 15)

In the Maori narratives, ethnic identity is treated as an 'omni-relevant device' (Sacks, 1966, lecture 6, pp. 313ff.) of sorts – a self-categorisation that permeates the Maori stories. It is evident in the sujects of the narrative and the background knowledge evoked for their understanding. On the other hand, the Pakeha narratives display no particular concern for ethnicity; nor is ethnic identity a relevant frame to comprehend their import. As Holmes comments, the different emphasis on ethnic identity reflects the positions of Maori and Pakeha in New Zealand society. As the dominant group, Pakeha treat their own values and practices as unmarked and valid for the entire society. Unlike Maori people, who reap from their enforced biculturalism an awareness of different cultural orientations and discourse-pragmatic practices, no social-structural forces impress on Pakeha the need to denaturalise their own ways of doing things.

As Holmes notes, her analysis is conducted from a Pakeha perspective. Her analytical framework, Labov's model of narrative structure, perfectly fits the Pakeha stories, which appear consistent with the American English narratives on which Labov developed his model. A model of story organisation based on Maori narratives would look quite different, and viewing Pakeha stories through its lenses would cast the overt, explicit elements in Pakeha speakers' and listeners' discourse as 'alienated' and marked. As it stands, Labov's model appears to provide an emic representation of Pakeha oral narratives but an etic account of Maori story discourse.

Chapter 9 by Diana Eades and Chapter 10 by Julie Kerekes adopt an interactional sociolinguistic approach in order to examine yet two more interview types, interviews conducted as criminal justice procedures and job interviews. Both studies clearly target their analysis at Level 6 in Coupland *et al.*'s model. During her extensive work on Aboriginal English in the Australian legal system, Eades has provided substantial evidence of incompatible discourse-pragmatic practices engaged by Aboriginal and white Australians in court cases and argued that the cross-cultural misunderstandings arising from different cultural assumptions contribute importantly to the legal discrimination suffered by Aboriginal people. In this study, she reports how legal professionals' understanding of Aboriginal discourse practices is essential to ensure fair process, but how such understanding can also be turned against Aboriginals involved in court cases. The two Aboriginal discourse practices examined here are silence and gratuitous concurrence. As shown in previous research (e.g. Jaworski, 1993; Tannen and Saville-Troike, 1985), the pragmatics of silence is cross-culturally and contextually variable. In Aboriginal discourse, silence is valued as a space for thinking about issues brought up during interaction and participants' right to silence is respected. In contrast, conversationalists in mainstream Anglo communities often experience discomfort with silence and routinely engage in silence-avoiding practices. Edmondson (1981) even deemed silence avoidance so pervasive that he graced it with its own conversational maxim – 'Plug any conversational gap' (p. 156).

The different cultural presuppositions associated with silence in Australian English and Aboriginal English work to Aboriginal people's serious disadvantage in a legal context when silence on the part of Aboriginal witnesses or defendants is interpreted according to its semiotics in Australian English. Gratuitous concurrence refers to a self-protective discourse strategy in responses to yes/no questions that Aboriginal people often have recourse to in interaction with white Australians – agreeing to whatever the Anglo Australian says, whether or not they understand the question or indeed believe the proposition to be true. This discourse strategy, itself indicative of the discrimination experienced by Aboriginal people, is particularly common in speech events consisting of repeated and fast-paced question–answer sequences, such as police and courtroom interviews. Importantly, it is precisely in such speech events that gratuitous concurrence can be turned against Aboriginal witnesses or suspects because, as Eades points out, unlike in ordinary conversation, agreements to propositions in police or courtroom interviews are legally binding and subsequent withdrawal of such agreements severely undermines the credibility of a witness or suspect. By showing how legal professionals' understanding of silence and gratuitous concurrence was pivotal in overturning a wrongful murder conviction in one case, but misused to manipulate the evidence of three Aboriginal witnesses in another, Eades powerfully demonstrates the potential and limits of interactional sociolinguistics as a tool for promoting non-discriminatory practices in gatekeeping encounters. When Roberts *et al.* (1992) assert that 'an understanding of the processes of interaction between people from different cultural and linguistic backgrounds does assist in heightening the perception of those who do not wish to discriminate' (p. 112), the last clause expresses a crucial caveat. When this condition is not met, awareness of ethnolinguistic differences can be exploited to the disadvantage of minority clients in institutional discourse, as demonstrated in the second court case that Eades discusses. Moving from the analysis of misunderstanding in cross-examination to the relationship between Aboriginal and Anglo Australians in the wider institutional and societal context, Eades argues with Fairclough (1989) that critical analysis must not stop with examining power *in* discourse but also needs to consider the power *behind* the discourse.

More evidence supporting this analytical strategy is provided in Chapter 10 by Julie Kerekes's study of employment interviews in the staffing industry in California. Consonant with the need for a flexible workforce on short-term assignments, one structural characteristic of the fast-paced and quickly changing economies in 'late modernity' (Giddens, 1991) is the 'outsourcing' of employee recruitment. Unlike company internal hiring, in which hiring decisions are primarily based on applicants' qualifications for a specific job, the hiring personnel in the staffing industry typically lacks expertise in the type of work sought by applicants. Consequently, staffing supervisors have to rely to a great extent on other assessment criteria than applicants' technical training or experience.

Kerekes identifies as a central emic assessment category 'trust' or 'trustworthiness', a complex notion comprising displays of sincerity, consistency, reliability and ambition. Successful applicants are those who manage to construct themselves as 'trustworthy'. Conversely, if applicants do not succeed in displaying such qualities in ways recognisable to the staffing supervisor, the resulting 'distrust' will be the basis for a negative placement decision. Centring on job interviews with two applicants, another type of high-stakes encounter with unequally distributed participant positions, Kerekes's chapter illustrates the second case. Through interactional-sociolinguistic analysis, she determines that in both interviews misunderstandings remain unrepaired and result in distrust. However, the source of the miscommunication is not a mutual misinterpretation of contextualisation cues but rather different understandings of the application and interview procedures. Even though the specific details of the application process that prove problematic for the two unsuccessful applicants are quite different, in both instances, the critical distrust-creating event is a discrepancy, in the staffing supervisor's view, between information supplied (or not supplied) by the applicants on the application form filled in prior to the job interview and their interview responses on the same issues. Kerekes's findings can usefully be conceptualised through the categories of 'pre-text' (Hinnenkamp, 1987) and intertextuality (e.g. Fairclough, 1992), here manifest in the significant role of the written application document for the success or failure of the oral employment interview.

Throughout this book, the reader is invited to act as a co-analyst and turn to the approaches engaged by the contributors on the presented studies and in particular the examined extracts of talk-in-interaction. While we hope that our volume opens up venues for further constructive dissent on the theory and analysis of problematic talk, we would be delighted if it also contributed to a better understanding of misunderstanding and, by implication, of the intricacies of spoken discourse.

References

Bazzanella, C. and Damiano, R. (1999). The interactional handling of misunderstanding in everyday conversations. In *Journal of Pragmatics*, 31, 817–836.

Berger, P. L. and Luckmann, T. (1966). *The social construction of reality.* New York: Doubleday.

Bremer, K., Roberts, C., Vasseur, M., Simonot, M. and Broeder, P. (1996). *Achieving understanding: Discourse in intercultural encounters.* London: Longman.

Byrnes, H. (1986). Interactional style in German and American conversation. In *Text*, 6, 189–206.

Coupland, N., Giles, H. and Wiemann, J. M. (eds) (1991a). *'Miscommunication' and problematic talk.* London: Sage.

Coupland, N., Wiemann, J. M. and Giles, H. (1991b). Talk as 'problem' and communication as 'miscommunication': An integrative analysis. In N. Coupland, H. Giles and J. M. Wiemann (eds), *'Miscommunication' and problematic talk.* London: Sage, 1–17.

Dascal, M. (1983). *Pragmatics and the philosophy of mind I: Thought in language.* Amsterdam: John Benjamins.

Dascal, M. (1999). Introduction: Some questions about misunderstanding. In *Journal of Pragmatics*, 31, 753–762.

Dua, H. (1990). The phenomenology of miscommunication. In S. H. Riggins (ed.), *Beyond Goffman.* Berlin: Mouton de Gruyter, 113–139.

Duranti, A. and Goodwin, C. (eds) (1992). *Rethinking context.* Cambridge: Cambridge University Press.

Edmondson, W. (1981). *Spoken discourse.* London: Longman.

Fairclough, N. (1989). *Language and power.* London: Longman.

Fairclough, N. (1992). Discourse and text: linguistic and intertextual analysis within discourse analysis. In *Discourse & Society*, 3, 193–217.

Giddens, A. (1991). *Modernity and self-identity. Self and society in the late modern age.* Stanford: Stanford University Press.

Goffman, E. (1974). *Frame analysis*. New York: Harper & Row.

Goffman, E. (1981). *Forms of talk*. Oxford: Blackwell.

Grice, H. P. (1968). Utterer's meaning, speaker's meaning and word meaning. In *Foundations of Language*, 4, 1–18.

Grimshaw, A. D. (1980). Mishearings, misunderstandings and other nonsuccesses in talk: A plea/or redress of speaker-oriented bias. In *Sociological Inquiry*, 50, 31–74.

Gumperz, J. J. (1982). *Discourse strategies*. Cambridge: Cambridge University Press.

Gumperz, J. J. (1992). Contextualization and understanding. In A. Duranti and C. Goodwin (eds), *Rethinking context*. Cambridge: Cambridge University Press, 229–252.

Heritage, J. and Greatbatch, D. (1991). On the institutional character of institutional talk. In D. Boden and D. Zimmerman (eds), *Talk and social structure*. Cambridge: Polity Press, 93–137.

Hinnenkamp, V. (1987). Foreigner talk, code switching and the concept of trouble. In K. Knapp, W. Enninger and A. Knapp-Potthoff (eds), *Analyzing intercultural communication*. Berlin: Mouton de Gruyter, 137–180.

House, J. (1996). Contrastive discourse analysis and misunderstanding: The case of German and English. In M. Hellinger and U. Ammon (eds), *Contrastive sociolinguistics*. Berlin: Mouton, 345–361.

Humphrey-Jones, C. (1986). An investigation of the types and structure of misunderstanding. Unpublished PhD dissertation, University of Newcastle-upon-Tyne.

Jaworski, A. (1993). *The power of silence*. Newbury Park, CA: Sage.

Kotthoff, H. (1993). Disagreement and concession in disputes: On the context sensitivity of preference structures. In *Language in Society*, 22, 193–216.

Labov, W. (1972). *Language in the Inner City*. Philadelphia: University of Pennsylvania Press. (Ch. 9).

Levelt, W. J. M. (1989). *Speaking*. Cambridge, MA: MIT Press.

Lieven, E. V. M. (1994). Crosslinguistic and cross-cultural aspects of language addressed to children. In C. Gallaway and B. J. Richards (eds), *Input and interaction in language acquisition*. Cambridge: Cambridge University Press, 56–73.

Long, M. H. (1996). The role of the linguistic environment in second language acquisition. In W. Ritchie and T. Bhatia (eds), *Handbook of research on second language acquisition*. New York: Academic, 413–468.

Ochs, E. (1991). Misunderstanding children. In N. Coupland, H. Giles and J. M. Wiemann (eds), *'Miscommunication' and problematic talk*. London: Sage, 44–60.

Roberts, C., Davies, E. and Jupp, T. (1992). *Language and discrimination*. London: Longman.

Sacks, H. (1966). *Lectures on conversation*. Ed. by G. Jefferson (1992). Oxford: Blackwell.

Schachter, J. (1991). Corrective feedback in historical perspective. In *Second Language Research*, 7, 89–102.

Schegloff, E. (1987). Some sources of misunderstanding in talk-in-interaction. In *Linguistics*, 25, 201–218.

Schegloff, E. (1992). Repair after next turn: The last structurally provided defense of intersubjectivity in conversation. In *American Journal of Sociology*, 97, 1295–1345.

Schegloff, E., Jefferson, G. and Sacks, H. (1977). The preference for self-correction in the organization of repair in conversation. In *Language*, 53, 361–382.

Shotter, J. (1993a). *Cultural politics of everyday life: Social constructionism, rhetoric, and knowing of the third kind*. Milton Keynes: Open University Press.

Shotter, J. (1993b). *Conversational realities. Constructing life through language*. London: Sage.

Tannen, D. and Saville-Troike, M. (1985). *Perspectives on silence*. Norwood, NJ: Ablex.

Tzanne, A. (2000). *Talking at cross-purposes*. Amsterdam: John Benjamins.

Tyler, A. (1995). The coconstruction of cross-cultural miscommunication. In *Studies in Second Language Acquisition*, 17, 129–152.

Van Dijk, T. (1998). *Ideology: A multidisciplinary approach*. London: Sage.

Vendler, Z. (1994). Understanding misunderstanding. In D. Jamieson (ed.), *Language, mind, and art*. Dordrecht: Kluwer, 9–21.

Watts, R. (1989). Relevance and relational work: linguistic politeness as politic behavior. In *Multilingua*, 8, 131–166.

Watzlawick, P., Beavin, J. H. and Jackson, D. D. (1967). *Pragmatics of human communication*. New York: Norton.

Weigand, E. (1999). Misunderstanding: The standard case. In *Journal of Pragmatics*, 31, 763–785.

White, H. (1978). *Tropics of discourse. Essays in cultural criticism*. Baltimore: Johns Hopkins University Press.

Wilkes-Gibbs, D. (1997). Studying language use as collaboration. In G. Kasper and E. Kellerman (eds), *Communication strategies: Psycholinguistic and sociolinguistic perspectives*. London: Longman, 238–274.   48.88   Amazon

2

Misunderstanding in intercultural university encounters

Juliane House

Introduction

In looking at misunderstandings in social life, one addresses a core question in the analysis of spoken discourse, i.e. how is it possible that two utterances by two different persons 'hang together'? We are here concerned with relationships on the linguistic surface that create cohesion as well as with thematic, content-related ties across larger stretches of discourse, in which rather more 'submerged' relations are set up along extended segments of talk. The amazing achievement of this 'texture' across turns-at-talk becomes most obvious when it breaks down – as is most patently the case in intercultural institutional misunderstandings, where the two interactants are not only tied up in differing institutionally imposed roles, but are also members of two different speech communities. Misunderstandings in intercultural talk can have manifold causes that often interact with one another in complex ways. We can try to filter out at least the following reasons for misunderstandings to occur.

Misunderstandings may stem from inadequate perception, or from inappropriate comprehension at different (and possibly interacting) levels of language, i.e. morphosyntactic, semantic, pragmatic and discoursal levels of language use. They may stem from gaps in one or both interlocutors' knowledge of the world, or from uncooperativeness on the part of one or both interlocutors, who may have understood perfectly well but simply behaved uncooperatively. Further, interlocutors may have perceived and comprehended correctly (on all conceivable levels) and also intended to cooperate, but were – for manifold reasons – unable to produce a well-aligned move in the fast give-and-take of the discourse.

Given these five potentially interacting reasons for intercultural misunderstandings, we are faced with an enormous multi-levelled complexity if we want to analyse concrete cases of misunderstanding. What we might hypothesise at this stage is that the most interesting and puzzling misunderstandings in intercultural interactions will not stem from mishearing, mispronouncing or misusing lexico-grammatical rules, rather they are likely to arise as a result of a failure to interpret alter's 'real meaning', her communicative conventions, which, as Goffman (1981) has pointed out, constitute hidden meanings underlying discourse structures. As work on communicative styles, politeness phenomena, indirect speech acts, Gricean implicatures and neo-Gricean relevance theory have revealed, much of 'normal talk' is indirect, which means, of course, that if we want to understand our interlocutors' contributions in any type of discourse, we must 'infer' their intentions in order to find out how the words they use are 'really meant'. Because indirectness is one major source of failed alignments, we may hypothesise that it also lies at the heart of many misunderstandings in talk. We may further assume that alignment failures and hidden differences in positioning and footing are more likely in talk between persons with different sociocultural backgrounds and institutionally imposed roles, where diverging or overlapping communicative conventions may trap interactants into illusions of comfortable likeness or insurmountable difference, which may influence their discourse behaviour in ways that puzzle both their communicative partner and the analyst.

Given the multi-levelled complexity of misunderstanding, attempts at 'defining' it in any facile manner are doomed to failure. Rather, it seems necessary to adopt what Halliday (1990) has called a 'transdisciplinary approach', i.e. an approach which transgresses traditional disciplinary boundaries and eclectically combines different research traditions, some of which I will now briefly outline before suggesting an integrative discourse processing model for the analysis of instances of misunderstanding. This model will then be tried out with an analysis of misunderstanding events in a university settting.

Ways of researching misunderstanding

Social views of analysing misunderstanding

There are two ways of looking at language and, by implication, at misunderstanding: an intra-organismic, cognitive-emotive and an inter-organismic, social one. Approaching language from a social viewpoint has a long and venerable tradition in Europe and in North America (and possibly in other parts of the world). Social conceptions of language can be traced back (in the twentieth century) to those linguists and literary critics in Russia (Russian Formalism) and Prague (Prague School of Linguistics) who differentiated between different functions of language and described functional styles, and in general stressed the interconnectedness of language and social contexts; to British linguists who emphasised the importance of 'the context of situation' in establishing meaning in language; to American sociologists of language and sociolinguists who also stressed the embeddedness of language in the context of culture and society.

Worthy of mention in this tradition is particularly Erving Goffman, whose distinction between a 'response' and a 'reply' in interaction is highly relevant to analysing misunderstanding. According to Goffman (1981, p. 35), a response emanating from an individual and inspired by what a previous speaker has said tells us something about that individual's positioning vis-à-vis, and alignment to, what is occurring now. In the context of an ongoing discourse, alignment implies that two interactional moves are brought in line with one another, and that an 'aligned' response is relevant here and now. A reply is a response in which the alignment and the object to which reference is made are conveyed through words or their substitutes. Replies, then, are directly verbally connected to what was said before. They achieve cohesion through explicit and overt surface connections on the utterance-expression level. For the comprehensive approach to misunderstanding which I am aiming at, it seems vital to take account of both the 'deeper' links achieved in responding via 'mental aligning' and the achievements of 'lower' surface-linguistic links.

Intercultural miscommunication

Another important strand of research is the seminal work by Gumperz (1982a, 1982b, 1992) on intercultural misunderstanding. In his work, the two per-spectives, the intra-organismic and the inter-organismic one, are combined. In Gumperz's view, misunderstandings frequently result from interactants' misuse of so-called 'contextualisation cues', i.e. prosodic, phonological and lexical choices which signal relevant interpretive 'frames' that are often culture-specific and thus open to misinterpretation by cultural outsiders. According to Gumperz, these linguistic cues are crucial for understanding because they act like signposts for the process of conversational inferencing, i.e. the context-bound, 'situated' process of interpretation interactants use when attempting to decode one another's intention. Another classic approach in this paradigm is Tannen's (e.g. 1979, 1993) investigation of interactions between members of different (sub)cultures. Building on Goffman's (1974) important concept of 'frame', Tannen looks upon cases of misunderstanding as a mismatch of 'frames', as frame breaking, or reframing, with frames being dynamically linked such that negotiated 'footings' in a chain of responding constantly change with interactants finding ever-renewed bases for making judgements about their interlocutors' intention, on which to base their response.

Further influential studies on intercultural communication include work on differences in communicative styles (Lakoff, 1990), indirectness and politeness (Blum-Kulka *et al.*, 1989; Kasper and Blum-Kulka, 1993). Indirectness in the realisation of speech acts in discourse is commonly linked with politeness – although some studies have shown that the relationship is often tenuous (Blum-Kulka, 1987; House, 1986). Politeness is important for misunderstanding analysis as it is commonly taken to be one of the basic social guidelines for any human contact and interaction, i.e. 'a system of interpersonal relations designed to facilitate interaction by minimizing the potential for conflict and confrontation inherent in all human interchange' (Lakoff, 1990, p. 34). Politeness has been discussed inside different frameworks: in its relation to certain social norms holding in a given society, which one must observe in order to be seen to display good manners; in the realisation of speech styles and formality (Fraser, 1990); as a pragmatic phenomenon, related to philosophical principles and maxims (Lakoff, 1990; Leech, 1983); and to the management of face (Brown and Levinson, 1987).

I do not wish here to go any further into the vast literature on politeness (see overview e.g. in Kasper, 1990), but simply stress that, when considering cross-cultural institutional talk and misunderstanding, one must have some understanding of politeness. What I therefore want to do here is suggest a tentative theory of politeness capturing a number of different levels (cf. also House, 1998, in press). Such a theory sets out to explain the tension between universal and culture-specific aspects of politeness. The model operates on three levels:

- a fundamental biological, psycho-social level based on animal drives ('coming-together' versus 'noli-me-tangere', cf. Brown and Levinson's distinction of negative and positive politeness)
- a philosophical level to capture the biological drives in terms of a finite number of principles, maxims or parameters
- an empirical descriptive level concerned with the fact that in cultures 1 to n, politeness operates in terms of a particular (open-ended) set of norms, tendencies or preferences.

The first two levels are universal ones; level three however is clearly variable. One might wish to argue that one can distinguish here between relatively negotiable rules and other, more normative, more or less fixed ones. This distinction relates to the issue of how far the language system as such imposes certain choices (e.g. honorific forms in a language such as Japanese).

Working top-down, one can pose the operation of a kind of 'negotiability parameter' in between the philosophical and the descriptive-linguistic levels, which would determine how relatively flexible any given culture is in terms of degrees of freedom concerning the realisation of certain maxims and principles. One might also be able to explain why a particular phenomenon appears to be so linguistically differentiated in one culture and so relatively inflexibly fixed in another culture. Working bottom-up, on the other hand, one may come up with principles and maxims which have no universal validity.

For my concern with constructing a model for analysing cross-cultural and institutional talk, it would be important to take account of level three, i.e. a detailed description of the linguistic-discoursal variation of communicative preferences and norms.

Pragmatic theory-based analyses of misunderstanding

Similar to work on intercultural miscommunication, studies of misunderstanding inside the pragmatic-theory-based research paradigm can be characterised by a dual consideration both of intra-organismic and inter-organismic phenomena. A further characteristic of this line of research is that its focus has been both on everyday interactions that take place between members of the same speech community and members of different speech communities (e.g. Blum-Kulka and Weizman, 1988; Blum-Kulka and Weizman, this volume; Dascal, 1985) with misunderstanding being analysed at different levels of pragmatic meaning. Participants in an interaction must continuously engage in a process of pragmatic reasoning guided by principles or maxims such as the Gricean ones in order to approach the gist of what the interlocutor may have meant. If a speaker's attempt to bridge the gap between what is said and what is meant, as well as her assessment of the role played by verbal cues and contextual constraints (such as role relationships and institutionally invested authority), goes wrong in the process of interpretation, she is faced with a 'misunderstanding'. Exactly what may 'go wrong' in the attempt to get at the 'meaning' of the interlocutor's utterance can be described with reference to at least the following questions: What did the speaker say (i.e. the propositional meaning of the utterance)? What was the speaker talking about (i.e. what did s/he say plus what was implicated, that is the extended semantic meaning of the utterance)? Why did the speaker bother to say what s/he said (i.e. the illocutionary force of the utterance)? Why did the speaker say what s/he said in the way s/he did (i.e. the 'key', tone or tenor of the 'message')? Following Searle (1983), Blum-Kulka and Weizman (1988, and this volume) make a further distinction between a speaker's meaning (the 'individual-I-meaning') and what they call the 'collective-we-direction' of the discourse. On one or several of these levels (or an interaction between them), misunderstandings can theoretically arise and in this pragmatic approach they can best be tackled in a context-sensitive, speech-event-specific approach to misunderstanding.

Philosophical views of the 'self-orientedness' of communication

As opposed to Grice's well-known inter-individual approach to analysing and explaining communication and miscommunication via the operation of the underlying principle of cooperation, another, less well-known research strand relates to the individual speaker's 'insular nature', her reliance on her own mode of interpretation and meaning creation and the attendant emotion evoked. Lévinas's (1961) theory is of interest here (in particular his notion of the conversationalist as a 'self-oriented' speaker) and its more recent interpretation by Jaszczolt (1996). Interaction is here interpreted as a relationship between two interactants, who are basically two separate entities. It is something 'doubly dynamic', which cannot be described using the metaphor of a dance with one conversational partner leading, the other one following. Rather, interaction is seen as a process in which each participant dances on his own, with meaning being created in between them, each speaker presenting his thoughts, without these thoughts necessarily penetrating to the ego of the other. Consequently, Lévinas maintains that we leave the 'otherness' of the other intact – thanks to language. In this view, language is used primarily as a self-defensive mechanism. Speakers appear to be strongly self-oriented. They trigger the production of meaning by speaking, hereby trying to reveal their own private worlds to the interactant. Communication is thus a self-centred affair, with the speaker leaving the hearer freedom of interpretation, and, in the last analysis, the freedom to create (rather than recover) assumptions. This 'selfishness' in talk, which has been downplayed in today's mostly mutuality-based theories of conversation (see e.g. Markovà et al., 1995), seems to be particularly suited for explaining misunderstandings. In fact, one might consider such a 'non-other-orientedness' to be a major reason for misunderstanding in that a concentration on oneself would prevent one from listening, anticipating and generally trying to throw oneself into one's interlocutor's mind.

In interpreting Lévinas's theory, Jaszczolt (1996) makes the important (and obvious) point that emotions tend severely to interfere with discourse interpretation. We may hypothesise that 'interfering' emotions tend to be exacerbated in the process of cross-cultural communication, because it involves interactants who habitually use different communicative styles.

Psychopathological views of misunderstanding

This approach is similar to the self-centred philosophical one in that it is also clearly intra-organismic and relates to speakers' mental processes and states. It can be traced back to Freud's famous writings about the 'psychopathology of everyday life' and especially his discussion of the genesis of 'slips of the tongue', and to the more recent investigations by Langer and her associates (see e.g. Langer, 1989) as well as the German psychologists Heckhausen and Beckmann (1990). The main point in this approach is that an attempt is made to relate misunderstanding to interactants' 'mindless', 'automatic', i.e. non-thoughtful behaviour. It is through interactants' routinised and automatised actions carried out without conscious mental control that 'interactional slips' or misunderstandings may and do occur.

This 'non-thinking' explanation of misunderstanding is supported by the extremely productive line of research on the packaging of knowledge in the mind suggesting that in many actions, speakers (must) rely on ready-made plans, schemata, scripts or social episodes in human memory, which enable them to predict upcoming moves. The consequence of such 'lean cognitive management' is that speakers often stop paying attention to interactants' real input. Speakers' illusion of being in control of the interaction is then only disrupted by misunderstandings, with which reality suddenly and forcefully intrudes.

Information processing approaches to analysing misunderstanding

These approaches, too, are clearly intra-organismic and linked to the psycho-pathological approach to misunderstanding in that here too the existence of scripted behaviour imprinted in the human mind is assumed, and cognitive plans, frames and schemata are postulated, which are conceived as representations of repeated behavioural patterns designed to alleviate cognitive work. Understanding language requires forming a mental model based on the language used, background knowledge and inferences. Cognitive models set up to predict and explain processes involved in discourse comprehension and production (e.g. Britton and Graesser, 1995; Kintsch, 1988) are therefore particularly relevant for explaining processes of misunderstanding. In Kintsch's 'construction-integration' model, for instance, comprehension is seen as initially bottom-up guided, with an integration process only later facilitating the selection of appropriate meaning. A minimally structured knowledge system is assumed, and particular on-line structures arise in the context of a particular interaction, gradually building up densely associative knowledge nets (see also the rich literature on speech production such as Dechert and Raupach, 1989; Levelt, 1989).

Information-processing models offer a fruitful way of approaching cross-cultural and institutional misunderstanding because they integrate the different insightful perspectives outlined above in a systematic way. Thus, even inter-organismic, social views of misunderstanding can be incorporated in that norms and conventions as well as behavioural tendencies must have cognitive substrates, and the interpretation of contextualised, situated meanings and misunderstandings can also be interpreted as an explication of underlying cognitive processing mechanisms.

It is therefore a cognitive discourse processing model which I take as an explanatory model in my analysis of misunderstandings. This model will be presented in the following section.

Using an integrative discourse comprehension and production model for the analysis of misunderstanding

The model assumes the existence of scripted behaviour imprinted in the human mind and postulates cognitive plans, frames and schemata – entities conceived as representations of repeated behavioural patterns designed to alleviate cognitive work. The model can therefore be described as a cognitive discourse processing model for which a claim is made that it can serve as an explanatory model for the analysis of cross-cultural misunderstandings. It is based on Edmondson's (1987, 1989) discourse model, and the version presented in what follows is a revised form of the adaptation of Edmondson's model presented in House (1993, 2000).

The model operates on two 'levels': a conceptual and a linguistic level, with the latter providing for the decoding of the linguistic input and the encoding of the output. These 'levels' must be conceived as being networked in a complex fashion, more complex, in fact, than any diagrammatic display (such as in Figure 2.1) is capable of revealing. In the light of more recent work on the important role emotional factors in discourse comprehension and production and in particular in the perception of, and reaction to, intercultural and institutional misunderstanding, the model presented in House (1993) is revised here to take account of the fact that emotional reactions – in the sense of 'spontaneous, unplanned physical externalisations of internal affective states' (Janney and Arndt, 1992, p. 27) – frequently accompany both revealed and hidden misunderstandings. In House (1996, 2000), for instance, I have shown that an emotional reaction is often the major factor responsible for a deterioration of rapport and for the mutual attribution of negative personal traits which, in turn, effectively prevents any recognition of real differences in cultural values and norms. Ochs (1989), Besnier (1990), Bloch (1996), Caffi and Janney (1994), Niemeier and Dirven (1997) among others have pointed to the crucial importance of emotion in interaction, and an increasing number of neurolinguistic studies (Damasio, 1999; Ledoux, 1996; Miall, 1995) have recently argued for the temporal priority and thus decisiveness of emotional reactions in the limbic system, i.e. emotions take effect before 'higher' cognitive 'construction-integration' can run its course. It is on the basis of findings such as these that the revised discourse comprehension and production model has been set up (Figure 2.1).

Briefly, the operation of the model in Figure 2.1 can be characterised as follows. In order to allow for the impact of discourse production and comprehension, one needs:

- to assume an awareness of self and other on the part of the system user
- to posit some sort of 'system equilibrium index', which indicates the level of emotional involvement or disengagement, i.e. type and nature of a language user's emotive stance.

Both awareness and equilibrium index have an impact on the entire system. Since they cannot be pinpointed or located at any single 'place' in the system, they are 'anywhere elements'.

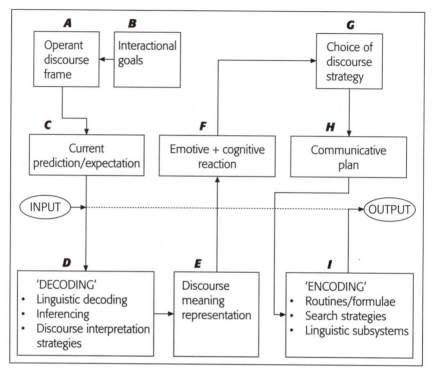

Figure 2.1   Discourse comprehension and production model

The individual 'boxes' of the model function and interact as follows. In Box A, a copy of the relevant stored situational constellation or schema is made and 'filled in' by knowledge derived from the current discourse situation. The result is a complex of both conceptual and linguistic representations making up the operant discourse frame. Note that the term 'frame' (Goffman, 1974; Tannen, 1993) is here used as distinct from 'schema', the latter providing the skeleton to be fleshed out in the ongoing discourse. In other words, a 'generalised' schema is built up into a particular discourse frame. In the ongoing discourse, however, it is always possible to call up alternative discourse schemata with the revision and reactivation of operant discourse frames leading to co-existent discourse frames (cf. the notion of 'co-existent discourse worlds' in Edmondson, 1981).

The representations in Box A allow, then, of both prospective anticipation and of retrospective adjustment or reinterpretation. Typically, the following elements are contained in a currently activated discourse frame:

1. Knowledge of the currently relevant interactional move constellation.
2. Knowledge of the currently relevant discourse topic.

3. A chunked representation of the discourse outcomes arrived at so far in the ongoing interaction, and the relevance of (1) and (2) to these, where appropriate, with the scope of such representations being affected by memory span, attention and emotional arousal.
4. A (partly or wholly) linguistic representation of the content and import of the precedingly relevant last turn, and here especially its rhematic content, which is held in working memory and can be accessed from the currently activated frame.

In terms of the pragmatic theory approach to misunderstanding (Blum-Kulka and Weizman, 1988 and this volume; Dascal, 1985), it is clearly the level of propositional meaning which is captured here.

Concretely, Box A features knowledge of intra- and cross-culturally variable norms such as at least the following four:

1. Contextual assessment norms, comprising, for instance, social role relationships and the concomitant degrees of power and familiarity, rights and obligations.
2. Socio-pragmatic and pragmalinguistic norms governing rapport management, such as preference or dispreference for overt expression of criticism or for using particular routine formulae in phatic and other discourse phases.
3. Underlying cultural and institutional communicative norms and values.
4. Rapport management devices, such as German and English means of indexing deference, politeness or distance via the *Du* and *Sie* distinction in German, and the quasi-equivalent use of first names in conjunction with other means of conveying social distance or alignment in English.

In intercultural institutional encounters, representations of the above four (and possibly more) aspects vary individually and culturally. This variation may be an important factor in interactants' mutual misinterpretation of their intentions and behaviour.

In Box B, the speaker's main goal plus any evolving subgoals for the ongoing encounter are accounted for. Just as Box A is made up of two elements (the basic schemata for interpretation and production and the accruing knowledge gained from the context), so Box B is also made up of an interaction between choices of interactional and illocutionary options (see Edmondson, 1981, 1987, for further details on this fundamental distinction between interactional and illocutionary moves). Interactional options concern whether the speaker will take a positive or a negative stance to her interlocutor's preceding or current discourse move, while illocutionary options concern the type of speech act (e.g. a request, an apology, a complaint) conventionalised for this purpose. In distinguishing between interactional and illocutionary categories, the system becomes highly efficient in that the categories of illocutionary acts can be economically restricted. Further, by including in Box B interactional moves and their combinatorial potential, a knowledge store is derived which may also be employed in non-verbal modes of interaction.

Integrating the distinctions made by pragmatic theorists such as Searle (1983) and Blum-Kulka and Weizman (1988), we can here further include two types of goals for the evolving interaction: an 'individual-I-point' (the 'speaker meaning') and a 'collective-we-direction', a sort of 'drift' in which the discourse is jointly propelled.

Box C marks the result of ongoing processing, where a more or less specific type of input is expected or predicted with particular inferences being drawn on the basis of background knowledge and incoming input.

Box D refers to the process of extracting a 'discourse meaning' involving complex subsystems of linguistic decoding, discourse interpretation strategies, inferencing procedures and politeness considerations, as well as incorporating concepts and distinctions elaborated inside work on intercultural institutional miscommunication such as participants' misinterpreting 'contextualisation cues' and communicative styles (see above, p. 24).

Box E marks the outcome of the decoding processes in D in the form of a tentative discourse meaning for the current input.

Box F is a critical one in this model. Here the interpreted input leads initially to a non-linguistic, emotive-cognitive 'gut reaction'. It is this central part of the model which – together with the system's emotion-related 'anywhere elements' – takes cognisance of the crucial role of emotion in discourse comprehension and production. In line with recent discourse theories such as the one proposed by Jaszczolt (1996), this model thus also explicitly accounts for the crucial role of human emotive reactions in discourse.

The determinants of the response in Box F are to a substantial degree personality-based depending on a person's ability for interpersonal adaptation in the ongoing interaction (cf. Burgoon et al., 1995). Personality traits impacting on a speaker's reaction in accordance with, or in violation of, expectation norms include factors such as cognitive flexibility, extroversion and introversion, risk taking and tolerance of ambiguity, many of which have recently been subsumed under the psychological construct of 'ego boundaries' (Ehrman, 1993).

In Edmondson (1989, p. 290), some 'reactive formatives' are posited which further concretise what is captured under (the non-linguistic) gut reaction to the current communicative situation in which a speaker finds himself. These 'formatives' include the following aspects:

- affective weight of the current discourse topic or preceding discourse contribution (e.g. balancing speaker and hearer interests)
- evocative associations as when a preceding turn triggers recollection from episodic memory

- degree of importance attached by the speaker to his own face in the ongoing interaction
- the result of cognitive-intellectual processes evaluating the propositional content of a preceding turn
- role relationship (power and intimacy) between interactants.

To elucidate the notion of 'reactive formative', Edmondson (1989, pp. 290–291) gives the example of a speaker producing the utterance 'You're late', which is interpreted in the ongoing discourse by the hearer as accusatory in tone. Here the system might, on the basis of some of the reactive formatives, derive an ensuing move by answering questions such as:

- Am I in fact late?
- Is my interlocutor in a social position to comment on my time of arrival in this way?
- Do I care what s/he thinks of me?
- Is punctuality something I value highly in others?
- Are there grounds why my arrival occurred just now, and not earlier?
- Have I met with such criticism before? How did I successfully handle it on previous occasions? and so forth.

Given such reactive formatives, the speaker has the options of 'ignoring' the utterance 'You're late' proceeding to plan an utterance that is (on the surface) non-coherent, she may feel insulted wishing to complain about the accusation and justify herself; or she may opt for an apology, and so on.

Box G: here the speaker may reconsider the 'gut' decisions made in F (which may not have surfaced to consciousness) and strategically manipulate them. The speaker may, for instance, choose to enact an intervening move which leads to looping inside the system, or she may decide to 'prepare the ground' for a felt reaction in anticipation of the hearer's next move.

Thus, the speaker in G resorts to strategic knowledge as a basis for choosing interactional strategies in order either to disguise the emotional gut reaction in F (if, for instance, this reaction is assessed as being potentially face threatening to the interlocutor), or to proceed immediately to reveal her emotional reaction. At this stage of the system the speaker may become aware of her own and her interlocutor's emotional state and also regain her emotional equilibrium and may, as a further option open to her, decide strategically to stall, i.e. delay any reaction. Alternatively she may resort to using a variety of politeness or indirectness strategies.

Box G resembles a 'filter' serving to mitigate or intensify illocutionary options under the constraints of perceived social conventions and/or contextual contingencies as well as anticipated potentially face-threatening reactions of the interlocutor, which themselves serve continually to adjust initial responses. Using strategic interactional knowledge will therefore commonly involve looping in the system. In the above example ('You're late') a gut reaction of exasperation may, for instance, be modified by considerations of politeness leading to the suppression of the initial intuitive reaction and to the production of a more strategically adequate discourse move.

In Box H we have arrived at a prelinguistic communicative plan, and finally at Box I this communicative plan is transformed into linguistic representations on the basis of a complex of linguistic resources, search strategies, prepacked chunks such as discourse markers or routine formulae.

Clearly, this model is not to be taken as depicting a straightforward linear-processing procedure, although the pathway mapped in Figure 2.1 and the numbering used here for expository purposes may well suggest such a procedure. Rather, the 'boxes' are interrelated in network fashion and the whole system operates in parallel and simultaneously. Various nodes, items and paths become activated at the same time and they also allow for a number of shortcuts, which cannot be elaborated here any further.

Case studies on intercultural university encounters

In order to demonstrate the operation of this model, I will now test it in a small empirical study of institutional discourse which is part of a larger ongoing project on intercultural misunderstanding between German and Anglophone speakers. Previous studies of interactions between German and Anglophone speakers provide some evidence for the hypothesis that differences in communicative preferences and styles as they are instantiated in everyday cross-cultural talk may cause considerable irritations. For instance, German speakers were found to 'attack one another more directly and likewise contradict one another more firmly' (Kotthoff, 1989, p. 13) in argumentative discourse, whereas Anglophone speakers were much less controversial in their moves. Disagreement sequences in German and Anglo-American disputes were also shown to differ in terms of expectation management and preference for overt disagreement (Kotthoff, 1993; Möhl, 1996). Further, the ritual dimension of talk tends to be given differential weight by German and Anglo-American speakers in many discourse events, such that, in phatic opening and closing phases, reciprocation of politeness rituals and routinised adjacency pairs differs both quantitatively and qualitatively, as Kotthoff (1994), House (1996, 1998, 2000) and Barron (2002) among others have demonstrated.

Would differences such as these also lead to misunderstanding sequences in intercultural institutional, specifically university, discourse between German and Anglophone speakers? How might such sequences be described and explained with the discourse processing model outlined in the previous section? Given these research questions, let us now examine the data.

The data consists of naturally occurring dyadic interactions between American exchange students studying at Hamburg University and their native German interlocutors, i.e. a university professor, a university administrator and a student friend. The American students were all between 20 and 28 years of age. They were given a recording device and asked to self-record their interactions in various university contexts. To triangulate this primary data, I conducted in-depth interviews with student participants in their native language. In these retrospective interviews, participants were asked to listen to the taped interactions and comment on them. Particular emphasis was given to 'critical incidents' – 'critical' originally in the analyst's opinion – which were substantiated or modified in the interactants' own assessment. Interactions were conducted in German (a foreign language for the American students). Glosses are provided for the transcriptions. All names are pseudonyms. (See Appendix for the transcription conventions.)

Extract 2.1: The exam

The interaction takes place in Professor Lehmann's (L) office. Amy is an American exchange student studying at the University of Hamburg for one academic year. She has knocked at the door of the office.

```
01 L:    Herein. {Amy enters office} Ja bitte nehmen Sie doch Platz. Was
02       kann ich denn für Sie tun
         $Come in. Yeah please have a seat. What can I do for you$
03 AMY:  erm guten Tag Herr Professor Lehmann ich nehme teil an Ihrem
04       Seminar II in diesem Semester und erm wissen Sie das Seminar
05       gefällt mir gut (0.1) es ist sehr ANDERS als was ich bei uns bei
06       meiner Universität zuhause besucht hab und [deshalb]
         $erm hallo Professor Lehmann I attend your Seminar II this
         term and erm you know I like the seminar (0.1) it is very DIF-
         FERENT from what I have attended at home and that's why$
07 L:                                              [ja das] das {embar-
08       rassed laughter} aber was (0.1) sagen Sie ich muss Sie fragen was
         ICH denn jetzt für Sie tun kann=
         $yes that that but what (0.1) tell me I must ask you what (0.1) it
         is that I can do for you$
09 AMY:  =ja ich meine das Seminar ist so ANDERS als (0.2) als die Kurse
10       die ich bei meiner Universität besucht habe und [ich ich]
         $yeah I mean the seminar is so DIFFERENT from the courses
         which I have attended at my university and I I $
11 L:                                                    [ja  also]   was
12       was nochmal meiner Frage was soll ICH damit=
                             $[yes so]what what again my question
         what shall I do with this$
```

13 AMY: =vielleicht (0.1) ich meine verstehn [Sie]
              $ maybe (0.1) I mean [you] understand
14 L: [was] was denn was
15   soll ich VERSTEHN
                                    $what what is it that I
        should UNDERSTAND$
16 AMY: aber Sie haben gesagt in der Klausur würde es wichtig sein
17   kritisch (0.2) KRITISCHES (0.1) ich weiss nicht ich lerne alles
18   (0.1) meine Notizen und die Artikel und (0.2) [und ich]
        $ but you have said in the exam it would be important to critical
        CRITICAL points (0.1) I don't know I am studying everything
        (0.1) my notes and the articles and [and I]$
19 L: [ja hmm]
                                        $[yeah erm]$
20 AMY: und ich entschuldigen Sie (0.2) ich meine es gibt ja noch
21   REFERATE aber ich weiss nicht vielleicht ist es besser (0.1) [dass ich]
        $and I I'm sorry (0.2) I mean there are TERM PAPERS but I
        don't know maybe it is better (0.1) [that I] $
22 L: [ja also]
23   ich habe ja bereits zu Beginn des Semesters die Unterschiede
24   dieser beiden Möglichkeiten für einen Schein klar gemacht, also
25   entweder Sie nehmen an der Klausur teil und beantworten die
        Klausurfra[gen]
                            $yeah well I have already at the
        beginning of term made clear the differences between these two
        possibilities for getting credits, so either you take the final exam
        and answer the questions$
26 AMY: [ja]ich weiss ich [wollte nur]
              $[yes] I know but I only wanted$
27 L: [wobei Sie] dies auch aus einer
28   KRITISCHEN Perspektive tun sollten oder aber Sie entscheiden
29   sich für eine bestimmte Fragestellung, die wir im Seminar nur
30   gestreift haben und das wäre dann die schriftliche Arbeit
                    $and you also have to do this from a CRITICAL
        perspective or you decide to tackle a specific question which we
        only treated cursorily in the course and that would be the written
        term paper
31 AMY: ja ich weiss (0.1) [das weiß ich]
        $yes I know I
32 L: [Sie wissen das] ja was soll ich denn DANN für
        Sie tun
                            $you know well in that case what can I do for
        you THEN$

33 AMY: ja ich ich wollte fragen wie so eine Klausur so (0.1) die Fragen
(0.2)
$yes I I wanted to ask how such an exam yeah (0.1) the questions
(0.2)

34 L: also über die FRAGEN kann ich Ihnen KEINE Auskunft geben

35   {laughs} aber na (0.1) Kopf hoch wird schon SCHIEF
gehen{shakes hands with Amy}
$well I can give you NO information on the QUESTIONS but
well (0.1) cheer up it can only go WRONG$

36 AMY: schiefgehn ja das glaube ich auch {sighs defeatedly}
$It'll go wrong I think so too$

In Extract 2.1, a German university professor interacts with one of his
students, an American exchange student, whom he has never met personally,
only 'at a distance' in one of his crowded seminars. The student, Amy, visits
Professor Lehmann wanting to inquire about course requirements, which
she, as an American, does not understand.

As the following analysis will reveal, misunderstanding in this excerpt is
both conceptually based (i.e. located in the upper 'boxes' of the model) and
procedural, where input is apparently ignored and 'short-cuts' are taken, in
that Boxes D and E are 'skipped', i.e. discourse frames are automatically
activated without 'reality intruding' – a case which, inside the psychopathological approach to misunderstanding (s. above), would count as a psycho-
pathological form of misunderstanding. However, there is also one case of a
language-based misunderstanding sequence (lines 34–36), where Amy's reaction (line 36) reveals that she has interpreted the idiomatic German phrase
('wird schon schiefgehen') in its literal sense, i.e. we are here dealing with a
formulaic quality implicature similar to the English routine 'break-a-leg' as a
well-wish. There seem to be differences in interactants' pragmatic knowledge, i.e. the operant discourse frame (Box A), as well as interactional goals
(Box B) and choice of discourse strategies (Box G). L and Amy, the student,
have different conceptions of appropriate communicative conventions governing the institutionalised speech event in which they are participating. For
instance, in the opening phase, Amy's ritual moves Greet (line 3) and Identification (line 3) are not reciprocated, her compliment move (lines 4 & 5)
is not acknowledged – omissions that would be marked lacunae had they
occurred in 'normal' everyday, non-institutional encounters. However, in
the asymmetrical role relationship professor–student and the speech event
during 'office hours' in the professor's own territory, they are deemed perfectly
'normal' and acceptable both by L and Amy – a situation clearly resembling
doctor–patient talk, where the doctor is expected to ignore reciprocal phatic
'inquiry-after-alter'. It is still noteworthy that it is only Amy – not the
professor – who transfers her conception of communicative conventions

holding for a non-institutional encounter into the institutional event. Thus, it is perfectly conceivable that instead of preparing her 'main business' by realising these polite preparatory moves, she might have launched into medias res by saying 'Ich wollte nur fragen ob . . . ' ('I only wanted to ask if . . .'), a common procedure used by German students in German professors' office hours. On another interpretation, Amy has transferred her knowledge of how to behave as a student in a North American office hours setting, where complimenting their professors on their professional conduct is an option students frequently use ('I really like your class').

L initiates the interaction using three requestive routine formulas in sequence (lines 1 and 2): ('Herein', 'Ja bitte nehmen Sie doch Platz', 'Was kann ich denn für Sie tun'), standard formulas in service encounters in many German administrative and public contexts. In the context of this university 'office hours' event, however, they are simply opening routines, impersonal rituals indexing already at this stage that L frames the encounter as one involving his professional competence alone and his non-awareness of the student as a person, just as a salesperson (normally) does not take cognisance of a customer as 'a person'. On the other hand, L's initial moves may count as an attempt to balance his quest for professional efficiency, competence and comprehensibility with a need to be polite and accommodating. Attempts to resolve the tension between these two motives are not uncommon in institutional environments (Thonus, 1999). This interpretation is also supported by L's assertion (during the interview) that he 'wanted to help the student come to the point'.

However, despite these professed 'collaborative ulterior motives', L effectively ignores his interlocutor's moves proceeding from his own interactional goal (Box B) immediately to his communicative plan (Box H) and its linguistic encoding (Box I) thus bypassing Amy's real input – a perfect example of procedural misunderstanding. True, and again indexing the institutionally induced balancing act, L does try to 'understand' (line 15) but he seems to merely verbalise this intention, since apart from some backchannel noises (line 19) he does not manage at all to align his responding moves in lines 22–25 and 27–30 to what Amy had asked him. Rather he elaborates on exam modalities in general but patently fails to address the student on a personal level, which means in effect that he fails to listen to what the student tries to tell him and what she 'wants from him'. In lines 3–6 Amy starts to prepare for her main move (a request for information which she manages to realise as late as line 33!), but since she is not helped on by her interactant at all, all her moves prior to line 33 can in fact be regarded as preparatory ones. After his opening routines, L keeps requesting information about Amy's 'business' in lines 7 and 8, lines 11 and 12, lines 14 and 15, and again in line 32 with increasing insistence (notice the upgrading particle 'dann' in line 32 'ja was soll ich denn DANN für Sie tun'), before proceeding to give her information she didn't need nor want to be given. Notice also the intensifying modal particle 'denn' which is an indicator of exasperation.

Amy's frustrated attempts to get her message through to her interactant do not make her produce an overtly negative emotional move until the very end of the interaction (line 36). But the overall emotional equilibrium and Amy's 'internal' emotional reaction (Box F) is strongly affected through the interaction. Amy's repeatedly thwarted attempts to make herself understood are evidence of this disequilibrium. L's emotive reaction is one of increasing overt impatience and frustration.

The misunderstanding event in Extract 2.1 cannot be located in any particular move or exchange, rather it is spread over the entire event (see Hinnenkamp, this volume, and descriptions of miscommunication sequences in Gumperz's work from a socio-interactive perspective). The differences in relevant knowledge representations (Box A), interactional goals (Box B) and choices of discourse strategies (Box G) as well as emotive-cognitive 'gut reactions' (Box F) widely diverge. Concretely, this divergence can be seen in the following particular instances: Amy's compliment (lines 4 and 5) followed by L's non-reciprocal move in lines 7 and 8; Amy's use of interpersonally active gambits (e.g. line 4: 'wissen Sie'; line 13: 'ich meine'; line 20: 'ich meine') and discourse strategies or supportive moves (e.g. cajolers, line 13: 'verstehn Sie', line 20: 'entschuldigen Sie') as compared to L's use of ideationally active supportive moves such as expanders (expanding on the topic chosen) in line 22–25, and topic introducers (line 8: 'ich muss Sie fragen').

The differences in relevant interpersonal and situational pragmatic knowledge (Box A) between the two interactants can now be specified. For L, the relevant discourse topic seems to be the transmission of information about an upcoming examination, for the student it is her anxiety and need to be reassured and put into a position where she can make a rational decision as to which exam form to take. Amy's attempts to introduce everyday (non-institutional) interactional norms emphasising the interpersonal function and preferring interpersonally active discourse mechanisms are pitted against L's emphasis of the cognitive-referential language function, which is given expression through using discourse devices focusing on 'message', 'content', or 'topic'.

L clearly acts within the constraints of the institution 'university'. His ascribed and accepted professional role as information-giver and information-eliciter informs all his turns – with the exception of his initial attempts at 'doing being polite', which may also be said to be part of professional communication in an academic context. The fact that he does not reciprocate the student's polite acts of greeting, complimenting, apologising are fully in line with his acceptance of his institutionally sanctioned role as provider of knowledge. Particularly revealing in this respect is L's last move (line 34: 'also ueber die FRAGEN kann ich Ihnen KEINE Auskunft geben . . .') which reveals his misunderstanding of Amy's interactional goal. We may hypothesise that he simply cannot imagine that a student – a foreigner to boot – does not know what type of exam a 'Klausur' is. He is unable to throw himself into another's mind. In terms of Blum-Kulka and Weizman's differentiation between 'individual-I-meaning' and 'collective-we-direction' of the interaction, Extract 2.1 is a good example of widely different individual-I-meanings leading to a non-existing collective-we-direction, or put differently, this lack of interpersonal alignment which characterises the interaction in this extract is evidence of participants' difference in perspective or intersubjectivity (Shea, 1994).

In the retrospective interview, L said that at first he did not understand what the student wanted from him, that he later began to believe the student being a foreigner did not know the difference between a 'Klausur' (a written final exam) and a 'Referat' (a term paper), and finally he came to think that the student simply wanted to pump him for the exam questions. Notice that L's assumptions about what the student wanted to see him about are exclusively concerned with the content of the seminar, never with the student as a person. It never strikes L that what the student really wanted from him had to do with guidance, reassurance and her need to combat her anxiety – a situation reminiscent of the incident described by Gumperz (1982a, pp. 135–136) where a black student who is (implicitly) seeking encouragement is left without any such support. L described his role in office hours sessions as dispenser of information on university regulations. Having the institutionally sanctioned power to gain and keep the floor in interactions with those who do not (yet) possess this information, he implied that he felt licensed to interrupt the student whenever the information flow was not progressing efficiently. L said he found it difficult to find out what Amy wanted because she did not express herself clearly. He fails to see that because he interrupts her as many as seven times (lines 7, 11, 14, 22, 27, 32) she is not given a chance to develop an uninterrupted train of thought. In his view, however, he does this 'um ihr zu helfen zum Punkt zu kommen (in order to help her come to the point)', i.e. he reframes his interruptions as an attempt to support his interactant through collaborative scaffolding. He commented on his non-reaction to the student's compliment saying that he had never heard a student compliment him before and he somehow thought it was not suitable ('finde ich irgendwie unpassend'). Apart from the revealing status consciousness in this utterance by a German university professor, the utterance can also be taken as confirming Holmes's (1988) and Miles's (1994) findings that compliment practices are preferred by female speakers, who – in contradistinction to Brown and Levinson's view of compliments as threats to H's negative face – interpret and use compliments as a solidarity strategy.

Amy said she had intended to find out about the nature of the exam (a 'Klausur'), which she assumed might be different from what she was used to from her home university, simply because the course as such had also turned out to be different from an American seminar. She was aware of the fact that she somehow 'didn't get through to the professor', who had seemed impatient and actually made her more anxious about the exam than she had been before her visit to his office. She had not noticed that her interactant had failed to reciprocate and/or acknowledge her moves greet, identification and compliment in the opening phase of the interaction.

Taken together, discoursal preferences held by two interactants in Extract 2.1 are revealed to differ not only cross-culturally but are also clearly overlayed by an institutionally sanctioned asymmetrical role relationship between a German professor and an American exchange student. The institutionalised power merges with the 'power' of the native speaker, making the communicative styles diverge even more markedly. Gender may also have played a role in influencing preferences for the realisation of certain speech act types.

Extract 2.2: Making a request

Fiona, an American exchange student at Hamburg university, has gone to a university office to inquire about scholarships for her German boyfriend. She is talking to Frau Gleich, an administrative assistant.

```
01 FIONA:   Ich hab gehört Sie haben eine neue BROSCHÜRE über
02          Stipendien und ich meine so für ein Studium im Ausland also
03          in den USA zum Beispiel [und ich]
            $ I have heard there is a new BROCHURE about scholarships
            and I mean well for studying abroad for instance in the US
            and [I just]$
04 FRAU G:                      [ach du] meine Güte das geht ja nun
05          schon den GANZEN Tag so (0.1) die Leute kommen hier
06          rein und erm fragen nach dieser Broschüre die ich die wir neu
07          zusammengestellt haben=
            $oh my goodness ALL day (0.1) people come piling in here
            and erm are asking about this new brochure that I that we
            have newly put together and yes$
08 FIONA:          = {embarrassed}Ich also ich habe gehört wissen Sie (0.1)
09          [ich]
                              $I well I have heard you know (0.1)
            [I]$
10 FRAU G: [ja es] gehört ja zu meinem JOB sie rauszugebn (0.1) aber was
11          ich Ihnen sagen wollte es is so es waren so viele so sehr viele
12          aber ich muss Ihnen sagen erm jetzt sind sie ausgegangen
13          [und ja]
            $yes yes it is my JOB to hand them out (0.1) but what I wanted
            to tell you is it is like this there were so many so very many
            but I must tell you erm now they are all gone now and yes$
```

14 FIONA: [oh ja so]
          $oh I see$
15 FRAU G: [also geben] Sie mir doch NAME und ANSCHRIFT und wir
16   schicken Ihnen eine Kopie der Broschüre zu erm ich hatte ja
17   NIE gedacht dass die so nachgefragt war so VIELE Leute
18   kamen da=
          $give me NAME and ADDRESS and later we'll send you a
          copy of the brochure erm I had NEVER expected this brochure
          to be so much in demand and so MANY people came$
19 FIONA: ={in a friendly tone} oh ja Sie haben ja viel zu tun ja (0.1) mit
20   diesen vielen Fragen und wo Sie [jetzt ja keine]
          $ oh yes you have lots to do okay (0.1) with all those
          inquiries and now [where none]$
21 FRAU G: {impatient} [was ich Sie] GEFRAGT habe
22   ist ich ich wollte eigentlich jetzt Ihren NAMEN und Ihre
          ADRESSE (0.2) [fürs]
          $ what I have asked you is I I really wanted your name and
          your address (0.2) [for]$
23 FIONA: [ja erm] oh ich ich
24   {silently writes down her name and address}
          $[yes erm] oh I I$

The most striking phenomenon in Extract 2.2 is the extent to which interactants' awareness of the evolving interpersonal relationship varies. While Frau G seems to be totally unaware of the deterioration of the relationship between herself and her interlocutor, Fiona is highly conscious of it. This becomes first evident in line 8, where Fiona is acutely 'embarrassed' by her interlocutor's realisation of a series of acts of disclosure (lines 4–7) – her embarrassment is indexed by her tone of voice and the way she is stumbling into her turn. The 'system equilibrium index' shows a marked imbalance pointing to cumulative interactional trouble, which can be explained by reference to differences in the pragmatic knowledge representations (of relevant discourse topics, and of the situation on hand and its context-internal and context-external variables), differences in interactional goals and choices of discourse strategies (Boxes A, B and G) resulting in diverging emotive-cognitive 'gut reactions' (Box F). The strength of Fiona's emotional reaction is such that, in the interview, she did not refer to an institutionally enforced social role constellation or culturally conditioned differences as partly responsible for the misunderstanding, instead she suggested 'personality deficits' ('Persönlichkeitsdefizite') in her interactant (level 3 in Coupland et al., 1991).

Indications of differences in pragmatic knowledge representations between the two interactants are first of all the markedly different weighting given to interpersonally-oriented illocutions. The moves realised by Frau G (lines 4–7, 10–13, 15–18) are all referenced back to her own person, her own experiences, feelings, circumstances. Frau G's moves are therefore marked by an absence of illocutionary acts, gambits and discourse strategies, which are typical of the discourse type 'small talk' as characterised by Edmondson (1981) (such as sympathiser, inquiry-after-alter, phatic remarks, uptakers, cajolers, appealers and disarmers), and which serve to concatenate interactants' moves into a texture characterised by give-and-take, reciprocation and the exploitation of shared knowledge and common context.

Frau G also concentrates on ideational (information-oriented) as well as self-disclosing discourse strategies, e.g. topic-introducers (lines 10–11: 'was ich Ihnen sagen wollte es ist so'; line 12: 'aber ich muss Ihnen sagen'; line 21: 'was ich Sie GEFRAGT habe ist . . .') as well as expanders, i.e. strategies with which one elaborates and repeatedly expands on a chosen topic (lines 11–13, 17–18).

By contrast, Fiona makes at least one half-hearted attempt to realise a sympathiser, a clearly other-oriented move (lines 19–20) in order to link herself up with Frau G's preceding series of acts of complaining and as a 'way out' of her 'recipient-only'-role. She even manages to produce this sympathiser in a 'friendly tone', which is remarkable since it transpired in the interview that already at this stage of the discourse, she no longer felt any sympathy for her interactant ('da hab ich mich ja schon nur noch über sie gewundert und geärgert'). Fiona realises a number of supportive moves (grounders) to support her requests for information (lines 1–3, 8–9) and also produces interpersonally-oriented discourse markers or gambits such as cajolers (line 2: 'ich meine'; and line 8: 'wissen Sie') and appealers (line 19).

Frau G's assessment of the role relationship evolving in the course of this interaction and the nature of the situation (Box A) is such that she believes she is licensed to realise a highly direct request, a raw imperative (line 15) which is further upgraded by the particle 'doch'. This licence may stem from the type of authority an institution bestows even on its lowliest member. Further, Frau G seems to be so wrapped up in her own discourse world that she appears not to listen to her interlocutor whom she consequently interrupts several times (lines 4, 10, 15, 21). In line 21, for instance, Frau G reverts to her previous request (line 15), but in doing so she manages completely to ignore Fiona's immediately preceding move, one in which Fiona expressed sympathy and positive politeness for her. This interruptive behaviour can also be taken as an outcome of the kind of internalised institutional authority common in interactants who are 'not themselves' but representatives of some organisation.

Due to these interruptions, which never occur at points of transitional relevance such that alter's train of thought is brutally cut apart, Frau G's moves are then no longer aligned with the preceding moves realised by her interlocutor. In line 5, for instance, Frau G sidetracks the student's nascent request by launching into a (non-sequitur) complaint about the crowds of people coming into her office and asking about the brochure. In line 10 she grudgingly admits that it is in fact her job to deal with the type of request the student had just put to her. However, this disclosure functions more as a self-revelatory and self-addressed aside than an other-directed apology.

While the core or peak of the misunderstanding is to be found in lines 17–24, the entire interaction is building up to this peak. The interaction may therefore be taken as a stretched-out 'misunderstanding event'.

Frau G's rejection of Fiona's attempt to proceed with her request and keep the floor (resulting, in particular, in the patent non-concatenation of moves 3 and 4, and 8/9 and 10) may also be interpreted as a short-cut in the processing route of the discourse reception and production system. By ostensibly not listening and producing a non-sequitur, Frau G jumps directly from her own interactional goal (B) to her own immediate communicative plan (H) and its linguistic encoding (I), thus bypassing not only her interlocutor's real input but also any strategic consideration of her own (G). This short-cut amounts to a type of procedural misunderstanding characterised by a series of initiations rather than a pattern of initiations and replies or responses. In other words, there is no 'real' interaction going on, in that Frau G stays, so to speak, 'within herself' ignoring the reality of alter's contributions to the discourse, a behaviour not only reminiscent of the psychopathology of talk, but also evoking Lévinas's claim of the self-centredness of communication. Such a behaviour is often displayed by somebody whose face is not at stake, because the self can hide behind an institutional role. As a result of this 'split', the individual-I-meanings in Extract 2.2 diverge so drastically that they prevent any development of a collective-we-direction.

In the post-hoc interview, Fiona said that she had gained the impression that she was reduced to a sounding board and at the end, when she tried to say something nice and 'got criticised for it', she felt as though she had been slapped in the face. In Fiona's interpretation, Frau G not only refused to pick up her offer of reciprocated 'friendly talk', but also put her down in a rude way. Fiona said she had sensed a strange disequilibrium of rights and privileges – the power invested in Frau G as a member of an institution – for which she had not been prepared. When Frau G talked about her own situation at length, Fiona, had thought of one way out of this situation, namely to commiserate with Frau G and express her sympathy. Why this move turned out to be so singularly unwelcome was incomprehensible to her, and it also partially explains her emotional reaction at the end of the interaction where she is effectively silenced and withdraws from the interaction.

Frau G stated that she had thought the student simply ignored her request to leave her name and instead distracted her by talking about something else, something 'personal'. She assumed that the student, a foreigner, had not understood her properly. Judging from the interview I conducted with Fiona, it was, however, quite clear that Fiona's linguistic competence was such that she was able to follow and respond to all of Frau G's moves.

In Extracts 2.1 and 2.2 foreign students interacted with representatives of the institution 'university'. By way of contrast, I will now present in Extract 2.3 an interaction between a foreign student and a German student.

Extract 2.3: Too much rice

Brian, an American student spending a year in Germany, has cooked a
meal for Andi, a German friend, who has recently helped him with his
German seminar paper. Brian and Andi have met several times before,
both in class and at social get-togethers. Andi has just arrived.

01 BRIAN: hallo Andi wie geht's?
          $hallo Andi how are you?$
02 ANDI: ja prima oh prima doch ja;
          $yeah fine oh fine really yeah$
03 BRIAN: so (0.1) es is alles fertig jetzt (0.1) ich hoffe es schmeckt dir gut
          (0.3) ich hab es selber gekocht [so weil]
          $so (0.1) everything's ready now (0.1) I hope you like it I have
          cooked it myself [so because]$
04 ANDI: [ja prima]
                                    $[yeah fine]$
05 BRIAN: isst man bei uns im Süden
          $that's what we eat in the South$
06 ANDI: {in a loud voice}aber das is ja so VIEL das is ja VIEL ZU VIEL
07   Reis
          $but that's so much that is FAR TOO MUCH rice$
08 BRIAN: das MACHT doch nichts (0.1) ich hab es ja bezahlt und ich hab
09   dich EINgeladen (.) [du hast]
          $that doesn't MATTER (0.1) I have paid for it and I have
          INVITED [you have]$
10 ANDI: [nein das] MACHT DOCH was DOCH
11   DOCH denk doch an die armen vielen hungernden Menschen
12   die sowas gern essen wuerden [also ich]
          $[no it] DOES MATTER it does IT DOES think of the many
          poor people who go hungry and would like to eat something
          like that   [well I]$
13 BRIAN: [ich ich]
14   glaube ich (0.1) ich [finde]
                                $[I I]$
          believe I (0.1) I [I find]$
15 ANDI: [ich finde] man sollte in dieser gemeinsamen
16   Welt in der wir alle doch leben (0.2) der Welt in der wir alle so
17   UNgleich mit materiellen Gütern ausgestattet sind sollten wir
18   uns   zumindest   in   kleinem   Maßstab   bemühen   keine
19   Verschwendung keine unnütze Ver[schwendung]
          $[I find] one should in this common world where we do all live
          (0.2) in which we are all endowed with material goods so
          UNequally we should at least in small scale try to produce no
          waste no useless [waste]$

20 BRIAN: [also Andi] ich bin nicht ich
21   (0.2) [glaube nicht]
                            $[well Andi] I am not I (0.2) [don't believe]$
22 ANDI: [keine Ver]schwendung zu produzieren und immer in unserem
23   Bewußtsein daran zu denken daß wir in der reichen westlichen
24   Welt etc. etc. {monologue continues for 1.5 minutes}
           $[no waste] to produce and always in our consciousness to think
           that we in the rich western world etc. etc.$

Extract 2.3 is a case of 'cross-talk', of misunderstanding emerging because of different communicative styles. The monologous and monothematic nature of the discourse is marked. Ample use is made by Andi of the supportive move type 'expander' (expanding information) in order to keep a particular topic in play. As a result of this one gains the impression that it is one participant who clearly 'hogs' the topic (Andi), with the other's (Brian's) two attempts (see lines 13/14 and 20/21) to gain the floor being overrun. Marked also is the non-reciprocity of the 'how-are-you move' in line 2, and the non-concatenation of lines 5 and 6. The move in line 5 is clearly a ritual move characteristic of a conversational opening phase or phatic talk in general, which would conventionally (in certain Anglophone discourse types) be coupled with either a follow-up request for information or another remark thematically linking turn 6 with turn 5, opening up a chain of sequentially relevant moves as contiguous replies in Goffman's sense. By contrast, what happens in turn 6 is an abrupt topic switch in the form of a complaint followed by a request in lines 11/12, with both these speech acts being produced at high levels of directness (for 'directness levels' see Blum-Kulka *et al.*, 1989; House, 1979; House and Kasper, 1981).

In terms of the discourse processing model, we can first of all state that the misunderstanding event revealed in the analysis and the retrospection is both conceptually based and procedural in nature. It seems to result from differences in the pragmatic knowledge base, interactional goals and choice of discourse strategies (Boxes A, B, G) but also from a process-internal short-cut. Andi and Brian have different conceptions of communicative conventions holding in a ritualised conversational opening phase, of the topics appropriate for a particular discourse event, a dinner table conversation, and of the appropriateness of turn allotment and floor holding during that event. Following Goffman, this difference is often analysed as 'frame conflict', e.g. by Gumperz (1992) or Tyler (1995). The moves produced by Andi thus strike Brian in their differentness as offensively self-oriented and preoccupied with a particular topic relentlessly, self-servingly and monologically pursued. Further, we may interpret Andi's rejection of Brian's attempts to gain the floor as a short-cut in the processsing route. By ostensibly not listening to Brian, Andi jumps directly from his own interactional goal (Box B) to an immediate communicative plan (Box H) and its linguistic encoding, thus bypassing not only his interlocutor's real input but also any strategic considerations of his own. This creates, in Goffman's (1981) terms, non-alignment, since Andi often produces neither a response nor a reply; he simply initiates. The individual-I-meanings seem to be widely divergent in this stretch of talk, a collective-we-direction is not discernible.

In the retrospective interview, Brian said that, in his role as host, he felt unpleasantly 'talked at' by his friend, who in his view acted like a 'know-all' teacher figure. He was disappointed that his friend did nothing to keep a 'real conversation' going. This, he said, happened to him quite often, i.e. in interactions with German friends he often felt that they did not want to, or were unable to, engage in 'harmless' small talk. It did not surprise him that there wasn't even a word in German for 'small talk'. He had got the impression that it often happened in German conversations that the topic was more important than the human beings discussing it, and that discussions therefore often turned out to be serious, 'deep', controversial. He thought there was often some sort of 'pressure' to talk about something important and weighty, 'even' with students. In informal social talk, such as Extract 2.3, he said that 'Americans prefer to engage in friendly chit chat', i.e. collaborative phatic talk wishing to establish common ground as a talking procedure. The German line of talk, he suggested, was rather to separate oneself from one's interlocutor as one gets 'sucked up by the theme of the conversation' (see Byrnes, 1986 and Watts, 1989, whose findings confirm this view).

It is interesting to note that Brian, despite these comments on what he thought were differences in German and American communicative norms, was nevertheless, in the concrete performance of this conversation, quite unable to apply this 'knowledge' in order to foster understanding and retain his emotional equilibrium. Rather he let himself be overcome by a sense of misunderstanding, he felt sad and disappointed and even 'took a dislike' to Andi, to whom he imputed inconsiderateness and 'selfishness' – and this despite the fact that this same Andi had 'selflessly' helped him before with his German essays, which, of course, also gave Andi the opportunity to display his competence.

Andi, on the other hand, said he thought they had an interesting discussion ('eine interessante Diskussion'). He said he was often surprised that Americans had a different outlook on the resources available in different countries and that this kind of 'overly generous' handling of the resources was also reflected in their often irresponsible behaviour vis-à-vis food and possessions. He was surprised that Brian had said so little and suspected that he was not interested in the topic.

The importance of emotion comes into play by Brian's feelings of being 'talked at', his disappointment, sadness and anger, all of which Brian attributed to Andi as a person, not to his culturally shaped communicative style (see Gumperz e.g. 1992 who demonstrates that cross-culturally divergent styles often result in negative attribution). The emotive-cognitive gut reaction (Box F) is strikingly negative for one of the conversationalists, with the 'system equilibrium index' indicating a strong disturbance of his equilibrium.

As concerns interactants' awareness of the existence and the causes of the emotional 'disturbance' resulting from the nature of the interaction in Extract 2.3, the retrospective comments clearly reveal that Andi lacks this awareness. It is only Brian who is acutely aware of how emotionally upset he is. At the same time, however, he is unable to 'proceduralise' his intuitions about how he and his friend differ in terms of internalised conventions holding for a particular discourse event. In the retrospective interview he never mentions the possibility that he and Andi may have acted upon divergent and conflicting expectations of how to socialise during a dinner invitation (see also Watts, 1989, for a similar point), and that these created different constraints for them in this particular activity type.

Having looked at two exemplars of institutional discourse and, by way of comparison, at one interpersonal encounter in some detail, we are now in a position to attempt some tentative conclusions.

Some explanatory hypotheses

With reference to the discourse processing model, we might say that the misunderstandings in Extracts 2.1, 2.2 and 2.3 derive essentially from incommensurable representations in Boxes A, B and D leading to negative gut reactions in F. The negative emotional reaction is, in a sense, unavoidable if we follow Jaszczolt's (1996) view that each interactant has the freedom to create assumptions and meanings and that emotions are liable to interfere with discourse interpretation. We may hypothesise that these interfering emotional states (Box F) are exacerbated by differences in institutionally prescribed status and cross-culturally variable communicative styles, which tend not to be diagnosed as such but rather as 'personal deficiencies and inadequacies' (cf. Coupland *et al.*'s, 1991, level 3, as well as Gumperz, 1982a and Thomas, 1983). In intercultural institutional interactions, then, speakers are apt (mentally) to redistribute their interlocutors' cognitive-emotive attributes and even, in a sense, 'create them anew' in the light of their own conventions. Put differently, it is through their 'self-centredness' that interactants gain the freedom to create their own assumptions. Given this freedom, the doors are wide open for misunderstanding which, in this interpretation (Jaszczolt, 1996, and above) appears to be a basically non-preventable part of intercultural interaction.

Taken together, the analyses of the three data extracts – both institutional and interpersonal ones – show that one important factor leading to misunderstandings seems to be the differential weighting given to the interpersonal functional component by German as opposed to Anglophone speakers. This difference is manifest in a greater focus on the ideational function of talk (Halliday, 1994), on the 'content' of the talk by German speakers

German speakers		Anglophone speakers
Directness	<------------------>	Indirectness
Orientation towards self	<------------------>	Orientation towards other
Orientation towards content	<------------------>	Orientation towards addressees
Explicitness	<------------------>	Implicitness

Figure 2.2   German and Anglophone speakers' contrasting discourse behaviour

(indexed by the use of particular linguistic devices, e.g. discourse markers and strategies, or a preference for a monothematic trajectory of discourse) as opposed to a more other-oriented discourse behaviour on the part of Anglophone speakers, evidenced, for instance, in the use of highly conventionalised reciprocal routines such the 'how-are-you move', interpersonally active discourse strategies such as disarmers, and a dialogic line of discourse.

In order to attempt some sort of 'deeper' explanation, one may invoke the results of contrastive German–English discourse analyses according to which German speakers tend to interact in both institutional and interpersonal discourse events in ways that can be described as more direct, more explicit, more self-referenced and more content oriented than Anglophone speakers in comparable events. This pattern of communicative preferences in different discourse events, which emerges from a series of German–English contrastive pragmatic and discourse analyses (summary in House, 1996), can be displayed along the dimensions shown in Figure 2.2.

The validity of the hypothesised dimensions in Figure 2.2 is supported by a number of German–English discourse analyses conducted in different communities of practice (Agar, 1992; Byrnes, 1986; Clyne, 1987; House, 1997; Kotthoff, 1989, 1994; Luchtenberg, 1994; Watts, 1989). They all point to similar differences in communicative preferences and styles.

Now, if we relate the hypothesised dimensional preferences to the differences in interactional discourse behaviour found in the three data extracts presented above, we can see that the dimensions may serve as explanatory hypotheses for these findings. In other words, interactants' discourse behaviour may be explained with reference to the operation of different empirically established communicative preferences displayed as a set of dimensions of variable discourse conventions.

It is however important to emphasise two points. First, we are here not dealing with clear-cut dichotomies. Rather, oppositions such as 'directness versus indirectness' represent end-points on different clines. The second point relates to the legitimacy of trying to relate misunderstanding events to culturally shaped discourse conventions phenomena. There seems to be some justification in trying to describe culturally influenced discourse behaviour from dialectically linked etic (culturally distant) and emic (culturally intrinsic) perspectives (see Hymes, 1996, for more detailed argumentation) – a procedure I tried to implement in my analyses. Further, as Ramathan and Atkinson (1999, p. 51) have pointed out, linking 'culture' to concepts like 'discourse' clearly reduces the risk of ethnic and national stereotyping through prescribed difference because the focus in a pragmatic-discourse approach is on particular social groups and particular individuals displaying patterned, cohesive verbal actions.

Returning to a discussion of German and Anglophone conventionalised discourse behaviour, we might hypothesise that Gricean maxims taken as rough guidelines of how speakers act in communicative interchanges are likely to be interpreted differentially in German and Anglophone contexts: The trend towards explicit verbalisation of content in German discoursal context has obvious repercussions for the quantity and relevance of talk, i.e. contributions of the German interlocutors in Extracts 2.1, 2.2 and 2.3 may appear more informative and less 'relevant' than is required from an Anglo-American point of view. Robin Lakoff (1990) has juxtaposed principles of informativeness with those of rapport, i.e. an orientation towards content versus an interpersonal orientation. In German–English intercultural institutional interactions, the tendency towards weighting the one differently from the other may have been partially responsible for the misunderstandings taking their course, and the emotional upsets and negative 'gut reactions'. Despite their non-empirical basis and thus untested generality, Lakoff's three politeness principles (don't impose; give options; make your hearer feel good) may also be adduced here. They seem to be given differential importance by native German and American interactants in the three data extracts, exacerbated, as we have seen, in Extracts 2.1 and 2.2 by institutionally determined discourse behaviour.

We may still want to ask why these tendencies in communicative choice should have come to be operative. For such a deeper explanation, it is necessary to link up differences in discourse styles with a richer macro-context of historical, political, philosophical and ideological developments, with legal and educational systems and other cultural practices, in order to examine how discourse patterns are anchored in cultural experiences in the sense of Sperber's (1996) socio-cognitive theory of culture. We would have to ask why it should be the case that in many discourse events in one culture, transactional language use (which is primarily message and topic oriented) tends to be valued differently from interactional language use, i.e. why, in Hallidayan terms, the ideational language function seems to be valued differently in one speech community's conventions of oral and written communicative practice at the expense of the interpersonal one.

In my own work, I started from a series of detailed pragmalinguistic analyses of spoken and written German and English discourse specimens and translations in both directions. These analyses have provided converging evidence for assuming certain German and English discoursal preferences, from which in turn I hypothesised differences in cultural conventions. In doing this, I implicitly support the view that language use is linked to culture and 'thinking for speaking' – a weak version of the linguistic relativity hypothesis in the sense of Slobin (2000). Tentative explanations of the roots of some of the German cultural preferences noticeable in the three extracts may point, inter alia, to an educational system that has traditionally placed greater emphasis on the transmission of content than on social skills. The result of this might be a dispreference of 'impression management' and the particular brand of an Anglo-American 'etiquette of simulation', where rules of verbal behaviour ('one must sound as if one meant it' when expressing thanks, apologies, compliments and other 'facelifts') are implicitly handed down from generation to generation. Other sources of communicative preferences include the legal system (negotiable case law versus prefixed statutes, Legrand, 1996) and predominant ideologies, which, as van Dijk has emphasised, may 'allow people, as group members, to organize the multitude of social beliefs . . . and act accordingly' (1998, p. 8).

Linking discourse behaviour to cultural practices in a community is, of course, at present speculative at best. What is clearly needed is inter-disciplinary research into this complex area. Such research seems to me a socially and ethically important supplement for localised micro-analyses of discourse.

Conclusion

I have suggested in this chapter that intercultural university encounters may be fruitfully analysed on the basis of a cognitive discourse processing model, which integrates different approaches in a transdisciplinary manner. A small number of authentic institutional and interpersonal dyadic interactions triangulated with interactants' subjective theories were analysed on the basis of this model. The hypothesis was put forward that the results of relevant contrastive pragmatic analyses may help to explain why misunderstanding occurs. It was suggested that a set of empirically derived dimensions of discoursal differences may be taken as guidelines to understanding some of the underlying reasons for the often emotionally charged nature of mis-understanding events in both intercultural and institutional interactions. The analysis also revealed that institutional constraints strongly influence the nature of encounters which take place in an institutional setting such as the university, producing tensions in interactants' discourse behaviour, which in turn interact with and exacerbate culturally conditioned discoursal differences.

The question of whether differences in cultural practices lead to unavoidable misunderstandings must be answered in a differentiated way. None of the types of misunderstanding (conceptual, procedural and language based) revealed in the above analyses can be completely avoided. It is only 'strategic misunderstanding' to do with lying, pretending, deceiving in a deliberate way, which can clearly be avoided. As concerns other misunderstanding events, it seems always possible simply to acquire more knowledge about one's interlocutor, about the institutional context and about discoursal preferences. Such knowledge can be shared in order to increase an awareness of the consequences of acting out one's own discourse style in ways that might give offence to one's interlocutor. For the extension of knowledge we need transdisciplinary work informing in-depth analyses of authentic intercultural interactions in different institutions and genres as well as introspective approaches, in which interactants' own voices are heard and related to relevant discourse practices. But knowledge is not enough, given the nature of language and communication and the nature of human beings. On the basis of the results of the sample analyses presented in this chapter and in line with Dascal's (1999) emphasis on the ethical aspect of misunderstanding, it might be suggested that one way of avoiding misunderstanding is to have (or acquire?) an 'openness of mind' and to give one's interlocutor a chance to understand before allowing misunderstanding to run its full course. To put it differently, participants in discourse might be well advised to start from the assumption that misunderstandings will occur despite increased knowledge of activity types in different institutional settings and discoursal conventions, simply because meaning is never laid out clean and neat but must be inferred, with inferences tending to be quick, automatic and fixed when they really need to be careful, considerate and 'revisable'. What interlocutors therefore might most need if they want to counteract the damaging personal recriminations and emotional scars suffered in many misunderstanding events, is not only what Janney and Arndt (1992) have so aptly called 'intercultural tact', but also some kind of 'revision mentality' with regard to the interpretation of intercultural institutional discourse. Just as rewriting is beneficial in written discourse, so might revising be helpful in spoken discourse if it is coupled with a flexible moving from micro to macro perspectives, keeping things in abeyance as far as possible and avoiding premature judging or prejudice.

Appendix

Transcription conventions

CAPITALS emphatic stress
[ ]   overlapping text
$ $ translation of the German original
(0.5)   pause of indicated length
=   latching, i.e. two utterances run together with no pause
{ }   descriptive comment.

References

Agar, M. (1992). Review of Werner Holly 1990. Politikersprache. In *Language in Society*, 21, 158–160.

Barron, A. (2002). *Acquisition in interlanguage pragmatics: Learning how to do things with words in a study abroad context*. Amsterdam: Benjamins.

Besnier, N. (1990). *Language and affect*. In *Annual Review of Anthropology*, 19, 419–451.

Bloch, C. (1996). Emotions and discourse. In *Text*, 16, 323–341.

Blum-Kulka, S. (1987). Indirectness and politeness in requests: Same or different? In *Journal of Pragmatics*, 11, 145–160.

Blum-Kulka, S. and Weizman, E. (1988). The inevitability of misunderstanding: Discourse ambiguities. In *Text*, 8, 219–241.

Blum-Kulka, S. and Weizman, E. (this volume). Misunderstandings in political interviews.

Blum-Kulka, S., House, J. and Kasper, G. (eds) (1989). *Cross-cultural pragmatics: Requests and apologies*. Norwood, NJ: Ablex.

Britton, B. K. and Graesser, A. C. (eds) (1995). *Models of text understanding*. Hilldale, NJ: Erlbaum.

Brown, P. and Levinson, S. (1987). *Politeness. Some universals in language usage*. Cambridge: Cambridge University Press.

Burgoon, J. K., Stern, L. A. and Dillman, L. (1995). *Interpersonal adaptation patterns*. Cambridge: Cambridge University Press.

Byrnes, H. (1986). Interactional style in German and English conversations. In *Text*, 6, 89–206.

Caffi, C. and Janney, R. (1994). Toward a pragmatics of emotive communication. In *Journal of Pragmatics*, 22, 325–373.

Clyne, M. (1987). Cultural differences in the organization of academic texts. English and German. In *Journal of Pragmatics*, 11, 211–247.

Coupland, N., Wiemann, J. M. and Giles, H. (eds) (1991). *'Miscommunication' and problematic talk*. London: Sage

Damasio, A. (1999). *The feeling of what happens: Body and emotion in the making of consciousness*. New York: Harcourt Brace.

Dascal, M. (1985). The relevance of misunderstanding. In M. Dascal (ed.), *Dialogue: An interdisciplinary approach*. Amsterdam: John Benjamins, 441–459.

Dascal, M. (1999). Introduction: Some questions about misunderstanding. In *Journal of Pragmatics*, 31, 753–762.

Dechert, W. and Raupach, M. (eds) (1989). *Transfer in language productions*. Norwood, NJ: Ablex.

Edmondson, W. J. (1981). *Spoken discourse. A model for analysis*. London: Longman.

Edmondson, W. J. (1987). 'Acquisition' and 'learning': The discourse system integration hypothesis. In W. Lörscher and R. Schulze (eds), *Perspectives on language in performance*. Tübingen: Narr, 1070–1089.

Edmondson, W. J. (1989). Discourse production, routines, and language learning. In B. Kettemann, P. Bierbaumer, A. Fill and A. Karpf (eds), *Englisch als Zweitsprache*. Tübingen: Narr, 287–302.

Ehrman, M. (1993). Ego boundaries revisited: Toward a model of personality and learning. In J. Alatis (ed.), *Georgetown University Round Table on languages and linguistics. Strategic interaction and language acquisition*. Washington, DC: Georgetown University Press, 330–362.

Fraser, B. (1990). Perspectives on politeness. In *Journal of Pragmatics*, 14, 219–236.

Goffman, E. (1974). *Frame analysis*. New York: Harper & Row.

Goffman, E. (1981). *Forms of talk*. Oxford: Blackwell.

Gumperz, J. (1982a). *Discourse strategies*. Cambridge: Cambridge University Press.

Gumperz, J. (1982b). *Language and social identity*. Cambridge: Cambridge University Press.

Gumperz, J. (1992). Contextualization and understanding. In A. Duranti and C. Goodwin (eds), *Rethinking context. Language as an interactive phenomenon*. Cambridge: Cambridge University Press, 229–252.

Halliday, M. A. K. (1990). New ways of meaning: A challenge to applied linguistics. In *Journal of Applied Linguistics*, 6, 7–36.

Halliday, M. A. K. (1994). *An introduction to functional grammar* (2nd edn). London: Arnold.

Heckhausen, H. and Beckmann, J. (1990). Intentional action and action slips. In *Psychological Review*, 97, 36–48.

Hinnenkamp, V. (this volume). Misunderstanding: Interactional structure and strategic resources.

Holmes, J. (1988). Paying compliments: A sex-preferential positive politeness strategy. In *Journal of Pragmatics*, 12, 445–465.

House, J. (1979). Interaktionsnormen in deutschen und englischen Alltagsdialogen. In *Linguistische Berichte*, 59, 76–90.

House, J. (1986). Cross-cultural pragmatics and foreign language teaching. In Seminar für Sprachlehrforschung (ed.), *Probleme und Perspektiven der Sprachlehrforschung*. Frankfurt: Scriptor, 281–295.

House, J. (1993). Toward a model for the analysis of inappropriate responses in native/non-native interactions. In S. Blum-Kulka and G. Kasper (eds), *Interlanguage pragmatics*. New York: Oxford University Press, 163–184.

House, J. (1996). Contrastive discourse analysis and misunderstanding: The case of German and English. In M. Hellinger and U. Ammon (eds), *Contrastive sociolinguistics*. Berlin: Mouton, 345–361.

House, J. (1997). *Translation quality assessment. A model revisited.* Tübingen: Narr.

House, J. (1998). Politeness and translation. In L. Hickey (ed.), *The pragmatics of translation.* Clevedon: Multilingual Matters, 54–71.

House, J. (2000). Understanding misunderstanding: A pragmatic-discourse approach to analysing mismanaged rapport in talk across cultures. In H. Spencer-Oatey (ed.), *Culturally speaking: Managing rapport through talk across cultures.* London: Continuum. 145–164.

House, J. (in press). Politeness in Germany. In L. Hickey and M. Stewart (eds), *Politeness in Europe.* Clevedon: Multilingual Matters.

House, J. and Kasper, G. (1981). Politeness markers in English and German. In F. Coulmas (ed.), *Conversational routine.* The Hague: Mouton, 157–185.

Hymes, D. (1996). *Ethnography, linguistics, narrative inequality. Toward an understanding of voice.* London: Taylor & Francis.

Janney, R. W. and Arndt, H. (1992). Intracultural tact versus intercultural tact. In R. Watts, S. Ide and K. Ehlich (eds), *Politeness in language.* Berlin: Mouton de Gruyter, 21–41.

Jaszczolt, K. (1996). Relevance and infinity: Implications for discourse interpretation. In *Journal of Pragmatics*, 25, 703–722.

Kasper, G. (1990). Linguistic politeness: Current research issues. In *Journal of Pragmatics*, 14, 193–228.

Kasper, G. and Blum-Kulka, S. (eds) (1993). *Interlanguage pragmatics.* New York: Oxford University Press.

Kintsch, W. (1988). The role of knowledge in discourse comprehension: a construction–integration model. In *Psychological Review*, 95, 163–182.

Kintsch, W. (1998). *Comprehension: A paradigm for cognition.* Cambridge: Cambridge University Press.

Kotthoff, H. (1989). *Pro und Kontra in der Fremdsprache.* Frankfurt: Lang.

Kotthoff, H. (1993). Disagreement and concession in disputes: On the context sensitivity of preference structures. In *Language in Society*, 22, 193–216.

Kotthoff, H. (1994). Zur Rolle der Konversationsanalyse in der interkulturellen Kommunikation. In *Zeitschrift für Linguistik und Literaturwissenschaft*, 93, 75–96.

Lakoff, R. (1990). *Talking power.* New York: Basic Books.

Langer, E. (1989). *Mindfulness.* Reading, MA: Addison-Wesley.

Ledoux, J. (1996). *The emotional brain.* New York: Simon & Schuster.

Leech, G. (1983). *Principles of pragmatics.* London: Longman.

Legrand, P. (1996). European legal systems are not converging. In *International and Comparative Law Quarterly*, 45, 52–81.

Levelt, W. J. M. (1989). *Speaking: From intention to articulation.* Cambridge, MA: MIT Press.

Lévinas, E. (1961). *Totalité et infini.* The Hague: Nijhoff.

Luchtenberg, S. (1994). A friendly voice to help you vs working through your manual: Pragmatic differences between American and German software manuals. In *Journal of Pragmatics*, 21, 315–319.

Markovà, I., Graumann, C. and Foppa, K. (eds) (1995). *Mutualities in dialogue.* Cambridge: Cambridge University Press.

Miall, D. (1995). Anticipation and feeling in literary response: A neuropsychological view. In *Poetics*, 23, 275–298.

Miles, P. (1994). Compliments and gender. *University of Hawai'i Occasional Papers*, 26, 85–137.

Möhl, S. (1996). Alltagssituationen im interkulturellen Vergleich: Realisierung von Kritik und Ablehnung im Deutschen und Englischen. MA thesis, University of Hamburg.

Niemeier, S. and Dirven, R. (eds) (1997). *The language of emotion*. Amsterdam: John Benjamins.

Ochs, E. (ed.) (1989). The pragmatics of affect. Special issue of *Text*, 9 (1).

Ramathan, V. and Atkinson, D. (1999). Ethnographic approaches and methods in L2 writing research: A critical guide and review. In *Applied Linguistics*, 20, 44–70.

Searle, J. (1983). *Intentionality*. Cambridge: Cambridge University Press.

Shea, D. (1994). Perspective and production: Structuring conversational participation across cultural boundaries. In *Pragmatics*, 4, 357–389.

Slobin, D. (2000). Verbalized events: A dynamic approach to linguistic relativity and determinism. In S. Niemeier and R. Dirven (eds), *Evidence for linguistic relativity*. Amsterdam: John Benjamins, 107–138.

Sperber, D. (1996). *Explaining culture*. Oxford: Blackwell.

Tannen, D. (1979). What's in a frame. In R. Freedle (ed.), *New directions in discourse processing*. Norwood, NJ: Ablex, 137–181.

Tannen, D. (1993). *Framing in discourse*. Oxford: Oxford University Press.

Thomas, J. (1983). Cross-cultural pragmatic failure. In *Applied Linguistics*, 4, 91–112.

Thonus, T. (1999). How to communicate politely and be a tutor, too: NS-NNS interaction and writing center practice. In *Text*, 19, 253–280.

Tyler, A. (1995). The coconstruction of cross-cultural miscommunication. In *Studies in Second Language Acquisition*, 17, 129–152.

van Dijk, T. (1998). *Ideology: A multidisciplinary approach*. London: Sage.

Watts, R. J. (1989). Relevance and relational work: Linguistic politeness as politic behavior. In *Multilingua*, 8, 131–166.

3

Misunderstandings: Interactional structure and strategic resources

Volker Hinnenkamp

If people who do not understand each other at least understand that they do not understand each other, then they understand each other better than when, not understanding each other, they do not even understand that they do not understand each other.

(Gustav Ichheiser 1949)

Misunderstanding is . . . a matter of degree.

(Jan Smedslund 1990)

Introduction: Misunderstanding as common sense category

Misunderstandings play an eminent role in everyday conversational conduct. Not only do we continuously misunderstand each other, but we also use dozens of routine constructions which give expression to our alertness vis-à-vis misunderstandings by their occurrence, their threatening potential, the damage they cause, and our endeavours to avoid or resolve them by either settling or simply removing them.[1]

The understanding of misunderstanding as serving as a 'strategic resource' may well be read in a double sense: first, as a particular kind of strategic exploitation of misunderstanding by participants in a conversational exchange; and second, in the sense of the notion of misunderstanding being strategically exploited by researchers as a passepartout outcome and as the raison d'être of intercultural communication research. My focus, however, will be on misunderstandings in general; that is, intercultural encounters will not be given prevalence. Essentially, this chapter is on method, on the methodical ways of misunderstanding – whether intercultural or intracultural. Writing as an interpretively and interactionlly orientated sociolinguist, my findings and reasoning will be strictly data-based, which means looking at and analysing what transpires as misunderstanding in talk-in-interaction. My database draws primarily on transcriptions, using about one hundred everyday conversational exchanges with some examples from university and other institutional settings. The bulk of my data is made up by my own audio- and video-recordings. However, conversations recorded and transcribed by others also serve as illustrating material.

Misunderstanding and intercultural communication

In linguistic pragmatics, misunderstandings have been subject to scrutiny particularly in the field of intercultural communication. Misunderstanding and more generally miscommunication seem to have become one of the most salient characteristics of this kind of communication (see Hinnenkamp, 1995). Mentions of 'misunderstanding' abound, and the analysis of its intrinsic dangers as well as its prevention or resolution into untroubled communicative harmony seem to have become the raison d'être of intercultural communication studies. Misunderstandings lurk in all kinds of intercultural communications, in international business as much as in international political relations. The former may lead to the loss of a good business deal, the latter to diplomatic crises or even war. Likewise in inter-ethnic minority–majority encounters, misunderstanding may lead to (additional) discrimination and disadvantages concerning allocation of work, housing, health and civil rights. These aspects have been shown particularly by the works of Gumperz and other researchers of intercultural, inter-ethnic and inter-racial communication.[2] Also native speaker–nonnative speakers' discursive endeavours are from an interlanguage pragmatist's perspective heavily determined by struggles with misunderstandings.[3] Although the literature on intercultural communication often focuses on misunderstandings, there are thus few if any critical reflections on the notion of misunderstanding itself. Misunderstanding and intercultural communication have become a mutually supporting couple. Such a coupling is well documented.[4]

Research questions

Four main questions seem to me to emanate from the paramount concern with misunderstanding. The first one is simply (1) 'What is a misunderstanding?' Admittedly, this seems trivial. Because we continuously experience misunderstandings, we even call them by their names: 'That was a misunderstanding.' or 'You must have misunderstood me there.'[5] Yet misunderstanding seems to have remained a lay, i.e. pre-theoretical category, transferred into linguistics and discourse studies without having been defined.

The second question to be answered is (2) 'How can we as observers know if, how and when people misunderstand?' That is, we clearly need criteria for misunderstanding, and we may combine this question with (1). Furthermore, we must be able to find observable criteria independent of lay concerns.

In view of the above-mentioned coupling, we may also have to ask (3) 'What is the particular relationship between intercultural communication and misunderstanding?' What is it that attracts the two, makes them a couple in much of the intercultural and interlanguage communication studies?

Finally, we have to investigate the possible abuse of misunderstanding (4) 'What is the relationship between misunderstandings in general and parasitic ones in particular?'

Questions (1) and (2) will be addressed in the next two sections. Question (3) will receive some attention but will not be of main interest here (see Hinnenkamp, 2002). The last two sections will be fully dedicated to 'parasitic misunderstandings', first on a more theoretical level and then exemplified by a transcript.

Misunderstanding as a category in its own right

The notion of misunderstanding usually does not go beyond a common-sense understanding of the term. It is furthermore often used as a strictly moral category in that it figures as a disturbing factor in communication which has to be removed in order to guarantee or recover smooth conduct. Such an interpretation of 'misunderstanding' reflects on and contributes to the ethics and norms of what constitutes 'proper', i.e. undisturbed and 'clean' conversational conduct. It is here that many conceptualisers of misunderstanding meet with many of those of the intercultural communication camp. Such an interpretation of misunderstanding is based on an idealistic view of language and communication, devoid of ambivalence and fuzziness. Thus, misunderstanding, trouble, breakdown and miscommunication in general are either presented as contradictable, counterproductive and suboptimal choices within the alleged consensual objective of talk and interaction as a cooperative and agreement-based enterprise, or as something which is structurally intrinsic to particular categories of encounters and situational constellations beyond interactional dimensions such as intersubjectivity and negotiation.

Rarely do we come across studies on misunderstandings as (pragma-)linguistic phenomena *in their own right*.[6] Even rarer are attempts at grounding misunderstanding empirically.[7] An absolute rarity is a real-life perspective on dialogue beyond experimental and fictional settings.

In those studies which focus on concrete misunderstandings in human conduct, we mainly find two different kinds of outlook on the problem. One approach aims to track down the sources of and reasons for misunderstandings (e.g. Allwood and Abelar, 1989; Falkner, 1997), while the other approach attempts to identify the interactional structure of misunderstandings

(Humphrey-Jones, 1986). At least one reasoning complex is accepted by both: the role that ambiguity and indirectness, the difference between speech and intended meaning and, more generally, coherence and mutual knowledge (or rather their disturbance) play in human speech. Apart from these global foundations of misunderstanding, there are attempts at systematising the possible semantic and pragmatic bases of misunderstanding on a local speech or dialogue level. Dascal, for example, argues that 'a first step in analyzing misunderstanding is to identify the layer [of significance] in which it arises' (Dascal, 1985, p. 443), thereby aiming at a taxonomy of the semantic and pragmatic grounds for misunderstanding. The interactive layers, however, where a misunderstanding might possibly arise, are as manifold as there are layers to be found. A taxonomy does not account for the working and treatment of misunderstanding, but rather tries to objectify misunderstanding as something to be grasped as exterior to the participants who are involved in an interaction. It identifies misunderstanding without drawing on the identifying work of the (mis)accomplishers involved.

What we need is clearly a perspective capable of showing that misunderstanding 'is best viewed as an interactional stance, something that can be claimed and disputed or agreed upon, rather than as an objective phenomenon existing independently of participants' claims and noticings' (Bilmes, 1992, p. 96). 'Treating something as a misunderstanding, then, is as much an interpretive accomplishment of speaker-hearers as treating something as a joke or story' (Schwartz, 1977, quoted in Humphrey-Jones, 1986, p. 21). A misunderstanding in my view may well be an interpretive accomplishment, but it may also be simply a unilateral interpretive matter and even just a feeling. In the following, I intend to approach the problem of misunderstanding by trying to exploit the interactional structure of different types of misunderstandings.

The interactional structure of misunderstanding

Seven types of misunderstanding

There are basically seven different types of misunderstanding (MU 1 to MU 7). They range from what Linell (1995) calls 'overt misunderstanding' (MU 1 and MU 2) to 'latent' ones (as MU 6 and 7), with the 'covert' type in between (MU 3 to 5). Only the overt and covert ones will be of empirical interest here, for two simple reasons: (a) As empirical linguists, we have no access to completely covert misunderstandings because they do not show up on the linguistic surface. Only psychotherapists or the like may have access to them. (b) The second reason is strongly related to the first. The majority of misunderstandings are interactionally managed.[8] They are solved in one way or another and will only very rarely lead to a complete breakdown of communication. Although the intercultural literature is full of such serious – and sometimes fatal – cases of communication breakdowns (for aircraft crashes see Cushing, 1994), in observed and analysed face-to-face interactions this is hardly corroborated.

This does not imply that misunderstandings might not have grave negative effects in interpersonal encounters or that misunderstandings might not be rooted in mutually incompatible properties due to intercultural differences – on the contrary. But as these misunderstandings most often show up in face-to-face communications and are mostly tackled by interlocutors, it is so much more important to come to terms with what is called 'misunderstanding': to regard misunderstanding not as an accident of communication but as a resource, as a 'rich point' in communication (Agar, 1993, 1994). Let us now take a look at some basic types of misunderstanding.

MU 1

There is an immediate recognition of a misunderstanding, which is indicated by a repair at the next possible opportunity and is then followed by a return to the status quo ante (Extract 3.1).

Extract 3.1: Fristen[9]

1 s:	°Ja, jaja°, aber wär halt ent**fris**tet, das ist das Beruhigende, ne(?)
	(Yeah, but it would be un**lim**ited, I'd be at ease, you know)
2 h:	Befristet- [naja] (Limited- well)
3 s:	[**ENT**fri]stet (**UN**limited)
4 h:	**Entfristet? (Unlimited?)**
5 s:	**Entfristet, mhm (Unlimited, ya)**
6 h:	Und die äh Habil machste aber trotzdem weiter(?)
	(But you'll still carry on with your dissertation, though(?))

In Extract 3.1 the whole shaded block of lines 2 to 5 could be omitted and there would not be a trace left of a misunderstanding. The shaded block constitutes a kind of minor subdialogue consisting of a repair cycle. Line 2 can be regarded as the repairable, as an indication of a mishearing. In line 3 an immediate correction of the misunderstood item takes place, and lines 4 and 5 comprise the reassurance by the mishearer and the ratification of the correction by the corrector. The misunderstood item in line 2 is identified as such in the next line by being corrected and in addition made intonationally salient. Speaker S says '**ENT**fristet' in line 3, thus putting contrastive weight on the exact source of misunderstanding. Note that the misunderstanding is not identified as such by the wrong ratification of speaker H in line 2, but in the retrospective identification of the repair turn position in relation to the alleged repairable in line 3.[10] The occurrence of a misunderstanding is thus located in a *vertical* order of sequentiality.[11]

MU 1a

Extended variant: the misunderstood segment may be reconstructed by virtue of identifying or localising it as such and may even become specified by an explicit 'diagnosis' (i.e. an indication of the features of the problem in question) or 'anamnesis' (i.e. case history) of the misunderstanding's trajectory. Such explicit diagnoses could be formulations like 'I think we have a misunderstanding there', 'That's not what I meant' or 'I don't mean X, I mean Y' etc. A 'case history' we find in examples where explanations or accounts are given to explain why the misunderstanding occurred: 'That was metaphorically meant, not literally', 'You missed that point' or, also interculturally, 'That's the way we do it', etc.

MU 2

There is an immediate recognition of a misunderstanding, which is indicated by a repair at the next possible opportunity, but there is no return to the status quo ante. The misunderstanding itself becomes a resource of continuation.

MU 2a

Extended variant: the misunderstood segment may be reconstructed by virtue of identifying or localising it as such and may even become specified by an explicit 'diagnosis' or 'anamnesis' of the misunderstanding's trajectory. Note: the more extended the misunderstanding's trajectory, the less likely is a return to the status quo ante. Instead, a continuation based on the misunderstanding is more likely.

MU 3

There is a gradual recognition of a misunderstanding, which may be indicated by disturbances in the flow of the conversational course, by signs of incoherence, by detours or recyclings (repetitions, paraphrases, circumlocutions, 'talking down' effects), by unresponded repair initiations, by suddenly or gradually developing traces of verbal, non-verbal, or paralinguistic insecurity, or simply by the indication or registration of what Erickson and Shultz (1982) have called 'uncomfortable moments', until one interlocutor becomes aware that some kind of misunderstanding has occurred. What may follow is the further treatment as described in MU 1 and MU 2 (including their extensions). But note: the more distant the recognition of a misunderstanding, the more effort is required to repair it and the less likely there will be an easy return to the status quo ante. The more distant the recognition, the less probable is the exact localisation and identification of the site of misunderstanding, particularly when the misunderstanding has built up over an entire stretch of turn-by-turn development.

MU 4

There is a gradual recognition of a misunderstanding, which may be indicated by disturbances in the flow of the conversational course, in signs of incoherence, by detours or recyclings (repetitions, paraphrases, circumlocutions, 'talking down' effects), by unresponded repair initiations, by suddenly or gradually developing traces of verbal, non-verbal, or paralinguistic insecurity, or simply by the indication or registration of 'uncomfortable moments,' until the misunderstanding is somehow recognised but is *not* treated as described in MU 1 and MU 2. That is, the misunderstanding will *not* be clarified by way of a repair with reference to the misunderstanding's anamnesis. It will, however, be solved. In short, interlocutors will overcome the misunderstanding without ever getting to its roots. There is no trajectory of the misunderstanding to be reconstructed, but rather particular lost threads of discourse will be made to fit together. This, of course, is also a kind of repair. It is like solving a complex mathematical problem without comprehending the individual steps that led to the solution. Extract 3.2, which I have taken from Williams (1985, p. 170), demonstrates the last two kinds of misunderstandings.

Extract 3.2: Canvassing[12]

1	IT:	What sort of work are you going to do when you finish the course?
2	V:	A few weeks ago ah (+) the school send me to factory doing
3		canvassing (+) canvassing (+) for two weeks' experience and ah the
4		boss say give me a position, but (. . .) when I will finish the course
5		because I have learned to do some more job and cannot take it

| 6a | IT: | So you've been canvassing for work |

| 6b | IT: | and who said that they'd give you a job? |
| 7 | V: | The boss |

| 8 | IT: | The boss of who, of what? |
| 9 | V: | The boss of factory ((laughs)) |

| 10 | IT: | What was the factory? |
| 11 | V: | Canvassing |

12	IT:	Oh, is that the **name** of the factory?
13	V:	Oh (+) Joyce (+) Joyce furniture, I think
14	IT:	Oh (+) Joyce (+) [furn- (+) Joy?
15	V:	[Furniture

```
                16  v:  Joyce
                17a iт:  Joyce

                17b iт:  They make beds?
                18  v:  Yeah (+) yeah

           19 iт:  Is that the place?
           20 v:   Yeah

                21  iт:  The place in (+) in (+) down near Fremantle?
                22  v:   In West O'Connor
                23a iт:  O'Connor. Yeah, that's right. The place that makes
                        beds.

  23b iт:  So he will give
  24       you a job, will he?
```

Participants in this encounter are IT, a counsellor at the Australian
Commonwealth Employment Service, and the client V, a Vietnamese man,
who is enrolled in a job-finding training scheme. IT obviously misinterprets
V's 'doing canvassing' (lines 2–3). It is not taken as the description of the
kind of work carried out in the factory, but is demonstrably understood in
the sense of canvassing for a job in that factory (line 6a). As this interpretation
is not questioned, the misinterpretation is not clarified. Thus, the factory
where V is offered a job remains underspecified and a step-by-step enquiry
into the specifics of this alleged offer follows. As V's answers do not seem to
observe the maxim of quantity (Grice, 1975), IT keeps on requesting more
and more details. Even in the exchange in lines 11 and 12 where 'canvassing'
is linked to the factory, the misunderstanding is not resolved. Instead, the
confirmation check reveals another misinterpretation because 'canvassing'
does not refer to the name of the factory but to a production process. Here
we have a second misunderstanding, of course. Finally, when the more general 'canvassing' is specified (or generalised) by 'that makes beds' (line 23a),
this does not clarify the first misunderstanding but eventually leads to an
understanding without ever having made the misinterpreted item a repairable.

The shaded and indented sequences of the exchange parts are all dependent on IT's assumption of being underinformed, whereas V's brevity may be
based on the assumption of having given sufficient information. We receive
a whole subdialogue, subdivided into various repair sequences (including
another misunderstanding), which are hierarchically dependent on each other.
The repairable, however, is not reached. If we skip the whole subdialogue
and imagine this exchange as smooth and uninterrupted, all that is left is the
following, shown in Extract 3.3.

Extract 3.3: Uninterrupted exchange

1	IT:	What sort of work are you going to do when you finish the course?
2	V:	A few weeks ago ah (+) the school send me to factory doing
3		canvassing (+) canvassing (+) for two weeks' experience and ah the
4		boss say give me a position, but (. . .) when I will finish the course
5		because I have learned to do some more job and cannot take it
23b	IT:	So he will give
24		you a job, will he?

MU 5

There is a gradual recognition of a misunderstanding, which may be indicated by disturbances in the flow of the conversational course, etc., in signs of incoherence, by detours or recyclings (repetitions, paraphrases, circumlocutions, 'talking down' effects), by unresponded repair initiations, by suddenly or gradually emerging traces of verbal, non-verbal, or paralinguistic insecurity, or simply by the indication or registration of 'uncomfortable moments', until the communication comes to a halt, dissolves, breaks down or is reinitiated by a change in topic. This is exactly the kind of misunderstanding Gumperz and his colleagues have worked on: 'Lack of shared background knowledge leads initially to misunderstandings, but since contextualisation conventions are not shared, attempts to repair these misunderstandings fail and conversational cooperation breaks down' (Gumperz, 1995, p. 120).[13]

MU 6

There is no obvious recognition of a misunderstanding, although an outside observer regards it as a misunderstanding; or one of the participants may have received particular information afterwards (even a long time after) that leads her to reassess the interaction (or parts of it) as a misunderstanding. However, the interaction in question remains untouched by this discovery or reinterpretation.

MU 7

To an outside observer there is no manifestation and no indication that a misunderstanding has occurred, yet one interlocutor (or even both interlocutors) may have the feeling that either s/he has or was or they have or were misunderstood. So the misunderstanding may have been noticed but remained unnegotiated.

Two kinds of misunderstanding: event and core

Of course, some reservations have to be added to this apparently clearcut division of misunderstanding types. One is that there is a gradation of variants between MU 2 and MU 3.[14] Likewise, the differentiation between the covert and the latent type will be analytically useful, but the deeper we get into the minutiae of the interactional structure, the more likely we are to find hints of doubts in understanding and hints of these doubts being negotiated. In particular, the Gumperzian approach of conversational inferencing, based on contextualisation cues and conventions, gives ample evidence of how even the mismatching of one or several contextualisation cues could develop into a disastrous interactional trajectory. These cues are at least analytically detectable as negotiated matters of discourse.[15]

One thing has to be re-emphasised and makes the continuum character of this typology clear: the greater the distance between a repair attempt of some misinterpreted item or sequence and its alleged source, the less explicit will be its manifestations (see Drummond and Hopper, 1991). Eventually, there will be no manifestations at all, solely stronger and weaker indications of misunderstanding. This also means that with weaker manifestations and with greater distance from the repairable, that is the item or sequence misunderstood, the more difficult will be reconstructions of the misunderstanding.

Our discussion of 'misunderstanding' so far is in some way irritating or even misleading because a misunderstanding comprises much more than an isolated item or intention or activity type. Speaking of misunderstanding – and this is a crucial point in my argumentation – comprises its recognition, its possible manifestation or indication and the reconstruction of its trajectory (by diagnosing, identifying, localising and even by reconstructing the motives of its occurrence). However, in actual practice it is often hard to gauge where a misunderstanding commences unless the case is so clearly manifest as in MU 1. A misunderstanding ceases where interlocutors either regain their status quo ante or come to a smooth continuation according to criteria of coherence. As we can see in MU 3 to MU 5, the misunderstanding will be quite extended or never end until the exchange collapses or is reinitiated.

Note that there are hence *two kinds of misunderstanding* at issue: a whole stretch of talk with an alleged beginning and end, as a speech event in its own right that is structurally and interactionally describable, and a particular (often identifiable) encoding or interpretation that is the alleged reason for the whole event. The latter I will call the *core misunderstanding*. The core in MU 1 was clearly the mishearing of the item 'unlimited' (line 1) and it is this item which was made the subject of the sequence to follow.

The misunderstanding event, on the other hand, comprises the whole grey-shaded sequence of the examples cited above. The core of the example for MU 4 was IT's misunderstanding V's 'doing canvassing' (line 2ff.). IT showed his (or her) misinterpretation in line 6a by the ratificatory statement 'So you've been canvassing for work', which was not corrected, however. The subdialogues created by the core misunderstanding comprise the managing (or handling) of this misinterpretation.

Whereas in Extract 3.2 there was no identifiable core for the interlocutors, the manifestation of the misunderstanding usually refers directly to the segment being misinterpreted. It is here that the misunderstanding really begins a transition back to the previous line of the prior interaction focus which is where it ends.

Thus when I speak of 'misunderstanding' I mean either the *whole misunderstanding trajectory as an event in its own right* or the alleged identifiable *core*: any misunderstanding in situated communication comprises the 'misunderstanding event' as a frame and embedded in it is the more or less identifiable 'core misunderstanding'. Note that the frame only exists by virtue of the core; the core however is not identifiable, localisable and repairable without the frame event because these activities are all part of the frame.

Let me summarise so far: a misunderstanding in a talk exchange is not simply a diffuse mismatching of alleged intention failure, but it is a *sequence*, a short, quite extended or even open-ended one where mismatching is retrospectively *negotiated* and most often repaired. Misunderstandings have a *beginning* and an *ending*. The beginning is sometimes not reconstructable. Furthermore, misunderstandings reveal a particular sequence of activities which may even comprise a whole *corrective cycle*. The repair itself sometimes includes a diagnosis with varying specificity, even an anamnesis more or less explicit, and additionally the mutual ratification of being back on the right track. It will include moves such as giving explicit relief to the producer of a misunderstanding or giving apologetic accounts or the like.

All this, I wish to repeat, is part of misunderstanding. This is why I talk about misunderstanding as an *event in its own right*.

Misunderstanding strategically

So far I have tried to describe the 'autonomous' character of misunderstandings in conversations as a cooperative and resourceful stretch of talk in its own right: one that doesn't end with the manifestation of a misunderstanding, what I have named 'core misunderstanding', but comprises a trajectory from retrospective discovery via a more or less successful repair or clarification to the return of the status quo ante. The mutual acknowledgement of some particular kind of trouble in a talk sequence by entering the repair cycle orientating back to something allegedly misinterpreted, misunderstood or mispronounced endows participants with particular rights and obligations. These include identifying whether it was self or other attributed, who is to start with clarification, whose and which face wants have to be taken into consideration, how intensively or extensively the misunderstanding should be dealt with, what kind of consequences the misunderstanding has for the return to the status quo ante and the continuation of the conversation. Clarification of a misunderstanding may be much more complicated than other en passant repairs as it does not automatically follow their preference structure (cf. Hinnenkamp, 1998).

Deviant (mis)understandings

Understanding in dialogues is manifestly indicated, hence it is 'demonstrably there' (cf. Linell and Luckmann, 1991). However, this does not say that all understanding is ultimatively of this kind. In working with authentic data from situated conversations, we can only empirically refer to and rely upon participants' displayed orientations towards each other. From these we infer the process of mutual understanding (and misunderstanding) as the participants of a conversation go along. Misunderstanding in dialogues is also of this kind. It is manifestly indicated, demonstrably there and often even more evident than understanding. A misunderstanding implies the cooperative accomplishment of making the misunderstanding, or rather one's putative misunderstanding or that of one's partner, a common problem for the continuation of the conversation at hand. This requires clarification and a solution without creating new problems (such as threatening a partner's face, legitimising dispreferred moves, etc.). The aim is to return to the main interactional focus as quickly and smoothly as possible.

Now there are myriad possibilities where the (trajectory of a) misunderstanding will not match this kind of cooperative ideal: (i) The declared misunderstanding may remain onesided (cf. MU 7 above). (ii) One conversationalist may question or even refute the manifestor's or corrector's interpretive demands. (iii) The misunderstanding may become overextended or even the new main focus and the prior focus may become irretrievable. It will thus transcend its transitory character and may function as a new resource for further continuation (cf. MU 2 above). (iv) The misunderstanding may be treated as a non-understanding and therefore will never enter into the clarification sequence, implying claims and counterclaims as to what should have been understood and what was actually or allegedly said. The misunderstanding is thus suspended in the identification and localisation phase, halfway towards clarification. (v) A misunderstanding may at the point of its unfolding be treated on a metalinguistic or metadiscursive level, that is, it may be topicalised as a phenomenon with a particular structure or with particular consequences.

Note that the more conversationalists there are involved in the talk and the course of a misunderstanding, the more possibilities there will be for treating it variously and the more complex will be its common coordination as one particular kind of conversational trouble.

Humphrey-Jones (1986, pp. 168, 276) supplies us with one such example (actually one of the few authentic examples in her data) in which all five types (there may be more, of course) are enacted in one way or another (Extract 3.4).

Extract 3.4: Zeppelins

1 c: He blew up my nose and he gave me a headache. It was nasty
2 a: It's supposed to be like a sort of zephyr
3 c: Well he was a phhhh-
4 a: A gale
5 d: Is that supposed to be romantic?
6 a: It gets dogs going I believe
7 b: Zeppelins aren't romantic
8 a: Pardon?
9 b: Zeppelins aren't romantic
10 a: Who mentioned zeppelins?
11 b: You just did (+) didn't you(?)
12 a: No
13 c: This is one of those conversations
14 d: ((towards B)) You did
15 b: I know (+) but only because I thought A did
16 d: No (+) you started that one
17 a: No, I'm afraid not, B
18 e: They could be thought extremely phallic
19 a: What can?
20 b: Phallic?
21 c: Zeppelins
22 a: Zeppelins
23 c: Oh ((extends arms wide)) those big things that go like that.

In Extract 3.4, the alleged understanding as demonstrated in lines 7 and 8 ('zeppelins') is explicitly refuted but not retrospectively checked with the original source (obviously 'zephyr' in line 2). We may regard the following section up to line 12 as the demonstrated manifestation of difficulties in identifying and localising the point of trouble. It is then made a resource for continuation, first on the metathematic level by C's commentary (line 13) and then is ratifiedly instantiated as the new subject by E picking up on B's misinterpreted item 'zeppelin' (lines 18–23).

Of course, to mention a further possibility (vi), something may be declared a misunderstanding in retrospect, e.g. in order to claim one's own right of interpretation or clarification vis-à-vis some other claim, *pretending* to have been misunderstood or trying to revise one's prior statement or make it more precise. Bilmes, an ethnomethodological sceptic as regards peering into an understander's mind, argued in this direction when he emphasised the general difficulty in establishing observer criteria for subjective understanding:

> There is a range of other possibilities. [(vii)] An accurate hearing may be rejected because the speaker has changed his mind about what he wants to be heard. [(viii)] An inaccurate hearing may be accepted because the speaker is satisfied to be understood in that way. [(ix)] Or a hearing may elaborate or specify a speaker's meaning in a way that the speaker never thought about, in a way such that the speaker cannot 'simply know' whether or not that meaning was what he had in mind. . . . [(x)] We may even experience our recipient's hearing as a revelation of what, after all, we had in mind in the first place.
>
> (Bilmes, 1992, p. 95)

I have added the enumeration of the various possibilities by inserting (vii)–(x) to the Bilmes quote. As we can see, there is quite a range of, as it were, *non-standard* trajectories of misunderstandings.

Knowing how to misunderstand

All the varieties mentioned in the first part (MU 1 to MU 7) and all the 'deviations' from the standard models discussed above require knowledge of *how* they work, i.e. conversationalists need to know the rules of the 'misunderstanding game'.[16] A common knowledge of the workings of a misunderstanding, even of its trajectory and its structure, is a prerequisite for all those taking part in the misunderstanding game, be it deadly serious, strategic or playful. There must be knowledge of how the particular type of misunderstanding functions, of how, for example, to coordinate the transition from the clarification sequence back to the main focus or, alternatively, of how to abuse the misunderstanding sequence by extending it, or of how a misunderstanding is creatively and playfully exploited. Mutuality, of course, may end at one point or another, so that for one participant clarification means to return to the status quo ante whereas for the other it may mean a step further, e.g. taking advantage of the situation and ridiculing one's partner. Whenever it becomes obvious that the 'knowing how to' of the misunderstanding game is converted into a 'knowing that', I will speak of a *strategic misunderstanding*. This does not mean that such a strategy can be mediated by its user: He or she may not be able to explain. I know that if I declare something to be a misunderstanding, I hereby insinuate to my partner that he or she has not interpreted, heard or understood me in the intended or 'correct' way, and that I, through this 'manoeuvre' regain the floor and can thus use the opportunity to rephrase or revise.

What is meant by 'strategic' is the analytic and conversational exploitation of a misunderstanding event. The term emphasises that conventional means of misunderstanding are not primarily used to serve clarification and return to the status quo ante, but demonstrate objectives external to conventional solutions. Such objectives could be a gain of prestige e.g. by showing one's wittiness by a word or language game or by threatening a partner's face. Hence, this kind of strategic action is to be regarded as counterproductive to the clarification and solution process of the misunderstanding. It is certainly not easy to decide what is external or specific to a misunderstanding event. It may also mean that during the development of a misunderstanding event some particular strategic function will compete with and/or (eventually) dominate the conventional function. The particular strategy will not necessarily have been planned a priori such as playing the misunderstanding card for opportunistic reasons, but rather will emerge during the negotiation of a misunderstanding as a 'good opportunity'.

A case study in parasitic misunderstanding

Let's take a look at a stretch of video-recorded talk from a seminar group discussion (Extract 3.5), an international workshop on intercultural communication, where after the clearance of a misunderstanding one of the conversationalists, the male locutor H, inserts a typical self-attributed misunderstanding diagnosis (lines 15 and 16) of the kind: 'I see (+) I'd understood, if she *isn't* **warm**, then she hasn't eaten.'

Extract 3.5: Warm essen (original German version)

1 A: Ich finde, was wichtig in der in der Thematik ist auch zum Beispiel in China, was äh für

2   eine **Rol**le das Essen hat überhaupt (+) zum Beispiel wenn äh + ä:h (+) meine Frau,

3   wenn sie **nicht warm** *i:sst*, sie hat nicht ge**ges**sen,

4 B: Mhm

5 A: sie hat nicht ge**ges**sen, zu Abend **auch**, das [ist, das ist unvor**stell**bar

6 C: [>Ist das {ne} Kinesin, oder?<

7 A: =Bitte?

8 C: °Deine [Frau?°

9 A: [°Ja, ja, aus Taiwan, ja°.= [Wenn es, wenn es mal (h)**Kä**:se oder-

10 ?:   [(. . . . . . [. . . .)

11 D: [°Seine Frau ist aus Taiwan°

12 E: °Wenn sie nich warm *isst*, dann hat sie nicht gegessen°
13 F: =Also wenns nichts Warmes is
14 G: =Als[o **KAL**tes Essen-
15 H: [Ach so (+) ich hab verstanden, wenn sie nich **warm** *is*, dann hat
16   sie nich ge**ges**sen
17   ((5.5 Sek. lang heftiges, sich steigerndes lautes Lachen, im Videobild
18   sichtbar lachen vor allem G, F, T7, T8, T9, T10. B schaut
19   orientierungslos in die Runde. H's Gesicht ist verdeckt. T7 und T8
20   lachen besonders heftig und mit vollem Körpereinsatz. A lehnt sich
21   zurück; er lacht zumindest nicht hörbar mit. – Im Ausklingen:))
21 G: **Kal**tes Essen ist kein Begri:ff

Extract 3.6: Warm meals (English gloss)

1 A: I find what's important on this on this topic as well is for example
2   that in China, what uh kinda **role** eating takes at all (+) for example
3   if uh + u:h (+) my wife, if she has **not** had a warm meal, she just
4   hasn't **eat**en,
4 B: Mhm
5 A: she hasn't **eat**en, **e**ven at night, that [is, that is unim**ag**inable
6 C: [>Is that {a} Chinese, right?<
7 A: =Sorry?
8 C: °Your [wife?°
9 A: [°Yeah yeah from Taiwan, ya°.= [Even if it's, if it's (h)**chee:se** or-
10 ?:   [(. . . . . . . [. . . . .)
11 D: [°His wife is from
12   Taiwan°
12 E: °If she hasn't had a warm meal, then she hasn't eaten°
13 F: =So if it isn't anything warm
14 G: =I mea[n **COLD** food-
15 H: [I see (+) I'd understood, if she *isn't* **warm**, then she hasn't
16   **eat**en
17   ((5.5 seconds of loud and uproarious laughter; visibly laughing are
18   G, F, T7, T8, T9, T10. B looks around disorientated. H's face is
19   hidden. T7 and T8's bodies are literally shaking with laughter. A
20   leans back; he doesn't give any signs of joining in with the laughter.
21   – While the laughter dies down:))
21 G: **Cold** food is no concept

From the reaction of the majority of the participants (lines 17–21), we can clearly assume that something funny must have happened immediately beforehand. This is indeed H's self-attributing misunderstanding diagnosis: 'I see (+) I'd understood, if she *isn't* **warm**, then she hasn't eaten' in lines 15–16. The English gloss unfortunately does not make clear what the pun of this utterance is. H's self-attributing misunderstanding 'confession' (lines

15–16) picks up on A's statements in line 3 'my wife, if she has **not** had a warm meal, she just hasn't **eaten**' ['*meine Frau, wenn sie **nicht warm** i:sst, sie hat nicht gegessen*'] and, again, on E's repetition in line 12 "°If she hasn't had a warm meal, then she hasn't eaten°" ["°*Wenn sie nich warm* isst, *dann hat sie nicht gegessen*°"]. What A and E try to explain here is that warm meals at every mealtime of the day are so important for A's wife that if she gets a cold meal instead she feels like not having had a meal at all.

H's alleged quote of A's statement (line 3) and E's repetition (lines 15–16) both have the typical format 'I understood X'. Note that speaker H does not say something like 'I thought you said X' which would have given a more subjective impression of the hearer's opinion. 'I understood X' is much more direct and also implies a much stronger right in stating one's understanding. H's taking the floor to state his prior misunderstanding and introduce another issue here is, after all, purely self-selected, without a prior summons. But what is it that H pretends to have understood and that gives him such an amused audience for more than five seconds?

H's statement 'wenn sie nich **warm** *is*' ['if she *isn't* **warm**'] (line 15) refers explicitly to A's utterance 'wenn sie **nicht warm** i:sst' ['if she has **not** had a warm meal', lit. 'if she does not *eat* warm'] (line 3) and E's repetition "°wenn sie nich warm *isst*°" ["°if she hasn't had a warm meal°", lit. 'if she doesn't *eat* warm'] (line 12). In German the third person singular present tense of the copula verb 'sein' (to be) is homophonous with the third person singular present tense of the verb 'essen' (to eat), although spelled differently: 'sein' (to be) and 'ist' (is) versus 'essen' (to eat) and 'isst' (eats). That is, 'sie isst' (she eats) and 'sie ist' in the existential sense 'she is' sound identical. The major difference between the two are in terms of pronunciation. Whereas the existential's final '-t' can be dropped, the final '-t'of 'isst' (eats) cannot.

It is exactly this dropping of the final '-t' in '**warm** *is*' (line 15) where speaker H marks the difference between the allegedly understood and the said to the other conversationalists. H thus exploits the intrinsic homophony of the two wordforms and in doing so creates a different context which gives rise to roars of laughter. This is corroborated by the possible double reading of the adjective 'warm', which in German has different meanings and different associations. Besides 'a warm meal' it is also used in the sense of 'being ready': a 'warm motor' is one ready to start. In a figurative sense 'warm' can also be understood as a sexual allusion of 'being ready', that is keen on sexual activity. Although this is not a highly conventionalised usage, 'hot' being generally used in such contexts, 'warm' can adopt this function as well – just one grade below 'hotness', so to speak.

In a way, this interpretation is rather far-fetched because the conversation so far definitely revolved around eating and food. But by way of recontextualising it in a newly marked and salient context, its sexual allusion has to be inferred. Such interpretation is particularly supported by the other participants' reaction. If we take a look at the prior sequence, we can see the critical development up to this point. Speaker A introduces his wife's national background in a rather down-toned side sequence, marking it as an example without wanting to give particular information about his private alliances (lines 1–3). Exactly this en passant manner of introducing his wife's nationality leads to C's question 'Is that {a} Chinese, right?' (line 6), which elicits A's immediate reaction: 'Sorry' (line 7). This is interpreted by C as a repair summons in that he corrects himself to: "°your wife?°" (line 8). A's response is clearly down-toned through a lowered voice and the direct continuation of the main strands of discussion by means of latching ('=') (line 9). His continuation in the prior mode of tempo and loudness is thus clearly distinguishable from the down-modulated information about his wife's national origin. This and the sequence to follow lead to some clarification about what A means to say about his wife's food needs by E's repetition: "°If she hasn't had a hot meal, then she hasn't eaten°" ["°*Wenn sie nich warm* isst, *dann hat sie nicht gegessen*°"] (line 12).

At the moment when G, herself Chinese, adds some further explanation (line 14), H advances his self-attributing confession of a misunderstanding. Note again, it is H's first turn. In doing so he makes use of a misunderstanding format, especially one of self-blame and self-responsibility, yet directing it towards a side-sequential topic which had been downplayed as much as possible. This kind of formulation is, of course, a very grave face-threatening attack because it not only overemphasises the issue, but also reverts to the private and intimate sphere of A's family life.

We can thus conclude that H makes use of a particular misunderstanding manifestation format in order to gain points at the cost of his fellow conversationalist. This is what I call 'parasitic'. By using a particular misunderstanding format, namely that of self-attribution at having misunderstood, H resorts to a typical introductory account which is part and parcel of a clarification sequence (see Hinnenkamp, 1998, p. 155; Schegloff, 1987, 1992). By using this particular format, H demonstrates that he is well aware of how a misunderstanding functions and that referring back to a prior utterance as 'misunderstandable' at this particular point of the conversational development entitles him to introduce a clarification sequence. However, as there is obviously nothing to be clarified, H's contribution is read as what it very likely means: a word game with a sexual allusion exploiting the homophonous and connotative correspondences between 'warm essen' (lit. 'to eat warm') and 'warm sein' (lit. 'to be warm').

Conclusion

The main argument I developed in the first part of this chapter essentially suggests that there are different kinds of misunderstandings. In turn, these can be ordered according to their interactional organisation. They are side-sequences in their own right and display an internal structure. The more explicit the manifestation of a misunderstanding, the more structured and formalised it will be. Misunderstandings have a *core*, which is mostly the retrospectively identified locus of the misunderstanding, and they have a trajectory which extends from the indication or manifestation to the return of the status quo ante. I have called the entire sequence from the trouble point in conversation up to the point of return to the main interactional focus the *misunderstanding event*.

Demonstrably, misunderstandings engender a particular kind of reciprocal activity in clarifying and solving the misunderstanding, a large amount of which is identical to Goffman's corrective cycle (see Goffman, 1971; Hinnenkamp, 1998, 2002). In particular, structures in misunderstanding display how next steps have been triggered by prior ones according to the treatment of the misunderstanding, in order to clarify it, remove it and get back to where the misunderstanding led to the deviating route, what I have called the status quo ante. The procedures described display participants' knowledge involved in handling misunderstandings. This 'knowing how to handle' a misunderstanding may be converted into a 'knowing that', perhaps less in terms of linguistic descriptions and more in terms of an awareness towards the functions a misunderstanding (or parts of the misunderstanding event) can have.

Implementing the knowledge of how a misunderstanding works for goals other than solving and clarifying the misunderstanding I have called '*strategic*'. Strategic exploitations are not based on anticipated decisions, but rather are spontaneous moves, such as jumping on a bandwagon. Strategic usage of misunderstanding also discloses that every dialogue is susceptible to turning into one where gaining points in a winner's game is all of a sudden at issue, often enough at the cost of the speaker's co-participant. Group discussions in particular are a wonderful playground for this kind of verbal rivalry, face gains, induced face threatens and losses. It is this latter kind of strategic exploitation of misunderstanding that I have called *parasitic*.

At the beginning of this chapter I posed several questions in need of an answer. 'What is a misunderstanding?' was my first question. It is a sequence to be described in its own right: how, I have shown above. I also asked 'How can we as observers know if, how and when people misunderstand?' I found some criteria which can be displayed through participants' ways of demonstrating their understandings and misunderstandings respectively. My third question, 'What is the particular relationship between intercultural communication and misunderstanding?', was not investigated very deeply here. However, it may have become clear that the relationship is not simply one in which the amount of misunderstandings become criterial for intercultural trouble points or, vice versa, that intercultural communication is mainly definable through misunderstandings. All misunderstandings are of the same kind – at least at one level. From another perspective there may be more covert and latent ones in intercultural communication. At least to some extent I have tried to answer the final question, 'What is the relationship between misunderstandings in general and parasitic ones in particular?' It is certainly a delicate one for those falling victim to the parasitic users. It is certainly a profitable one for those who are winners in the game of reciprocal face threats. This is part and parcel of everyday conversational conduct and it shows interlocutors' susceptibility to playing games, creativity and taking advantage. At the same time, however, it also opens another side of conversation which is characterised by non-cooperation and competition.

Appendix

Transcription conventions

{comes}	doubtable reconstruction
(. . . .)	incomprehensible
(( ))	commentary, e.g. ((1.5 sec.)), ((laughter))
how-	abortion of utterance
so:, ru::::de	lengthening of vowel, degree of lengthening
eating	stressed, emphasised
THIS	high volume
THAT	emphasised and high volume
°there°	low volume
>beyond<	fast tempo
word	analytically salient (no surface realisation symbol)
+	pause, below 1 second
(+)	micropause
(h)	hesitation (e.g. he (h)comes)
=	fast connection, latching
come [in]	
[go]	overlap, point of overlap and its extension

Acknowledgements

This chapter is based on a presentation given at the AILA-Symposium 'Misunderstanding in Everyday Life', Jyväskylä, Finland, 4–9 August 1996. I gratefully acknowledge that my research on misunderstanding was financed by the University of Augsburg and that the presentation of the paper at the AILA-Symposium was made possible only through the generous support of the Kurt-Bösch-Foundation, Augsburg.

Notes

1 These associations can be nicely revealed by scrutinising the use of the word 'Missverständnis' (misunderstanding): out of a text corpus of 30 million text words I have tried to isolate a set of stereotypical concepts that comprise the different usages of the noun 'Missverständnis' as occurring in collocational and functional contexts. I thus arrived at stereotypes of the kind: 'One has to protect oneself from misunderstandings', 'misunderstandings can be intentionally created, promoted and provoked', 'misunderstandings can be dealt with, they can be revealed, cleared up and removed', but also 'misunderstandings can be exploited to one's own advantage, such as by reducing one's own responsibility, euphemising one's own faults etc.' (cf. Hinnenkamp, 1998, Ch. 4).

2 Cf. Gumperz (1982a, 1982b); Gumperz and Cook-Gumperz (1981); Gumperz and Roberts (1978, 1991); Gumperz et al. (1979); Erickson and Shultz (1982); Hinnenkamp (1989, 1991); Roberts et al. (1993).

3 Cf. e.g. Bremer (1996); Bremer and Simonot (1996a, b); Gass and Varonis (1991); House (1993a, 1993b, 1996); Varonis and Gass (1985).

4 Take a reader like *Analyzing intercultural communication* (Knapp et al., 1987) as an example; the term 'misunderstanding' is used about 20 times (including 3 references in my own contribution to the volume) and 'miscommunication' about 15 times. Both are in frequent company with 'awkward moments', 'inherent ambiguities', 'communication conflict', 'communication breakdown' and 'communicative failure'.

5 The English usage of 'misunderstanding', however, does not fully match the German 'Missverständnis'. In addition to the enquiry into the usage in German (cf. Note 1), a student of English at Augsburg University, Sarah K. Dietl, made a comparative analysis in English, the results of which differ widely, however, in terms of frequency and relevance from the German stereotypes. Whereas in German 'Missverständnis' collocates most strongly with the verb 'vorbeugen' (to prevent), there is no such strong collocation for 'misunderstanding'. Here stative and assertive constructions such as 'there is a misunderstanding' are clearly the most prominent ones. The prevention schema on the other hand is very rare. If there is a correspondence between the naming practice and the kind of attitude towards misunderstanding, then we can easily imagine the handling and managing of misunderstandings as a source of intercultural conflict (or misunderstanding?).

6 Cf. e.g. such attempts as Dascal (1985); Grimshaw (1980); Mudersbach (1987); Weizman and Blum-Kulka (1992); Zaefferer (1977).

7 Here we find case studies on lexical ambiguity between students' discussion (Loretz, 1976), an experimental study on successful and failed intention attribution (Dobrick, 1985), and speech act pragmatic corpus research into misunderstandings in fictional dialogues (Falkner, 1997).

8 But how can we finally know this, in view of (a)? We must simply exclude latent misunderstandings from our consideration.

9 Original German version in which the English gloss follows each line. The legend for transcribing conventions is in the Appendix.

10 This pertains of course only to such an understanding of misunderstanding where the encoding of a word that was misheard, for example, is regarded as the repairable. But one might as well regard such mishearing itself as the repairable.

11 For Schegloff, misunderstanding, at least this overtly manifest type, is seen to stand in close relation to the repair device, because sequentially a misunderstanding – as we can see in the above example – can only be repaired from the third position onward, as 'repair after an interlocutor's response (second position) has revealed trouble in understanding an earlier turn (the "repairable" in first position)' (Schegloff, 1992, p. 1301). Schegloff has furthermore mentioned that devices of a misunderstanding manifestation ('composition of third position repair'), those of *horizontal* sequentiality, appear in a kind of canonical order (in English, at least, and similarly in German, see Hinnenkamp, 1998): first, prefatory 'no'; second, a less obligatory kind of acceptance token; third, a rejection component; fourth, 'the repair proper', which is then subcategorised into various kinds of accounts, one of them typically starting with 'I mean' (Schegloff, 1992, p. 1310).

12 The mode of transcription has been adapted to the transcription system I use.

13 The studies of Gumperz and his colleagues abound in examples. See Gumperz (1982a, 1982b, 1989, 1992a, 1992b, 1995), or Gumperz and Roberts (1991).

14 For example, what Schegloff (1992) has named 'third position repair' as being typically indicative for a misunderstanding may also become a 'fourth or fifth position repair'. But the more distant the repair, the more likely manifestations will be less explicit, the more likely will there be implicit indications with harder reconstructions. 'Canvassing' is a good example for this.

15 See Gumperz (1982a, 1989, 1992a, 1992b, 1995), or Auer (1986, 1992).

16 Except for latent and one-sided misunderstandings, all misunderstandings depend on conversationalists' mutual work, i.e. they are based on ratification and negotiation of the item under suspicion of having been misunderstood.

References

Agar, M. (1993). *Language shock. Understanding the culture of conversation.* New York: William Morrow.

Agar, M. (1994). The intercultural frame. In *International Journal of Intercultural Relations*, 18, 221–237.

Allwood, J. and Abelar, Y. (1989). Lack of understanding, misunderstanding and language acquisition. In G. Extra and M. Mittner (eds), *Studies in second language acquisition by adult immigrants. Proceedings of the ESF/AILA symposium held on the 9th of August in Brussels.* Tilburg: Tilburg University, 27–55.

Auer, P. (1986). Kontextualisierung. In *Studium Linguistik*, 19, 22–47.

Auer, P. (1992). Introduction: John Gumperz' approach to contextualization. In P. Auer and A. di Luzio (eds), *The contextualization of language.* Amsterdam: John Benjamins, 1–37.

Bilmes, J. (1992). Mishearings. In G. Watson and R. M. Seiler (eds), *Text in context. Contributions to ethnomethodology.* Newbury Park, CA: Sage, 79–98.

Bremer, K. (1996). Causes of understanding problems. In K. Bremer, C. Roberts, M.-T. Vasseur, M. Simonot and P. Broeder (eds), *Achieving understanding: Discourse in intercultural encounters.* London: Longman, 37–64.

Bremer, K. and Simonot, M. (1996a). Preventing problems of understanding. In K. Bremer, C. Roberts, M.-T. Vasseur, M. Simonot and P. Broeder (eds), *Achieving understanding: Discourse in intercultural encounters.* London: Longman, 159–180.

Bremer, K. and Simonot, M. (1996b). Joint negotiation of understanding: Procedures for managing problems of understanding. In K. Bremer, C. Roberts, M.-T. Vasseur, M. Simonot and P. Broeder (eds), *Achieving understanding: Discourse in intercultural encounters*. London: Longman, 181–206.

Cushing, S. (1994). *Fatal words. Communication clashes and aircraft crashes*. Chicago: University of Chicago Press.

Dascal, M. (1985). The relevance of misunderstanding. In M. Dascal (ed.), *Dialogue – an interdisciplinary approach*. Amsterdam: John Benjamins, 441–459.

Dobrick, M. (1985). *Gegenseitiges (Miß-)Verstehen in der dyadischen Kommunikation*. Münster: Aschendorff.

Drummond, K. and Hopper, R. (1991). Misunderstanding and its remedies: Telephone miscommunication. In N. Coupland, J. M. Wiemann and H. Giles (eds), *'Miscommunication' and problematic talk*. London: Sage, 301–314.

Erickson, F. and Shultz, J. (1982). *The counselor as gatekeeper. Social interaction in interviews*. New York: Academic Press.

Falkner, W. (1997). *Verstehen, Mißverstehen und Mißverständnisse*. Tübingen: Niemeyer.

Gass, S. M. and Varonis, E. M. (1991). Miscommunication in nonnative speaker discourse. In N. Coupland, J. M. Wiemann and H. Giles (eds), *'Miscommunication' and problematic talk*. London: Sage, 121–145.

Goffman, E. (1971). *Relations in public. Microstudies of the public order*. New York: Harper & Row.

Grice, H. P. (1975). Logic and conversation. In P. Cole and J. L. Morgan (eds), *Syntax and semantics 3: Speech acts*. New York: Academic Press, 41–58.

Grimshaw, A. D. (1980). Mishearings, misunderstandings, and other nonsuccesses in talk: A plea for redress of speaker-oriented bias. In *Sociological Inquiry*, 50 (3/4), 31–74.

Gumperz, J. J. (1982a). *Discourse strategies*. Cambridge: Cambridge University Press.

Gumperz, J. J. (ed.) (1982b). *Language and social identity*. Cambridge: Cambridge University Press.

Gumperz, J. J. (1989). Contextualization cues and metapragmatics: The retrieval of cultural knowledge. In B. Music, R. Grascyk and C. Wiltshire (eds), *CLS 25, Papers from the 25th annual regional meeting of the Chicago Linguistic Society. Part Two: Parasession on language in context*. Chicago: Chicago Linguistic Society, 77–88.

Gumperz, J. J. (1992a). Contextualization revisited. In P. Auer and A. di Luzio (eds), *The contextualization of language*. Amsterdam: John Benjamins, 39–53.

Gumperz, J. J. (1992b). Contextualization and understanding. In A. Duranti and C. Goodwin (eds), *Rethinking context*. New York: Cambridge University Press, 229–252.

Gumperz, J. J. (1995). Mutual inferencing in conversation. In I. Marková, C. F. Graumann and K. Foppa (eds), *Mutualities in dialogue*. Cambridge: Cambridge University Press, 101–123.

Gumperz, J. J. and Cook-Gumperz, J. (1981). Ethnic differences in communicative style. In C. A. Ferguson and S. B. Heath (eds), *Language in the USA*. Cambridge: Cambridge University Press, 430–445.

Gumperz, J. J. and Roberts, C. (1978). *Developing awareness skills for interethnic communication*. Southall: NCILT (also published 1980 as Occasional Papers No. 12 of the SEAMEO Regional Language Centre, Singapore).

Gumperz, J. J. and Roberts, C. (1991). Understanding in intercultural encounters. In J. Blommaert and J. Verschueren (eds), *The pragmatics of intercultural and international communication. Selected papers of the International Pragmatics Conference, Antwerp, August 17–22, 1987, Volume 3, and the Ghent Symposium on Intercultural Communication*. Amsterdam: John Benjamins, 51–90.

Gumperz, J. J., Jupp, T. C. and Roberts, C. (1979). *Crosstalk. A study of cross-cultural communication. Background material and notes to accompany the BBC film*. Southall: NCILT.

Hinnenkamp, V. (1989). *Interaktionale Soziolinguistik und Interkulturelle Kommunikation. Gesprächsmanagement zwischen Deutschen und Türken*. Tübingen: Niemeyer.

Hinnenkamp, V. (1991): Talking a person into interethnic distinction: A discourse analytic case study. In J. Blommaert and J. Verschueren (eds), *The pragmatics of intercultural and international communication. Selected papers of the International Pragmatics Conference, Antwerp, August 17–22, 1987, Volume 3, and the Ghent Symposium on Intercultural Communication*. Amsterdam: John Benjamins, 91–110.

Hinnenkamp, V. (1995). Intercultural communication. In J. Verschueren, J.-O. Östman and J. Blommaert (eds), *Handbook of pragmatics 1995*. Amsterdam: John Benjamins.

Hinnenkamp, V. (1998). *Mißverständnisse in Gesprächen*. Opladen: Westdeutscher Verlag.

Hinnenkamp, V. (2002). The notion of misunderstanding in intercultural communication. In J. Allwood and B. Dorriots (eds), *The diversity of intercultural communication. Selected papers. 5th NIC Symposium Gothenburg, Sweden. (= Papers in Anthropological Linguistics 28)*. Göteborg: Göteborg University, Dept. of Linguistics, 55–88.

House, J. (1993a). Mißverstehen im interkulturellen Diskurs. In J. P. Timm and H. Vollmer (eds), *Kontroversen in der Fremdsprachenforschung*. Bochum: Brockmeyer, 178–196.

House, J. (1993b). Towards a model for the analysis of inappropriate responses in native/non-native interactions. In G. Kasper and S. Blum-Kulka (eds), *Interlanguage pragmatics*. New York: Oxford University Press, 161–183.

House, J. (1996). Contrastive discourse analysis and misunderstanding: The case of German and English. In M. Hellinger and U. Ammon (eds), *Contrastive sociolinguistics*. Berlin: Mouton de Gruyter, 345–361.

Humphrey-Jones, C. (1986). An investigation of the types and structure of misunderstandings. Dissertation, University of Newcastle upon Tyne.

Ichheiser, G. (1949). Misunderstanding in human relations: A study in false social perception. [Supplement] In *American Journal of Sociology*, 55(2), Pt. 2.

Knapp, K., Enninger, W. and Knapp-Potthoff, A. (eds) (1987). *Analyzing intercultural communication*. The Hague: Mouton de Gruyter.

Linell, P. (1995). Troubles with mutualities: Towards a dialogical theory of misunderstanding and miscommunication. In I. Marková, C. F. Graumann and K. Foppa (eds), *Mutualities in dialogue*. Cambridge: Cambridge University Press, 176–213.

Linell, P. and Luckmann, T. (1991). Asymmetries in dialogue: Some conceptual preliminaries. In I. Marková and K. Foppa (eds), *Asymmetries in dialogue*. Hemel Hempstead: Harvester Wheatsheaf, 1–20.

Loretz, N. (1976). *Verständigung und Missverstehen: Versuch einer semantisch-pragmatischen Analyse an schweizerdeutschen und hochsprachlichen Texten*. Frauenfeld, Stuttgart: Huber.

Mudersbach, K. (1987). Kommunizieren als Übersetzungsproblem. Über Mißver-ständnisse und deren Verhinderung. In F. Liedtke and R. Keller (eds), *Kommunikation und Kooperation*. Tübingen: Niemeyer, 239–247.

Roberts, C., Davies, E. and Jupp, T. (1993). *Language and discrimination. A study of communication in multi-ethnic workplaces*. London: Longman.

Schegloff, E. A. (1987). Some sources of misunderstanding in talk-in-interaction. In *Linguistics*, 25, 201–218.

Schegloff, E. A. (1992). Repair after next turn: The last structurally provided defense of intersubjectivity in conversation. In *American Journal of Sociology*, 97(5), 1295–1345.

Schwartz, H. (1977). Understanding misunderstanding. In *Analytic Sociology*, 3 [quoted by Humphrey-Jones, 1986].

Smedslund, J. (1990). A critique of Tversky and Kahneman's distinction between fallacy and misunderstanding. In *Scandinavian Journal of Psychology*, 31, 110–120.

Varonis, E. M. and Gass, S. M. (1985). Miscommunication in native/nonnative conversation. In *Language in Society*, 14, 327–343.

Weizman, E. and Blum-Kulka, S. (1992). Ordinary misunderstanding. In M. Stamenov (ed.), *Current advances in semantic theory*. Amsterdam: John Benjamins, 417–432.

Williams, T. (1985). The nature of miscommunication in the cross-cultural employment interview. In J. B. Pride (ed.), *Cross-cultural encounters. Communication and mis-communication*. Melbourne: River Seine, 165–175.

Zaefferer, D. (1977). Understanding misunderstanding: A proposal for an explanation of reading choices. In *Journal of Pragmatics*, 1, 329–346.

4

Repetition as a source of miscommunication in oral proficiency interviews

Gabriele Kasper and *Steven Ross*

If you don't repeat, you forget.

(MILAN KUNDERA, THE BOOK OF LAUGHTER AND FORGETTING)

Introduction

Misunderstandings in gatekeeping encounters frequently sabotage clients' access to social privileges. This applies, a fortiori, to an activity type whose purpose is to assess a candidate's communicative ability in a second or foreign language, known as oral proficiency interview (OPI). Even OPIs involving candidates at fairly advanced levels of second language proficiency are susceptible to pragmatic misunderstandings (Ross, 1998), reflecting mismatches in the interviewer's and candidate's language use that may be interpreted as shortcomings in the candidate's target language ability. Additionally, and no less seriously in their possible consequences for interview outcomes, misunderstandings can also emerge from the interaction itself. This study examines misunderstandings arising from a pervasive interactional practice – the use of repetition.

Oral proficiency interviews (OPIs)

OPIs are speech events designed to measure a candidate's speaking ability in a target language. The first antecedents of OPIs were developed in the 1950s by various US state agencies (e.g. Foreign Service Institute, Defense

Language Institute, Central Intelligence Agency, National Security Agency). In the 1970s, language testing professionals began to call for test instruments capable of informing on candidates' ability to use the target language functionally and spontaneously in authentic contexts through direct samples of oral proficiency. Since 1980, OPIs, in one variety or another, have been the dominant assessment format used also by non-governmental test agencies such as the Educational Testing Service (ETS), the American Council on the Teaching of Foreign Languages (ACTFL) and the First Certificate in English of the University of Cambridge Local Examinations Syndicate (see Clark and Clifford, 1988, for the history and development of OPIs).

As the use of OPIs as the major apparatus for assessing second language performance became more widespread, the need for interviewer training and standardisation increased. The major emphasis for training of interviewers for standardised interview procedures as seen in the interview formats adopted by the Foreign Service Institute, Defense Language Institute, ETS and ACTFL has to date been focused on the structuring of the interview procedure in four main phases, comprising a boundary transaction at the beginning and end and two interlocking central transactions. The initial Warm-Up serves a predominantly phatic function but also allows the interviewer a preliminary check of the candidate's proficiency level. During the subsequent Level Check, the interviewer seeks to determine the highest sustainable level of the candidate's speaking proficiency. The Probes serve to provide confirmatory evidence of the hypothesised proficiency level. To this end, the candidate is given tasks whose execution requires proficiency one level above the level established in the Level Check. If the candidate performs adequately at this level, the Level Check–Probe cycle is repeated at the new level. The final phase is the Wind-Down, whose function, parallel to that of the Warm-Up, is predominantly phatic, but it also provides the interviewer with a last opportunity to assess yet incompletely tested components of the candidate's oral proficiency (ETS, 1982). In actual practice, interviewers adhere to the generic OPI format somewhat variably, and the Level Check may embed several subphases serving such purposes as identifying a topic on which the candidate can talk extensively (Ross, 1995).

A second measure to promote standardisation was to establish a hypothetical scale of proficiency on which candidates' performance could be evaluated. These scales comprise a number of levels, specifying functional, formal, and situational criteria by which increasing target language performance can be described in putatively implicational fashion. The widely used *ACTFL Proficiency Guidelines* (1986) include nine levels, ranging from Low Beginner to Superior; the scale has recently been revised and expanded to ten levels (ACTFL, 1999). The earlier Defense Language Institute provisional definitions of oral proficiency distinguished seven levels (ETS, 1982). For instance, Level 2 (Advanced), the category relevant to the study reported below, is defined as follows:

Able to satisfy routine social demands and limited work requirements. Can handle with confidence but not with facility most social situations including introductions and casual conversations about current events, as well as work, family, and autobiographical information; can handle limited work requirements, needing help in handling any complications or difficulties. (Can get the gist of most conversations on non-technical subjects [i.e. topics which require no specialised knowledge]). Can give directions from on place to another. Has a speaking vocabulary sufficient to respond simply with some circumlocutions; accent, though often quite faulty, is intelligible; can usually handle elementary constructions quite accurately but does not have thorough or confident control of the grammar.

(ETS, 1982)

'Proficiency' is here operationalised in vaguely domain-specific and topic-oriented terms and comprises a rather unprincipled assortment of pragmatic, discourse, lexical and morphosyntactic indicators, as well as pronunciation and fluency. Based on the elicited speech samples, the interviewer's task is to provide a holistic assessment of the candidate's integrated target language ability.

The OPI format and rating scales are employed in academic, business, government and military contexts in the United States and internationally. Test outcomes can be decisive for a candidate's admission to tertiary education or fulfilment of programme requirements, promotion and foreign assignments. While all tests must provide reliable and valid measures, this is a particularly urgent requirement when a test is instrumental to the distribution of life chances and social selection. In the OPI, reliability is promoted through the predetermined interview structure and proficiency levels. Trained interviewers are periodically recertified in order to ensure uniformity in administering the interview and in the inferences drawn on candidates' proficiency from the elicited language samples.

As is common in the field of educational measurement, reliability has traditionally been more of a concern than validity. Rather than examining how well candidates' performance in the OPI matches their performance in speech events outside the test contexts, it was assumed that OPIs – as an interactive, oral activity type – bear sufficient resemblance to authentic target discourse to permit valid inferences on candidates' spoken language ability. Since the mid-1980s, data-based studies of OPI discourse have cast doubt on the construct validity (the degree to which test scores are interpretable in terms of the measured construct) and authenticity (the correspondence between test tasks and target tasks) of the test format (Bachman and Palmer, 1996; He and Young, 1998; Johnson, 2001; Kormos, 1999; Young, 2002). Of course, determining the construct validity of any test presupposes a definition of the construct. Many problems with the OPI as a test *format* can be traced to an ill-defined (or ill-understood) test *construct*. Since its inception, 'oral language proficiency' had been treated as a taken-for-granted concept rather than a notion requiring theoretical explication and empirical substantiation (Kramsch, 1986). Significant progress was made when the pre-theoretical notion of proficiency was replaced by increasingly more elaborate constructs of communicative competence (Bachman, 1990; Bachman and Palmer, 1996; Canale and Swain, 1980). Recent theory and research have resulted in yet a further specification of the construct to be measured in the OPI. Developing the intra-individual construct of communicative competence into the inter-individual concept of interactional competence, He and Young (1998) propose a constructivist, intersubjective, situated and practice-oriented view of speaking ability which cannot be reduced to an individual participant's linguistic and cognitive resources. Consequently, the interaction between interviewer and candidate (rather than isolated candidate contributions) must be the prime locus for proficiency assessment.

On the criterion of authenticity, many commentators have noted substantial differences between the OPI and ordinary conversation, summarised aptly by He and Young:

(1) as interviews, the topical structure and turn-taking systems of LPIs (OPI) differ from ordinary conversation, (2) as instances of institutional discourse, the speech exchange system and the goal-orientedness of LPIs differ from ordinary conversation, and (3) as cross-cultural encounters, participants in LPIs often have different understandings of what is going on in the LPI, a situation that may not occur in ordinary NS-NNs conversations.

(He and Young, 1998, p. 9)

As will be shown below, all of these activity-type specific features impact the interaction in the examined OPI. (1) and (2) point to the fundamental paradox of the OPI: it is a test format designed to test candidates' foreign language proficiency in contexts when they are not being tested. With reference to (3), misunderstandings in OPI interaction are both well-attested (Egbert, 1998; Katona, 1998; Ross, 1998; Young and Halleck, 1998) and a particular liability because they can result in negative evaluations of the candidate's target language skill. As in all types of interactive discourse, misunderstandings in OPIs can be overtly displayed through repair (Schegloff, 1987), indexed implicitly through participants' conduct but without resulting in redressive action, or lack any manifest discourse-internal indication. In the latter case, misunderstandings may be recognisable with reference to the activity type and the activity-type specific trajectory of expected actions (Ross, 1998). Misunderstood discourse practices in this category that warrant particular attention are pervasive, multifunctional 'system constraints' of interaction (Goffman, 1976). One such system constraint is repetition in discourse.

Repetition in discourse

Repetition, the reproduction of a prior occurrence of some form or function, is pervasive in discourse. Studies of the structure and function of repetitions include such discourse domains and activity types as aviation discourse (Cushing, 1994), therapeutic discourse (Ferrara, 1994), TV interviews (Nofsinger, 1994), instructional discourse in bilingual classrooms (Bean and Patthey-Chavez, 1994) and tutor–student interaction in early second language acquisition (Tomlin, 1994), native–nonnative speaker discourse (Knox, 1994) and OPIs (Kim and Suh, 1998). Repetition is a dialectical process in the sense that it operates anaphorically on the original segment and derives (much of) its 'meaning' by virtue of being another instantiation of the original – *plus ça change, plus c'est la même chose*. By isolating a prior segment of talk from its original co-text and re-presenting it, attention to that segment's formal features or its semantic, pragmatic or interactional meaning is maintained or refocused. Simultaneously, the reiteration produces additional or different meanings. On the meaning altering function of repetition, Johnstone *et al.* (1994) note: 'It is in fact a theoretical principle that, when something is repeated, its meaning changes. It's got a new box around it, because it happened a second time' (p. 12). They point out that repetition is fundamentally metalinguistic because 'it focuses attention on the makeup of both the repeated discourse and the earlier discourse' (p. 13). It is presumably due to its metalinguistic properties that repetition plays an important part in language acquisition and educational discourse. As an interactional strategy, repetition has been credited with such conversational functions as:

> getting or keeping the floor, showing listenership, providing back-channel response, stalling, gearing up to answer or speak, humor and play, savoring and showing appreciation of a good line or a good joke, persuasion . . . linking one speaker's ideas to another's, ratifying another's contributions (including another's ratification), and including in an interaction a person who did not hear the previous utterance.
>
> (Tannen, 1989, p. 51)

Merritt (1994) notes that repetition functions as a cognitive and interactional resource in classroom discourse, serving to 'provide more processing time, facilitate ongoing rhythm in the encounter, provide another opportunity to perceive the information accurately, gain the interlocutor's attention, focus that attention, or even display attentiveness to what the interlocutor has contributed' (p. 31). In fact, these roles of repetition extend beyond the classroom to other interactions involving participants of differential expertise, such as interviewer and candidate in the OPI.

Repetitions have been classified according to various formal and functional criteria (Johnstone *et al.*, 1994; Merritt, 1994; Norrick, 1987; Tannen, 1989). Cushing (1994) has offered the following comprehensive (though not exhaustive) categorisation:

> A *genuine* repetition is an utterance that replicates some previous utterance and is intended by the speaker to be a replication of that earlier utterance; a *virtual* repetition is an utterance that resembles some previous utterance in significant respects, but is not intended by the speaker to be such. A *correct* repetition is an utterance that substantially replicates an earlier utterance in all relevant features; an *incorrect* repetition is an utterance that fails to replicate some key feature of an earlier utterance that it otherwise matches. A *full* repetition is an utterance that replicates all of a previous utterance; a *partial* repetition is an utterance that replicates only part of an earlier utterance. A *literal* repetition is an utterance that replicates the words of a previous utterance, regardless of the meaning; a *conceptual* repetition is an utterance that replicates the meaning of an earlier utterance, regardless of the words. A *spontaneous* repetition is one that arises from a speaker's own initiative based on his or her judgment of a prevailing situation; an *obligatory* repetition is one that a speaker is required to utter by regulation or convention. An *effective* repetition is one that succeeds in having the impact on the hearer that the speaker intends it to have, or that a post hoc observer takes the speaker to have intended to have or considers that it might have had; an *ineffective* repetition is one that does not have such an impact.
>
> (Cushing, 1994, p. 55)

The repetitions we will consider for analysis are genuine, correct, partial, literal and spontaneous. Some of them meet the criterion of effectivity as defined by Cushing (1994) while others do not. It is those 'ineffective' repetitions that are a source of misunderstanding in the OPI data.

Data

The assessment interviews in English as a foreign language examined in this study were selected from an archive of over 400 OPIs conducted in-house at a large Japanese multinational electrical components manufacturing corporation, which we call Morimoto. The majority of the candidates were fully employed at Morimoto in various research or overseas retail positions, or as trainees in the overseas training division, a technical training facility for new employees in the company. All candidates were native speakers of Japanese, holding at least a bachelor degree from a Japanese university, usually in engineering, computer science or a natural science. Approximately one-third of the candidates held masters degrees in international business management or a natural science. The interviewers were native speakers of different varieties of English (Canada, New Zealand, UK, US) who had been trained initially by an Educational Testing Service representative and had recently been recertified. Most of them held bachelor degrees, usually in the humanities; less than half had a masters degree in Teaching English as a Second or Foreign Language. All of the interviewers were English as a Foreign Language teachers employed primarily as part-time instructors at one of the company's language training programmes for full-time Japanese employees. The profile of the interviewers closely matches that of English language teachers in Japanese corporate programmes – considerable practical teaching experience in the classroom, but little formal exposure to theory and research in applied linguistics and second language studies.

The interviews, conducted on-site in company offices in Osaka and Tokyo, were part of the regular testing schedule at the company's in-house language training programme. They were audiorecorded for reliability and validity checks as part of the standard interview procedure, with the recording equipment in full view of interviewers and candidates. The interviews are authentic in the sense that they served language assessment not research purposes and were recorded irrespective of any secondary purposes beyond quality control. The policy of recording all interviewers came from the need for programme administrators to review the contents of the OPIs for cross-checking and verification of rating outcomes in high-stakes interviews leading to overseas postings or awards of promotions within the corporation. In addition to the high-stakes interpretations of interview results, assessments of speaking proficiency were routinely used for decisions about employee placement into overseas programmes, technical school graduation requirements and overseas assignment potential.

For the present study, we selected 25 interviews, conducted by 11 different interviewers. Candidates in these interviews were rated as Advanced (Level 2) on the Defense Language Institute proficiency scale, defined above. The interviews varied between 15 and 30 minutes in length.

Analysis

Our object of enquiry is limited to 'instances in which a second speaker reproduces a phrase or clause spoken by another participant (the "first" speaker) in the adjacent turn and uses substantially the same words as that first speaker' (Nofsinger, 1994, p. 84). The subset of repetitions to be considered can thus be categorised as 'other-repetitions in the turn immediately subsequent to the repeated talk' (p. 85), referred to as repeats (Merritt, 1994; Sorjonen, 1996). As documented in the conversation analytic literature

(Sorjonen, 1996, for a recent study), repeats are multiply ambiguous in the interactional jobs they can do. As repair initiators, they identify the repeated material as somehow troublesome; as displays of the repeat speaker's hearing or comprehension, they request confirmation, whereas repeating formulations of indirectly conveyed actions serves to 'confirm allusions' (Schegloff, 1996); as indices of the repeat speaker's epistemological stance towards the repeated material (Sorjonen, 1996), they display epistemic positions such as surprise or disbelief; as neutral receipts and 'go-ons' (Edmondson, 1981; Schegloff, 1990), they request the recipient to continue the line of talk she is currently engaged in; as requests for elaboration, they project further conversational treatment of the repeated material beyond confirmation. Especially in the latter function, repeats have an active topic-developmental import in that they foreground the repeated information and thus cast it as a candidate topic or topic component. In this function, repeats are one procedure of the stepwise transition of topics ('topic shading', Schegloff, 1990).

Previous studies of OPI discourse (He & Young, 1998) have established that repeats are frequently used interactional routines in this activity type, serving any and all of the functions listed above. Because of the multiple interactional purposes for which they may be deployed, interviewer and candidate may not always see eye to eye on the actions performed by a repeat at a particular moment in the interview. This is the case with most of the repeats that we will now examine. (I = interviewer, C = candidate; see p. 104 for transcription conventions.)

Our analysis will focus on seven repeats produced by the interviewer in a 70-line-long transcript. While the clustering of repeats in this segment may seem extreme, it is not untypical of the interviews in our corpus. Most of the repeats follow an answer given by the candidate to an interviewer question, that is, they occur in the third position of a three-part sequence.

Extract 4.1.1a

```
 7 I:   Ah hm. How big is the school.
 8 C:   .hh oh:: the students- uh the students who:: come-
 9      >who come< to my house is (.) about, (.) uh, over
10      one hundred,
11      (1.0)
12 → I:  Over one hundred.
```

Extract 4.1.2a

```
31   I:   Mm. (0.8) Good= and, uh, how about yourself?=
32        What kind of work do you do at Morimoto?
33   C:   Uh I'm doing planning.
34        (0.8)
35 → I:   Planning.
```

Extract 4.1.3a

(continued answer to questions in 31 and 32)
```
50      c: =uh (.) so I (.) uhh (.) I did (.) I'm doing now
51         (.) umm (.) rather hehehhhe rather boring job.
52 → i:  Boring job.
```

Extract 4.1.4a

```
54      i:  SO, what kind of- uh (.) I don't- planning is
55          planning. Are you- are you planning, uh, company
56          recreation [trips or::]
57      c:             [No hehehe]
58      c:  Uh (.) planning (.) uh (.) new products.
59 → i:  Planning new products.
```

Extract 4.1.5a

```
63      i:  What kind of products?
64      c:  Um, our company is produc-, producing uh (.) video
65          videos,
66 → i:  °Videos°.
```

In the last turn of each segment, the interviewer repeats, with falling intonation, the final elements from the candidate's turn, which include the new information that answers I's question. The falling intonation contour indexes, minimally, acknowledgement of the receipted item(s), yet it does not convey alignment with the speaker or any particular affective stance. However, the repetitions perform different actions, as a closer look at their preceding discourse context and prosodic composition reveals.

The interviewer's question in Extract 4.1.1a, line 7, is preceded by a long exchange about the candidate's parents and their professions. In line 10, C delivers the final element of her utterance with level intonation, suggesting that she has not finished her answer but is possibly pausing for a receipt token by I at the transition relevant place following her last turn-constructional unit (TCU). The candidate's orientation to some receipt response is all the more plausible as I cannot have expected the information just provided by C about the size of her family's language school. Furthermore, according to Japanese discourse practices, a listener response would be almost normative at this point. The interviewer, on the other hand, by not producing any vocal action, appears to be waiting for C to continue her turn, as projected by the prosodic contour of C's last TCU. The gap of silence (line 11) can itself be taken as indicative of a minor misunderstanding of what the next action due is in the understanding of each participant. I ends the one-second silence by repeating the last two elements of C's preceding turn, which include the information requested by I in line 7 (the size of the language school). By virtue of its sequential placement after the pause follow-ing C's incomplete turn, the repeat invites C to resume the topical talk.

Extract 4.1.2a has a parallel structure to Extract 4.1.1a. The candidate's response is followed by a gap of silence, which is terminated by the inter-viewer's repeat of the last element in C's turn. But the sequence differs from 4.1.1a in several respects. Whereas 4.1.1a was situated in the context of an ongoing topic, the candidate's family, the interviewer's question in lines 31–32 introduces a new topic, the candidate and her work at Morimoto. The question is designed as a two-part construction. The first part nominates the new general topic with the formula 'how about yourself', thereby contrasting the new topic with the previous subject matter, C's family. The immediately following specification narrows down the general solicit to a particular ques-tion about C's work at Morimoto. While the candidate's answer (line 33) is relevant to the question, the gap of silence (line 34) suggests that the inter-viewer is waiting for her to elaborate her brief response before he produces the repeat (line 35). Through the repeat, the interviewer treats the response as underelaborated, and the special emphasis on the first syllable (<u>Plan</u>ning.) can be heard as indexing doubt about what exactly the candidate means by 'planning'. If the repeat displays anaphorically, as it were, the interviewer's understanding of the candidate's response, then its cataphoric import is a solicit for elaboration.

Unlike Extracts 4.1.1a and 4.1.2a, the repeats in the remaining extracts are not preceded by a gap of silence but follow immediately upon the candi-date's prior turn. The repeats in Extracts 4.1.3a and 4.1.4a give emphatic stress to the new information from C's answer – '<u>Bor</u>ing job.' (line 52) and 'Planning new <u>pro</u>ducts.' (line 59) In her turns preceding the repeats, C described her job as boring but did not explain what her job was or why it was boring (Extract 4.1.3a), and she did not specify the kinds of product that she 'plans' (Extract 4.1.4a). The repeats request elaboration of the underspecified responses.

The repeat in Extract 4.1.5a ('Videos') contrasts with the previous four in its prosodic composition: those were articulated at a normal volume and gave emphasis to (part of) the repeated segment, whereas the repetition in line 66 is delivered sotto voce and without special emphatic stress. If both the candidate's immediately preceding answer and the interactional context a few turns before are taken into consideration, the repeat can be understood as doing double duty as a confirmation of C's self-repair in line 65 and a receipt token. The repeat might be heard as doing a repair confirmation by virtue of its adjacent placement to C's self-repair ('video – videos'). At the same time, its position in the transition space (Sacks *et al.*, 1974) following

C's turn in lines 64–5 is also a prime location for a receipt token. The receipt reading is further supported by the fact that the interviewer twice solicited information about the topic component 'products "planned" by the candidate' – less directly, and unsuccessfully, by the repeat 'Planning new products.' in line 59 and directly, and successfully, by asking 'What kind of products?' in line 63. When the candidate finally offers the information (lines 64–65), the interviewer acknowledges receipt – but through the prosodic design of the repeat, he also indexes the information as barely newsworthy. As the interviewer and the candidate are both Morimoto employees, they share the knowledge that videos are one of the company's main product lines. The candidates treatment of the repeat supports the reading, as evident from the continuation of the segment in Extract 4.1.5b.

Extract 4.1.5b

```
63      I:  What kind of products?
64      C:  Um, our company is produc-, producing uh (.) video-
65          videos,
66  →   I:  °Videos°.
67      C:  so:: um (.) all- MOST videos are camcorders or
68          veeceeuh or teevee veeceeuh combina↑tions.
69      I:  Mm. Mm.
70      C:  That kind of things.
```

We noted earlier that the candidate, in certain environments, appears to expect a receipt and upon its absence does not resume her turn. Following the repeat in 66, by contrast, she continues her line of talk as initiated in 64. Further support for the receipt function of the repeat may also be gleaned from the last two turns of the segment. Upon the interviewer's topic non-implicative receipt tokens ('Mm. Mm.') in line 69, C shuts the topic down by producing a prototypical concluding statement (Maynard, 1980), the general extender 'That kind of things' (Overstreet, 2000). In this segment, then, interviewer and candidate treat the repeat as doing the same action.

On the sequential evidence in the interaction prior to the repeats and their formatting characteristics, we have observed that the interviewer performs four of his repeats as requests for elaboration. While confirmation of I's hearing of the repeated items may serve as a relevant initial uptake, confirmation without subsequent elaboration would not sufficiently match the repeats' response trajectory. After having focused on the actions carried out by the interviewer through repeating material from the candidate's preceding turn in Extracts 4.1.1a to 4.1.4a, we shall now examine how the candidate treats the interviewer's repeats in her subsequent turn and the interactional consequences ensuing from her responding action.

Extract 4.1.2b

```
31      I:  Mm. (0.8) Good= and, uh, how about yourself?=
32          What kind of work do you do at Morimoto?
33      C:  Uh I'm doing planning.
34          (0.8)
35  →   I:  Planning.
36      C:  Planning, yes, planning section. >I belong to
37          planning section< (.) .hh but uh: (.) our company is
38          rather (.) uh (.) >our company< is originally (.) uh (.)
39          productu company, so:: (.) uh (.) they first (.) uh (.)
40          produced, uh uh=>manufactured< (.) um (.) productions,
41          so: .hh they- they can't (.) uh (.) they can't plan (.)
42          um (.) their original production= >product<. So hhh.
43          rather (.) umm (.) in that sense (.) th- we are not (.) we
44          are not doing planning [job,]
45      I:                          [°Mm°]
46      C:  I think.
47      I:  °Mm°. So.=
48      C:  =SO um hehehe=
49      I:  hehe
50      C:  =uh (.) so I (.) uhh (.) I did (.) I'm doing now
51          (.) umm (.) rather hehehhhe rather boring job.
```

In her response turn to the interviewer's repeat, the candidate first confirms
I's hearing of the repeated material. The confirmation is done emphatically,
by first re-repeating the repeated element 'planning', followed by the agreement token 'yes', and finally by extending 'planning' to 'planning section'.
By quickly adding 'I belong to planning section', I offers a clarification of
what she referred to earlier as 'I'm doing planning', a bit of information that
ostensibly puzzled the interviewer. The candidate now proceeds to provide
some historical detail about Morimoto and the role of 'planning' at the company. In so doing, she shifts the focus from the topic of *her* work at Morimoto
(the focus of the interviewer's question in line 32) to the department she
works in and the company at large. She first returns to her own work at
Morimoto in lines 50–51, where she describes her job as 'boring' – without,
however, having specified what that boring job is. Her elaborate response is
receipted rather unenthusiastically by the interviewer's sotto voce "°Mm°'s,
which can be heard as dissatisfaction with her response (see the contrasting
actions that different response tokens and their formatting can perform, e.g.
Jefferson, 1984, 1993). Nevertheless, the candidate did elaborate the repeated
item and thus treated it as a request for elaboration. So in this sequence, the
interviewer and the candidate displayed agreement on the actional import of
the repeat 'Planning.' in line 35, although they did not concur about the
topical relevance of C's elaboration, as will become clearer shortly.

The remaining repeats that we have analysed as soliciting elaboration are not treated as such by the candidate, as the actions subsequent to the repeats reveal.

Extract 4.1.3b

```
(continued answer to questions in 31 and 32)
50      c:  =uh (.) so I (.) uhh (.) I did (.) I'm doing now
51          (.) umm (.) rather hehehhhe rather boring job.
52  → i:  Boring job.
53      c:  Yes.
54      i:  SO, what kind of- uh (.) I don't- planning is
55          planning.
```

Extract 4.1.4b

```
54      i:  SO, what kind of- uh (.) I don't- planning is
55          planning. Are you- are you planning, uh, company
56          recreation [trips or::]
57      c:              [No hehehe]
58      c:  Uh (.) planning (.) uh (.) new products.
59  → i:  Planning new products.
60      c:  Yes, but hehehe uh (.) our- our company is rather (.)
61          uh (.) NEW at- at that point, so they can't do the
62          planning (.) uh (.) >very well<, so (.) um
63      i:  What kind of products?
```

Extract 4.1.1b

```
07      i:  Ah hm. How big is the school.
08      c:  .hh oh:: the students- uh the students who:: come-
09          >who come< to my house is (.) about, (.) uh, over
10          one hundred,
11          (1.0)
12  → i:  Over one hundred.
13      c:  Over one hundred.=
14      i:  =Mm.=
15      c:  =Yes.
16      i:  Do they teach any other subjects be-, besides, uh,
17          English?
```

In Extract 4.1.3b, the continuation of 4.1.2b, the sole response offered by the candidate to the interviewer's repeat 'Boring job' is the agreement token 'Yes.', even though the emphatic marker invites commentary as to what is boring about C's job. We suggest that C abandons the candidate topic component of why her job is boring because in lines 50–51, her turn prior to the repeat, the unfavourable assessment of her job concluded C's telling of her workplace. Moreover, the concluding assessment is indexed as such by the concluding marker 'so' (Schiffrin, 1987) in lines 50 and 48. By confirming the interviewer's hearing rather than offering an elaboration, the candidate treats the attribution of her work as boring as a conclusion rather than a new piece of information, as the interviewer did in his repeat.

From the interviewer's following turn lines 54–56, it transpires that at this point, he is less concerned with the uninspirational nature of C's job than with finding out what her job is in the first place. After his high-volume turn-initial 'SO' (resuming his aborted 'so.'-marked turn in line 47), I starts on a soon-to-be-aborted question about the kind of planning that C's job involves, followed by hesitation tokens, another aborted TCU 'I don't-' and the tautological 'planning is planning'. The composition of the turn thus far conveys distress, not to say exasperation. The interviewer ends the turn with a 'pushed-down' question, a self-repair whereby he redesigns the initial wh-question as a yes–no question that offers up a candidate planning activity. Upon her overlapped negative response to the proposed planning job, C reveals 'new products' as the target of her 'planning' (in line 58), a response that the interviewer's repeat (line 59) treats as underelaborated and in need of specification. The candidate, however, does not elaborate on the kinds of products that she plans. Rather, she first confirms the interviewer's hearing of 'planning new products' with an agreement token ('Yes,') and then resumes her earlier assessment of Morimoto's planning ability. So, unlike her response in Extract 4.1.2b, even though C produces extended topical talk, she does not provide the elaboration of 'products' as requested by the interviewer, as evident from I's follow-up question 'What kind of products?' (line 63).

Extract 4.1.1b, too, demonstrates that the interviewer and candidate orient to the repeat differently. Although the topic component 'size of the language school' is strongly foregrounded through the adjacent repeats of 'Over one hundred.', C does not add further topic-developmental talk beyond the confirmation. Rather, the topic component is laid to rest immediately after the confirmation through the paired exchange of the topic nonimplicative acknowledgment tokens ('Mm.' – 'Yes.').

The remaining two repeats in this OPI segment differ from the ones discussed so far.

Extract 4.1.6a

```
16    I:   Do they teach any other subjects be-, besides, uh,
17         English?
18    C:   Uh: my step- hehehe stepbrother is uh teaching-
19         >teaching them< (.) Japanese.
20  → I:   Your stepbrother.
21    C:   Yes.= My, uh, my bigger sister's husband.
22    I:   OH (.) oh (.) that's your BROTHER, your brother-in-law.
```

```
23      C:  Yea-, hehe ((embarrassed)) I'm so[rry.]=
24      I:                                [I see.]
25      C:  = °Brother-in-law° ((laughing voice)).
26          (0.5)
27  →   I:  Brother-in-law uh?=
28      C:  =Yes. Yes=
29      I:  =Mm. Mm.=
30      C:  =Mm.
31      I:  Mm. (0.8) Good= and, uh, how about yourself?=
```

Although the interviewer's repeat in line 20 is located in the same sequential position as the previous repetitions, that is, in the third turn following a question–answer exchange, there are several indicators that it performs a different action. A first, structural observation is that unlike the other repeat instances, the repetition 'Your stepbrother.' takes up an element that occurs earlier, not turn-finally in C's response. Second, this element is not the new information elicited by the preceding question. In lines 16–17, I initiated a new topic component, i.e. other subjects taught at the language school run by C's family besides English. In her response, the candidate foregrounded the new information 'Japanese'. The utterance-final placement of 'Japanese' in line 19 positions it in the same slot as 'English' in 17 and thus accentuates the common category membership. Therefore, the candidate item for a repeat with a view to continuous topic development is 'Japanese', not 'stepbrother', since 'Japanese' is the information solicited by I's question in 16 and 17. Third, C's hesitation token in 18 and her abandoned first attempt at 'stepbrother', followed by laughter, flag the item 'stepbrother' as potentially problematic. Fourth, parallel to C's indexing of 'stepbrother' as troublesome, the interviewer repeats precisely this item in line 20, marking the first element of the compound 'stepbrother' with special emphasis. Fifth, going further back into the preceding interactional context, when asked about the members of her family earlier in the interview, C mentioned her parents and bigger sister, but no stepbrother. The sudden emergence of the stepbrother as a teacher in the language school is therefore suspect. All of these sequential aspects and design features conspire to cast the repeat of 'Your stepbrother.' as an other-initiated repair. In her initial response, the candidate treats the repeat as a request for confirmation, as evident from her confirmation token 'yes' (line 21) and the latched-on reference term 'my bigger sister's husband'. The falling intonation on both 'yes' and 'husband' mark the reformulation as periphrastic to 'stepbrother' rather than as a self-repair. It is first after the interviewer's correction (line 22) that the candidate, by doing 'accountings' (Jefferson, 1987), orients to the repair activity.

I's comprehension token 'I see' in line 24 could have terminated the repair sequence and provided the occasion to resume topical talk. But C lingers on the repaired element, softly repeating '°Brother-in-law°' in line

25. We now see a sequence structurally parallel to the repeat sequence in Extract 4.1.1b: none of the participants continues to produce topic developmental talk. Following the half-second silence in line 26, I repeats 'Brother-in-law uh? this time followed by a question tag with rising intonation, which biases response options towards a confirmation. Neither the original topic component 'other subjects taught at the school' nor the candidate topic component 'the Japanese teaching brother-in-law' are pursued in further topical talk, although through the extended foregrounding via the repair, the brother-in-law practically presented itself as a topic component on a silver platter. Instead, through the sequence of topically non-implicative acknowledgment tokens in lines 28–31, the coparticipants perform a multiple transition exchange – 'multiple' because the exchange closes the repair sequence, the current topic component 'other subjects', and the entire topic 'C's family'.

The seven interviewer repeats occurring in the OPI segment functioned as receipt, repair initiator, request for confirmation and request for elaboration. Which of these interactional jobs a particular repeat was doing depended on its sequential environment and structural properties, especially its prosodic composition. That intonation contributes significantly to the meaning of repetition has been recognised in several studies (Ferrara, 1994; Norrick, 1987; Simpson, 1994; Sorjonen, 1996). By far the most frequent prosodic pattern in the OPI corpus is falling intonation, a structural feature shared with repetition in casual conversation (Simpson, 1994). Falling intonation suggests that 'a repetition is to be interpreted as either positive, as in answering questions and in supportive backchanneling and shadowing, or negative, as with corrections and imitations' (Simpson, 1994, p. 48). A falling intonation contour appears to be heard as 'less threatening than a rising or more exaggerated, emphatic intonation', 'calling attention to the phrase in a noncommittal way' (Simpson, 1994, p. 47).

As summarised in Table 4.1, a single repeat can do more than one job at the same time and participants may orient to different conversational roles of the same repeat. This was particularly apparent in participants' treatment of the interviewer's repeats as requests for confirmation and elaboration. On several occasions, the interviewer oriented to elaboration rather than mere confirmation of his hearing or understanding. The interviewer thus attended to the capacity of repeats to generate further topical talk. This function of repeats parallels strikingly a type of repetition used by psychotherapists in therapeutic discourse, referred to as mirroring (Ferrara, 1994).

Extract 4.2: Therapy (Ferrara, 1994, p. 75)

CLIENT: When I went home last week I made a discovery.↘
THERAPIST: A discovery.↘

Table 4.1   Interactional roles of repeats

Repeat token	Treated by I as	Treated by C as	Same	Different
over one hundred.	Elaboration request	Confirmation request		✓
your stepbrother.	Repair initiator	Confirmation request		✓
brother-in-law uh?	Confirmation request	Confirmation request	✓	
Planning.	Elaboration request	Confirmation and elaboration request*	✓	
Boring job.	Elaboration request	Confirmation request		✓
Planning new products.	Elaboration request	Confirmation request		✓
°videos°.	Receipt and repair confirmation	receipt**	✓	

* Categorised as 'same' because initial confirmation of I's hearing as displayed in the repeat is consistent with treating the repeat as elaboration request.
** Categorised as 'same' because the repeat is ambiguous between a receipt and repair confirmation, thus allowing treatment as either action.

Ferrara summarises the interactional work of mirroring as follows:

> Mirrored speech tends to replicate shorter segments, usually salient phrases or key words rather than clauses or entire utterances. Mirroring, like back channel cues such as *Mhmhmm*, is a most minimal response intended to insure that the previous speaker continues an extended turn with little interruption. Mirroring serves to quickly return the 'turn at talk' . . . to the prior speaker and has the added advantage that it signals attentiveness and invites continuation of a topic. By selecting a key word or phrase for repetition, and by delivering it either in a monotone or with downward intonation, a discourse recipient indicates that he or she is in fact listening . . . the technique of mirroring appears to foster rapid resumption by the prior speaker and a continuation or elaboration of topic . . . the result of a minimal speech unit produced by the therapist is client continuation or elaboration of the previously initiated topic.

> (Ferrara, 1994, pp. 77–79)

The structural and functional isomorphism of mirroring and elaborative repeats results from the similarities between the two activity types in which they have been observed. Psychotherapy and OPIs share with many other types of institutional discourse their asymmetrical participant structure, endowing the therapist/interviewer with control over turn allocation and topic management. Although topics in therapeutic discourse are usually client generated whereas topics in the OPI are proposed by the interviewer, the effectiveness of both activities hinges critically on clients' and candidates' production of extended talk. In the OPI, continuation of the current topic ensures that the candidate produces more target language samples for assessment while facilitating the interviewer's job – the longer a current topic can be maintained, the less the need for the interviewer to generate new topics. But unlike the clients in Ferrara's (1994) corpus of therapy sessions, who appeared to respond to mirroring repetitions by elaboration and topic continuation – i.e. the repetitions were 'effective', in Cushing's (1994) sense – the candidate in Extract 4.1, just like many of her colleagues throughout the examined OPI interactions, responded only occasionally as mandated by the activity-type specific demands of the OPI. As evident from C's responses, C treated the opportunity space opened by I's repeats as more restricted. C only engaged in elaboration where there was a substantial indication in the sequential environment of the repeat that extended topic-relevant talk was required, as was the case in 'Planning'. C only engaged in elaboration where there was a substantial indication in the sequential environment of the repeat that extended topic-relevant talk was required, as was the case in 'Planning'. When this condition did not obtain, C treated the repeat as a request for confirmation and thereby as a possible pre-closing of the current topic or topic component. As apparent from the actions following 'Planning new products', the sequential implicativeness of repeats-as-confirmation requests for topic shift or change is no iron-clad law, but it evidently is one of the topic management roles that repeats can play in the OPI.

The ambiguity of repeats as eliciting topic-non-implicative talk and resulting in topic shift or change versus eliciting topic-developmental talk and thus keeping the current topic going is something like a mixed blessing in the OPI context. By focusing on material in the candidate's preceding turn, the interviewer's repeat casts this material as possible matter for further topical talk. Moreover, because the candidate offered the material in the first place, it is likely to refer to a matter that the candidate is comfortable to talk about. As reported in the interlanguage literature, topic expertise is a major factor in interlanguage performance (e.g. Douglas and Selinker, 1985; Zuengler, 1993). Therefore, repeats – as requests for elaboration or 'tell me mores' – can be an effective conversational technique to elicit optimal performance from the candidate. But since the candidate's understanding of which repeat counts as an elaboration request may be considerably more restricted than the interviewer's, repeats may not be heard as inviting talk on a matter offered by the candidate, but rather as a means of closing down the current topic. As a consequence of the fundamental exchange structure of the OPI, where the interviewer asks the questions and the candidate gives the answers (Schegloff, 1992, on the fundamental exchange structure of interviews), nomination of the next topic is invariably performed by the interviewer. Repeats are thus highly potent devices for topic control, yet as their multifunctionality may give rise to divergent understandings of their interactional import on the part of interviewers and candidates, they can also be hazardous undertakings in an institutional setting where such divergent orientations may have adverse consequences for interview outcomes.

Misunderstood repeats: towards an explanation

Previous research on OPI discourse suggests several – complementary rather than mutually exclusive – explanations for the divergent understandings of repeats observed above. A first interactional account refers to Kim and Suh's (1998) observation that Korean Language Proficiency Interviews exhibit a five-turn exchange structure, in which a confirmation sequence provides the transitional exchange to the next question:

1st I: Question
2nd C: Answer
3rd I: Confirmation request
4th C: Confirmation
5th I: Follow-up assessment/question

(Kim and Suh, 1998, p. 302)

This exchange structure – together with others – occurs in our OPI data as well (Extract 4.3).

Extract 4.3: OPI Morimoto

```
 1      I:  [. . .]Okay, what did you do last weekend?
 2      C:  Last weekend. Uh, I have a test, I had a test.
 3      I:  What kind of test?
 4      C:  Mm, (0.5) general education and English and
 5          competition in (.) Japanese. It's for journalist.
 6      I:  Mm.
 7      C:  Yeah.
 8      I:  How did you do?
 9      C:  Awful.=
10  →   I:  =Awful?
11      C:  Yeah.
12      I:  You don't think you passed?
13      C:  Not really.
14      I:  When do you find out?
15      C:  It's on the newspaper.
16  →   I:  It's in the newspaper?
17      C:  Yeah.
18      I:  Mm, um, if you are interested in journalism, does
19          that mean that you read a lot of newspapers
20          yourself?
```

Lines 8–12 and 14–18 map perfectly on the exchange structure identified by Kim and Suh (1998). Although I's third-turn confirmation requests (lines 10 and 16) are designed as repetitions (disregarding the correction in 16 for the present analysis), they differ in their prosodic composition from six of the seven repeats in Extracts 4.1.1 to 4.1.6. Their rising intonation suggests that these repetitions may be treated as confirmation requests. As a first explanatory hypothesis why candidates may treat elaborative repeats as confirmation requests, we suggest that candidates with little exposure to oral target language discourse may tend to focus their attention on the interviewers' words without also processing the prosodic composition of repetitions. They therefore miss decisive contextualization cues (Gumperz, 1982) which index the *actions* implemented by the *practice* of repetition in the OPI context (Schegloff, 1997, for the distinction between practices and actions). In the light of interactional sociolinguistic studies on culturally divergent form–function matches of prosodic cues (e.g. Gumperz, 1992), one might suspect that the differential interactional role assigned to repeats by interview participants reflects candidates' own practices in using repeats. We have therefore compared candidates' repeats of interviewer contributions with the interviewer repeats of candidates' utterances examined in this study. Unsurprisingly, candidates frequently check their understanding of interviewers' contributions by requesting confirmation. These confirmation requests are almost invariably produced with rising intonation, as in Extract 4.4.

Extract 4.4: OPI Morimoto

```
 1      I:  Mm. (.) Can you describe your house to me please?
 2  →   C:  .hh °house°?=
 3      I:  =Yeah.
 4          (0.5)
 5      C:  My house is, um, (.) manshon.
 6      I:  Um.=
 7      C:  manshon
 8      I:  Uh-huh
 9      C:  A::nd, my father and my mother (.) and I lived in (.)
10          there. hehe
11      I:  Uh-huh.
12          (0.5)
13      I:  Can you describe your apartment?
14  →   C:  Apartment? Um, (0.8) apartment is near (.) by, eh, Baji
15          Koen
16      I:  Uh-huh=
17      C:  =It is, (.5) horse, mm, *many* *horses* in, many horses in
18          the:: park,
19      I:  Uh-huh=
20      C:  very near, um, to my house.hhe
21      I:  Is your, is your house very big?
22      C:  hehe. ↑U::MM, not so biggu.
```

```
23      I:  How many rooms are there?
24  →   C:  Rooms? (.) One (0.5) f-, four rooms and dining kitchen,
25          and bathroom
26      I:  Uh-huh
27      C:  that's all.
```

The repeats in Extract 4.4 illustrate two of several formats deployed by candidates in the OPI – turn-initial repeats followed by a delayed response in the same turn (lines 14, 24) and a repeat whose production is delayed from turn-initial position (2) without subsequent same-turn response to the interviewer's question. Unlike the repeats in lines 14 and 24, this repeat works as a practice to implement a next-turn repair initiation, as evident in the composition of the repeat turn as a display of comprehension trouble and the interviewer's confirmation of the candidate's proffered understanding (3). Unfortunately, the audiorecords do not capture possible non-verbal interviewer responses to the turn-initial repeats in lines 14 and 24. It is not unlikely that the interviewer treated the repeats as confirmation requests by signalling confirmation non-verbally, such as by headnod, immediately subsequent to their production. While these and other repeats performed by candidates in next turn after interviewer questions await detailed analysis, they are predominantly formatted with rising intonation. Considering candidates' own practices of repeat production, one might assume that they would treat the *absence* of rising intonation on interviewer repeats as indexing an interactional role different from confirmation checks, but evidently this is not the case. Highly routinised strategies in discourse production do not automatically translate to equivalent routines in comprehension and vice versa.

Finally, candidates' treatment of elaboration repeats as confirmation requests may be a transfer of L1 discourse practices. Previous studies found that Japanese OPI candidates as a group – individual differences notwithstanding – tend to under-elaborate their interview contributions (Ross, 1998; Young and Halleck, 1998). The minimalist style (Ross, 1998) displayed by interview candidates seems related to a culturally informed dispreference for volubility in hierarchically structured encounters. Self-disclosure and trivial factual information are not seen as appropriate in interaction with unfamiliar interlocutors. Even speakers with the highest proficiency ratings, who are demonstrably capable of producing extended discourse, may adhere to the culturally preferred minimalist style, as the candidate in Extract 4.5 from Young and Halleck (1998, p. 376):

Extract 4.5: OPI (Young and Halleck, 1998, p. 376)

```
I:  Mhm (.) so you will live in Tokyo?
C:  Yes.
I:  Mhm where is your family now?
C:  Oh in (  ) Prefecture.
```

I: How far is that?

C: Uh it's about six hundred or seven hundred kilometers away so it's very far.

I: Far away.

C: Very far.

As is often the case in unequal power encounters, divergence from institutional norms and expectations can become a liability for the candidate. The Japanese candidates' reticence towards elaboration may under-represent their ability to produce topical talk in the target language. Analysis of 80 OPIs from the Morimoto interview archive revealed that under-elaboration of responses to interview questions typically resulted in accommodative moves on the part of the interviewer, and such accommodation was correlated to ratings of candidates' proficiency (Ross, 1995). Although candidates doubtless understand that the OPI serves no other purpose but language assessment, the discourse requirements arising from the goal of the activity do not seem apparent to them – or are overridden by highly overlearnt interactional practices extant in the community outside the OPI context.

A complementary analytical strategy to the one pursued in this chapter is to examine misunderstandings of elaborative repeats in the OPI corpus against the backdrop of frame conflicts (Ross, 1998) or Rich Points (Young and Halleck, 1998, following Agar, 1994). Such analysis suggests that under-elaboration, while available as avoidance strategy and part of a discourse survival kit to cope with overtaxing demands on candidates' target language ability irrespective of their cultural background, may be a culturally preferred strategy that militates against the candidates' best interest in the high stakes context of the OPI. As Young and Halleck (1998) have demonstrated, cultural differences in candidates' interactional style favour those whose discourse practices are more consonant with the activity-type specific goals of the OPI and disadvantage others. Making the OPI a more equitable assessment instrument for candidates from different speech communities will require a considerable research effort. In fact, it is not at all clear whether the OPI as an assessment procedure will survive such a project.

Appendix

Transcription conventions	
(0.8)	Time gap in tenths of a second
(.)	Brief time gap
=	Latching of utterance segments
[ ]	Overlapping talk
.hh	In-breath

hh	Out-breath
(( ))	Transcriber comment
-	Cut-off
:	Elongated sound
!	Emphatic tone
.	Falling intonation
,	Continuing intonation
?	Rising intonation
↑	Marked rise of immediately following segment
<u>Under</u>	Emphasis
CAPITALS	Increased volume
°	Decreased volume
><	Increased speed
→	Line discussed in text

Acknowledgements

Thanks are due to Jack Bilmes and Johannes Wagner for their insightful comments on an earlier version of this chapter.

References

Agar, M. (1994). *Language shock*. New York: Morrow.

American Council on the Teaching of Foreign Languages (ACTFL). (1986). *ACTFL proficiency guidelines*. Hastings-on-Hudson, NY: Author.

American Council on the Teaching of Foreign Languages (ACTFL). (1999). *ACTFL proficiency guidelines* (revised). Hastings-on-Hudson, NY: Author.

Bachman, L. (1990). *Fundamental considerations in language testing*. Oxford: Oxford University Press.

Bachman, L. and Palmer, A. (1996). *Language testing in practice*. Oxford: Oxford University Press.

Bean, M. S. and Patthey-Chavez, G. G. (1994). Repetition in instructional discourse: A means for joint cognition. In B. Johnstone (ed.), *Repetition in discourse* (Vol. 1). Norwood, NJ: Ablex, 207–220.

Canale, M. and Swain, M. (1980). Theoretical bases of communicative approaches to second language teaching and testing. In *Applied Linguisitics*, 1, 1–47.

Clark, J. L. D. and Clifford, R. T. (1988). The FSI/ACTFL proficiency scales and testing techniques: Development, current status, and needed research. In *Studies in Second Language Acquisition*, 10, 129–147.

Cushing, S. (1994). 'Air Cal three thirty six, go around three thirty six, go around': Linguistic repetition in air-ground communication. In B. Johnstone (ed.), *Repetition in discourse* (Vol. 2). Norwood, NJ: Ablex, 53–65.

Douglas, D. and Selinker, L. (1985). Principles for language tests within the 'discourse domain' theory of interlanguage: Research, test construction, and interpretation. In *Language Testing*, 2, 205–226.

Edmondson, W. (1981). *Spoken discourse*. London: Longman.

Egbert, M. M. (1998). Miscommunication in language proficiency interviews. In R. Young and A. W. He (eds), *Talking and testing. Discourse approaches to the assessment of oral proficiency*. Amsterdam: John Benjamins, 147–169.

ETS (1982). *Oral proficiency testing manual*. Princton, NJ: Author.

Ferrara, K. (1994). Repetition as rejoinder in therapeutic discourse: Echoing and mirroring. In B. Johnstone (ed.), *Repetition in discourse* (Vol. 2). Norwood, NJ: Ablex, 66–83.

Goffman, E. (1976). Replies and responses. In *Language in Society*, 5, 254–313.

Gumperz, J. J. (1982). *Discourse strategies*. Cambridge: Cambridge University Press.

Gumperz, J. J. (1992). Contextualization and understanding. In A. Duranti and C. Goodwin (eds), *Rethinking context*. Cambridge: Cambridge University Press, 229–252.

He, A. W. and Young, R. (1998). Language proficiency interviews: a discourse approach. In R. Young and A. W. He (eds), *Talking and testing. Discourse approaches to the assessment of oral proficiency*. Amsterdam: John Benjamins, 1–24.

Higgs, T. V. (1984). *Teaching for proficiency, the organizational principle*. Lincolnwood, IL: National Textbook Company.

Jefferson, G. (1984). Notes on a systematic deployment of the acknowledgements tokens 'Yeah' and 'Mm hm'. *Papers in Linguistics*, 17, 197–216.

Jefferson, G. (1987). On exposed and embedded correction in conversation. In G. Button & J. R. E. Lee (Eds), *Talk and social organisation* (pp. 86–100). Clevedon: Multilingual Matters.

Jefferson, G. (1993). Caveat speaker: Preliminary notes on recipient topic-shift implicature. In *Research on Language and Social Interaction*, 26, 1–30.

Johnson, M. (2001). *The art of non-conversation. A reexamination of the validity of the oral proficiency interview*. New Haven and London: Yale University Press.

Johnstone, B. *et al.* (1994). Repetition in discourse: A dialogue. In B. Johnstone (ed.), *Repetition in discourse* (Vol. 1). Norwood, NJ: Ablex, 1–20.

Katona, L. (1998). Meaning negotiation in the Hungarian oral proficiency examination of English. In R. Young and A. W. He (eds), *Talking and testing. Discourse approaches to the assessment of oral proficiency*. Amsterdam: John Benjamins, 239–267.

Kim, K-h., and Suh, K.-h. (1998). Confirmation sequences as interactional resources in Korean language proficiency interviews. In R. Young and A. W. He (eds), *Talking and testing. Discourse approaches to the assessment of oral proficiency*. Amsterdam: John Benjamins, 297–332.

Knox, L. (1994). Repetition and relevance: Self-repetition as a strategy for initiating cooperation in nonnative/native speaker conversations. In B. Johnstone (ed.), *Repetition in discourse* (Vol. 1). Norwood, NJ: Ablex, 195–206.

Kormos, J. (1999). Simulating conversations in oral-proficiency assessment: a conversation analysis of role plays and non-scripted interviews in language exams. In *Language Testing*, 16, 163–188.

Kramsch, C. (1986). From language proficiency to interactional competence. In *Modern Language Journal*, 70, 366–372.

Maynard, D. W. (1980). Placement of topic changes in conversation. In *Semiotica*, 30, 263–290.

Merritt, M. (1994). Repetition in situated discourse – exploring its forms and functions. In B. Johnstone (ed.), *Repetition in discourse* (Vol. 1). Norwood, NJ: Ablex, 23–36.

Nofsinger, R. E. (1994). Repeating the host: An interactional use of repetition by guests on televised episodes of *Computer Chronicles*. In B. Johnstone (ed.), *Repetition in discourse* (Vol. 2). Norwood, NJ: Ablex, 84–95.

Norrick, N. R. (1987). Functions of repetition in conversation. In *Text*, 7, 245–264.

Overstreet, M. (2000). *General extenders*. Oxford: Oxford University Press.

Ross, S. (1995). Aspects of communicative accommodation in oral proficiency interview discourse. Unpublished PhD dissertation, University of Hawai'i at Manoa.

Ross, S. (1998). Divergent frame interpretations in oral proficiency interview interaction. In R. Young and A. W. He (eds), *Talking and testing. Discourse approaches to the assessment of oral proficiency*. Amsterdam: John Benjamins, 333–353.

Sacks, H., Schegloff, E. A. and Jefferson, G. (1974). A simplest systematics for the organization of turn-taking for conversation. In *Language*, 50, 696–735.

Schegloff, E. A. (1987). Some sources of misunderstanding in talk-in-interaction. In *Linguistics*, 25, 201–218.

Schegloff, E. A. (1990). On the organization of sequences as a source of 'coherence' in talk-in-interaction. In B. Dorval (ed.), *Conversational organization and its development*. Norwood, NJ: Ablex. 51–77.

Schegloff, E. A. (1992). On talk and its institutional occasions. In P. Drew and J. Heritage (eds), *Talk at work*. Cambridge: Cambridge University Press, 101–134.

Schegloff, E. A. (1996). Confirming allusions: Toward an empirical account of action. In *American Journal of Sociology*, 102, 161–216.

Schegloff, E. A. (1997). Practices and actions: Boundary cases of other-initiated repair. In *Discourse Processes*, 23, 499–545.

Schegloff, E. A., Jefferson, G. and Sacks, H. (1977). The preference for self-correction in the organization of repair in conversation. In *Language*, 53, 361–382.

Schiffrin, D. (1987). *Discourse markers*. New York: Cambridge University Press.

Simpson, J. M. (1994). Regularized intonation in conversational repetition. In B. Johnstone (ed.), *Repetition in discourse* (Vol. 2). Norwood, NJ: Ablex, 41–49.

Sorjonen, M.-L. (1996). On repeats and responses in Finnish conversations. In E. Ochs, E. A. Schegloff and S. A. Thompson (eds), *Interaction and grammar*. Cambridge: Cambridge University Press, 277–372.

Tannen, D. (1989). *Talking voices. Repetition, dialogue, and imagery in conversational discourse*. New York: Cambridge University Press.

Tomlin, R. S. (1994). Repetition in second language acquisition. In B. Johnstone (ed.), *Repetition in discourse* (Vol. 1). Norwood, NJ: Ablex, 172–194.

Young, R. (1995). Conversational style in language proficiency interviews. In *Language Learning*, 45, 3–42.

Young, R. (2002). Discourse approaches to oral language assessment. In *Annual Review of Applied Linguistics*, 22, 243–262.

Young, R. and Halleck, G. B. (1998). 'Let them eat cake!' or how to avoid losing your head in cross-cultural conversations. In R. Young and A. W. He (eds), *Talking and testing. Discourse approaches to the assessment of oral proficiency*. Amsterdam: John Benjamins, 352–382.

Young, M. and Milanovic, M. (1992). Discourse variation in oral proficiency interviews. In *Studies in Second Language Acquisition*, 14, 403–424.

Zuengler, J. (1993). Explaining NNS interactional behavior: The effect of conversational topic. In G. Kasper and S. Blum-Kulka (eds), *Interlanguage pragmatics*. New York: Oxford University Press, 184–195.

5

Misunderstandings in political interviews

Shoshana Blum-Kulka and
Elda Weizman

Introduction

The chapter is concerned with the notion of misunderstanding in institu-tionalised discourse. It explores the objects and processes of misunderstand-ings in political discourse in the media, analyses the ways in which they differ from the discourse of misunderstanding in ordinary conversations and argues for the need for a context-sensitive theory of misunderstanding. We are concerned here only with misunderstandings on the pragmatic and discursive levels, excluding cases of linguistic misunderstanding, and in developing our argument will build on the relevant theories in pragmatics and discourse analysis, including our former work. Specifically, the question we address here is: Are misunderstandings in news interviews inherently different from misunderstandings in everyday life?

In what follows, we will set up the theoretical framework for the analysis (section 1), posit some theoretical observations we have made in our previ-ous work on misunderstandings in everyday talk (section 2), argue for the specificity of misunderstandings in political news interviews (section 3) and discuss some of their implications (section 4).

Understanding and misunderstanding: a sample dialogue

Consider the following extract from Shakespeare's *Richard II*:

Extract 5.1: Richard II (Act V, Sc. IV)

EXTON: 1. Didst thou not mark the king, *what words he spake*?
2. 'Have I no friend will rid me of this living fear?'
3. Was it not so?
SERVANT: 4. These were his very words.
EXTON: 5. 'Have I no friend?' quoth he. *He spake it twice*,
6. And urg'd it twice together, did he not?
SERVANT: 7. He did.
EXTON: 8. And, speaking it, *he wishtly look'd on me*,
9. As who should say 'I would thou wert the man,
10. That would divorce this terror from my heart',
11. **Meaning** the king at Pomfrec. Come, let's go.
12. I am the king's friend, and will rid his foe.

Extract 5.2: Richard II (Act V, Sc. VI)

EXTON: 1. Great King, within this coffin I present
2. Thy buried fear. Herein all breathless lies
3. The mightiest of thy great enemies,
4. Richard of Burdeaux, by me hither brought.
BOLING: 5. Exton, *I thank thee not, for thou has wrought*
6. **A deed of slander** with thy fatal hand,
7. Upon my head and all this famous land.
EXTON: 8. *From your own mouth, my lord, did I this deed.*
BOLING: 9. They love not poison that do poison need,
10. Nor do I thee. *Though I did wish him dead,*
11. *I hate the murtherer, love him murthered.*
Note: Authors' emphasis

Extracts 5.1 and 5.2 illustrate the process by which misunderstanding can be triggered. For our purposes at this point, it does not matter whether the exchange involves a 'real' misunderstanding. As we know, it had grave consequences, leading to the murder of Richard by Sir Pierce of Exton, an act Henry Bolingbroke later denies giving instructions for. Both extracts illustrate some crucial insights about how communication works and how misunderstandings might occur. These insights have their counterparts in pragmatic theory, as follows:

1. *Pragmatic misunderstandings occur in cases of potential ambivalence or indirectness.* The distinction between 'what words he spake' (Exton, Extract 5.1, line 1) and 'as who should say' (Exton, Extract 5.1, line 9) is parallel to the pragmatic differentiation between sentence meaning and utterer's meaning (Grice, 1968), or between utterance meaning and speaker's meaning (Dascal, 1983).

2. *Communicators need to engage in 'acts of reasoning'.* As Gardiner insists, 'the listener's interpretation is always a matter of reasoning' (Gardiner, 1932, p. 199, quoted in Taylor, 1992, p. 124). Such acts of reasoning are conducted within a model that by necessity assumes some type of communication obligations participants need to abide by, like Grice's (1975) model of cooperativeness and conversational maxims. In this particular case, the acts of reasoning that led Sir Pierce towards the assigned meaning are clearly displayed, since he endeavours to explicate them.

3. *Communicators rely on verbal and non-verbal cues and clues for interpretation* (Dascal and Weizman, 1987; Weizman and Dascal, 1991). First, in deciphering the deictics of an utterance, interpretation rests on mutually known contextual parameters. Here, mapping the protagonists (e.g. 'he' in 'he spake it twice' (5) as referring to 'the king' (1), and 'this living fear' (2) as well as 'his foe' (12) as 'meaning the king at Pomfrec' (11)) draws on extralinguistic specific and shallow *clues* such as the power relationships between them as well as the history of these relationships. Second, *cues* are employed to detect indirectness, or a mismatch between various levels of meaning: Exton considers Bolingbroke's repetition ('he spake it twice' (5)) as a cue for indirectness, that is, as an indication that the king's speaker's meaning (i.e. what he meant to convey) diverges from his utterance meaning (i.e. from what his words meant in the context of utterance). Third, clues are exploited for the construction of the intended meaning. For example, the king's gaze ('wishtly look'd on me' (8)) provides him with a clue as to the nature of the speaker's meaning, i.e. to its indirect requestive value ('As who should say "I would you wert the man/ That would divorce this terror from my heart"' (9–10)). Of course, assigning a requestive function in the first place to what seems at first blush to be a rhetorical question rests on contextual constraints 'brought along' to the situation. It is only against the background of the given political situation and the asymmetrical power relations between the actors that such seemingly innocent words can have such grave consequences.

4. *Pragmatic ambivalence allows for potential misunderstanding and carries a high potential of deniability.* Thus, Bolingbroke can engage in further equivocal communication (as politicians often do), dodging responsibility for giving instructions to murder Richard ('Exton, I thank thee not', Extract 5.2, line 5; 'I hate the murtherer' (11)).

5. *A possible source of misunderstanding might be that words spoken in public could have a double articulation,* being targeted at different audiences, and

interpreted differentially by them. Media talk, as shown by scholars of communication, is a prime case of double articulation (Scannell, 1996).

The last three points suggest that the meanings conveyed and inferred in any given speech situation are constrained by the repertoire of language games socially permissible in that type of situation. For instance, the same words would not have resulted in murder, had the speaker not been in Henry Bolingbroke's position, or had they been addressed to another hearer.

Ordinary misunderstanding

Taylor (1992) posits three aspects of understanding:

- *whether* communicators generally understand each other
- *what* it is for communicators to understand each other
- *how* understanding in communication occurs.

In our former work on misunderstanding in ordinary talk (Blum-Kulka and Weizman, 1988; Weizman and Blum-Kulka, 1991), we have addressed the issue of whether generally people understand each other by suggesting that misunderstandings can have two types of existence: one, mental only; two, both mental and discursive. In other words, they can be *negotiated or non-negotiated*. Since misunderstandings that exist only on the mental plane are not negotiated in discourse, we need to talk about them always in terms of potential misunderstandings. We have argued that in everyday talk it is often the case that the pragmatic ambivalence inherent in a given utterance is left unattended to, since for social considerations the interpreter prefers not to go on record. This would be the case, for example, if A makes a request for information, intending it as a request for action ('I realise now that we won't have the car today. Could you tell me how to get to your place by bus?'). When B replies to the direct request for information and does not comply with the indirect request for a ride ('It's bus number 7'), A should choose between assigning to the reply the illocutionary value of a refusal to comply, or assume that her question was misinterpreted as a genuine request for information. Considering the loss of face involved in admitting a requestive intent, A may attempt no clarification and the potential misunderstanding would remain unattended to. We have argued that in non-public, interpersonal communication participants tolerate a high degree of non-acknowledged, unresolved potential misunderstanding (Blum-Kulka and Weizman, 1988).

At the other end we have *negotiated* misunderstandings, where a misunderstanding is publicly admitted metadiscursively (by a phrase such as 'I don't think you understand me correctly'), or hinted at by various verbal and non-verbal cues (for example, by reformulations of a question or by an increase in its degree of specification that may serve as cues for clarifying a suspected misunderstanding). In negotiated misunderstandings, the sequential location of the metadiscursive talk is important: if it concerns the first speaker, its location is by necessity at the third turn slot, since it is only by the response to the first turn that the first speaker can have evidence for an apparent misunderstanding. This point needs to be borne in mind when we look at political interviews, and particularly at the way both sides choose to signal misunderstandings.

In considering *what is being understood or misunderstood*, we postulated three dimensions of understanding: aboutness, purpose and key (Weizman and Blum-Kulka, 1991). Roughly, *aboutness* concerns discourse propositions and topics, *purpose* concerns the illocutionary point and *mode* relates to the tone of the interaction (as serious, playful, sarcastic, etc.). Furthermore, building on work by Searle (1992), Dascal (1992), Dascal and Berenstein (1987) and Dascal and Idan (1989) that looks at conversations as sites of collective action, with shared intentionality, we suggested that misunderstandings can occur at two levels: not only the level of 'I', the individual participant, but also at the 'we' level shared by all participants engaged. These levels may conflict, as when misunderstandings at 'I level' do not exclude the possibility of an understanding at the 'we level', endowing the conversation with a shared, collective direction (Weizman, 1999).

Our approach to '*how communication occurs*' assumes with Grice individual agency and intentionality. Taking into account the work of Goffman and much ethnomethodological and interactional sociolinguistics, as well as discourse analytical work, this approach also looks for overt, demonstrable public practices of the process of understanding or misunderstanding.

Misunderstandings in televised political discourse

We turn now to misunderstandings in broadcasted political interviews.[1]

Certain basic features of misunderstandings seem to be shared across different genres of talk. Misunderstandings derive from some level of potential ambiguity and in all the discourse may bear witness to varying levels of successful or futile, indirect or overt, metapragmatically indicated attempts of resolutions. Yet we would like to suggest that there are basic ways in which both the process and object of misunderstandings in news interviews, or in all political discourse in the media, are different in essential ways from the way they enfold in everyday talk. These differences will become clear as we consider three of the unique features of mediated, institutionalised, political discourse centred speech events:

1. High levels of tolerance for equivocal talk in political discourse in general, including media talk.

2.   A tendency to focus on disputable events on the public agenda.
3.   Given a specific geography of the situation that requires adaptation to two spaces simultaneously.

Non-negotiated misunderstandings: high level of tolerance for equivocal talk

Political discourse in general is well known for its high level of equivocation. As Bavelas *et al.* (1990) found, politicians readily describe their own communication as 'ambiguous', 'vague' and 'wishy-washy' and are not apologetic about such responses. From their point of view, the situation does not allow for simple, direct communication. In the view of Bavelas *et al.*, since they must cope with avoidance of conflicts of many kinds (such as having a divided electorate on a given issue, or policy contradictions between aspects of the party platform) equivocation is the only solution. This interpretation is supported by experimental studies from the mid-1970s (reviewed in Bavelas *et al.*, 1990, pp. 21–22) which show that equivocation 'worked' in the sense that equivocal messages attributed to public figures elicited more agreement and resulted in better character ratings than did clear messages on difficult topics. The question that needs to be asked is: What are the consequences of such in-built vagueness for the notions of understanding or misunderstanding? Given that clear talk is not normally expected from politicians, is the phenomenon of misunderstanding relevant at all for political discourse and, if it is, in what sense?

First, let us consider non-negotiated, potential misunderstandings. We posit that though political discourse operates within the constraints that govern communication in general – it is based on the assumption of intentionality and needs to abide by the cooperative principle and the conversational maxims – the criteria by which adherence to the conversational norms is judged are not the same as in everyday communication. In political discourse, including political interviews, the norms of conversation are flexed to the point of suspension. The degree of adherence to truth (Quality), informativeness (Quantity), clarity (Manner) and Relevance (Relation) in political discourse takes into account that equivocation is inherent to this genre of discourse. One of the consequences of this flexing of norms is a transformation in the expectations for misunderstanding. Whereas in everyday talk a lack of adherence to the norms raises both the possibility that a misunderstanding has occurred and the possibility that the speaker is intentionally exploiting the maxims to generate an implicature, in political discourse the second possibility is the preferred one. Unless otherwise indicated, both interviewers and audiences work with the assumption that no misunderstandings occur and the lack of adherence to the norms is intentional. In other words, no matter how unrelated a politician's response to a question seems, the general assumption will be that the politician is flouting the maxims intentionally. The task of the interpreters is to decipher the implicatures generated by his or her talk. Consider Binyamin Netanyahu's response to a question during the debate between himself and Shimon Peres (Extract 5.3), the two candidates for prime minister, before the 1996 elections in Israel (Blum-Kulka and Liebes, 1999). (See Appendix to this chapter for transcription symbols.)

Extract 5.3: Netanyahu–Peres debate

| 1 Interviewer: | Thank you, Mr Peres, and the next question now is for eh [1.10] Mr Netanyahu. You are willing to invest in the settlements [0.8] less than 1.3 billion shekel, but this is still a considerable sum. At the same time you say that you are aware of the reality [0.8] and you accept the Oslo agreement. You say that you accept the Oslo agreement **but** you [0.7] will not retreat now or redeploy [0.5] in Hebron. You say that despite your refusal to redeploy immediately in Hebron, under certain conditions you will be willing to meet with Yassar Arafat. You are willing to meet with Arafat **but** you are committed to close down the Orient House [Palestinian political headquarters in East Jerusalem], something that even Shammir's [right wing Likud] government did not do. I am asking you, in this mixture, what is policy [0.7] and what is election smokescreen? | toda raba lexa mar Peres. ve-ha she'ela overet el mar e::: [1.10] Netanyahu. ata muxan lehashkia ba-hitnaxaluyot [0.8] paxot me-exad nekuda shlosha miliyard shkalim aval ze, sxum nikar. yaxad im ze, ata omer she-ha-meciut [0.8] mukeret lexa ve-ata mekabel et heskemey oslo. ata omer she ata mekabel et heskemney oslo **aval** ata [0.7] lo tisog axshav o lo tearex me-xadash be [0.5] e:: be-xevron. ata omer im zot lamrot she-lo te'arex me-xadash kvar axshav be-xevron be-tna'im mesuyamim tihiye muxan lifgosh et yaser arafat, tihiye muxan lifgosh et arafat **aval** ata mitxayev lisgor et ha-orient haus davar she-lo asta gam memshalto shel icxak shamir. ani sho'el otxa ba-blil ha-ze, ma medinyut [0.7] u-ma miksam shav shel bxirot? |
| 2 Netanyahu: | [answer, 90 seconds] | |

3 Interviewer:	[Camera focused on interviewer]: Mr Netanyahu, here we'll stop your answer and I would like to ask you a follow up question and the question is, and I have asked this before **and the answer was as it was** [0.6]. And if as a result of your policies the Intifada [the Palestinian uprising] is renewed (.), will you then, against your will, return the soldiers of the IDF to the Cassba of Nablus, to the alleys of Gaza and its refugee camps?	mar Netanyahu, kan anu na'acor et ha-tshuva shelxa ve-ani roce lish'ol otxa she'elat hemshex. ve-ha-she'ela hi zo ve-gam hicagti ota kodem **ve-ha-tshuva hayta kshe-hayta** [0.6] ve-im ke-toca'a mi-medinyutxa titxadesh ha-intifada (.) az ha-im xeref kol reconxa taxzir et xayaley cahal la-kasba shel shxem u-le-simta'ot shel aza u-le-maxanot ha-plitim shela?
4 Netanhayu:	[turning to interviewer]: I must tell you that from my experience with the Arabs, with Arab representatives and generally, both at the UN and at the foreign office, the office of the Prime Minister and during public contacts, the Arabs are much more realistic [1.0] than generally depicted. [*using a lot of hand movements*] When they see a weak government like Mr Peres's government they demand everything [0.7], get everything and demand more. Mr Peres has promised them half of Jerusalem [0.7] now they are demanding forty percent of West Jerusalem as well. But when they come up against a government that knows how to take a firm stand (.)	ani muxrax lehagid lexa she-hanisayon sheli im ha-aravim im ha-necigim ha-aravim u-bixlal ha-hitnasut im ha-aravim gam ba-um ve-gam be-misrad ha-xuc, misrad rosh ha-memshala u-ve-magaim pumbiyim ha-aravim hem harbe yoter meciutiyim [1.0] mi-ma she-meta'arim otam. kshe-hem roim memshala xalasha kmo ha-memshala shel mar Peres hem tov'im et ha-kol [0:7] mekablim et ha-kol ve-dorshim yoter. mar Peres hivtiax lahem xaci yerushalayim [0.7] axshav hem dorshim gam arba'im axuz mi-ma'arav yerushalayim. aval kshe-hem nitkalim be-memshala she-yoda'at

	– [/] [literally: insist on the red lines], and we know how to do that then [0.7] they eventually calm down. When we entered the Madrid talks the Intifada was already behind us. I mean to [0.5] conduct peace talks. [0.9] I intend to lead Israel in security [0.7] and I am convinced that all the Arab leaders, with no exception [0.6] – the Palestinians [0.6], the Syrians [0.6], the Jordanians [0.7], the Saudis – will conduct peace talks with me [0.6] and it will be a lasting peace. A *secure* peace.	la'amod al ha(.) – [/] al ha-kavim ha-adumim ve-anaxnu yod'im la'amod al kavim adumim [0.7] hem be-derex klal, nirgaim be-sofo shel davar. kshe-halaxnu le-veidat madrid kvar ha-intifada hayta me-axorenu. ani mitkaven [0.5] lenahel masa u-matan le-shalom [0.9] ani mitkaven lehovil et medinat israel, be-vitxa [0.7] ve-ani meshuxna, she-*kol* ha-manhigim ha-arvim, bli yoce min ha-klal [0.6] ha-palestinaim [0.6] ha-surim [0.6] ha-yardenim [0.7] ha-sa'udim, hem omrim et ze yenahalu iti masa u-matan le-shalom [0.6] ve-ze yihye shalom *amiti* she-yaxzik ma'amad. shalom batuax.
5 Interviewer:	Thank you very much Mr Netanyahu. **The two candidates have answered the questions with the degree of specificity they chose to**, and as I said before the elections in Israel this time are personal and hence as difficult it is for the host there is no evading the personal questions [. . .]	toda raba lexa mar Netanyahu. **shney ha-muamadim heshivu et asher hem heshivu la-she'elot be-ramat ha-partanut she-hem baxaru** va-ani kvar amarti she-habxirot ha-pa'am be-israel hen bexirot ishiyot u-lefixax ke-xol she-ze kashe la-manxe ein manos gam mi-she'elot ishiyot [. . .]

Source: Israeli Television, Channel 1, 27.5.1996. Interviewer: Dan Margalit. Broad transcription, our emphasis.

Consider the host's question (3) and Netanyahu's answer (4). The question ostensibly asks about a hypothetical course of events and queries Netanyahu's response to these events, implying that they are bound to happen. In a way it can be read as a yes/no-challenging question: I am putting it to you that this is what will happen and asking you to confirm or contest my proposition. Netanyahu does not answer directly to the challenge. At first glance, his response seems completely unrelated to the question: no cohesive ties; no reference to the IDF, or to the possibility of an outbreak of the Intifada in the future. How are we to account for what seems to be a blunt violation of the maxim of relevance? One reading can be that Netanyahu chooses to ignore the question completely in order to articulate a pre-prepared message. But this is a simplistic interpretation. A more accurate account in our view is that Netanyahu is engaged in a classic example of maxim exploitation, flouting a maxim in Grice's original sense. He is exploiting the maxim of relevance – instead of relating to the scenario proposed by the host, he sketches an alternative scenario, one in a which the Arabs 'relax' and there is 'secure peace'. Assuming the cooperative principle is adhered to, providing the answer in this specific slot as a 'response' can be read as deliberately designed to generate an implicature. On this account, the response is a blunt rejection of one aspect of the proposition implied by the question: the question implies that y (namely Netanyahu's policies) are to be condemned because they will lead to x (namely the renewal of the Intifada). The response indirectly answers to the challenge that the policies are to be condemned by painting a rosy picture of the future under these policies (i.e. 'secure peace') and thereby cancelling the need to relate to what could happen if the policies were indeed condemnable.

Thus, an implicature is assigned where misunderstanding could have been attributed. This interpretation is strengthened by two metapragmatic cues in the interviewer's talk. First, by drawing attention to the need to repeat the question ('I have asked you this before', (3)) the interviewer implies that the question has been answered unsatisfactorily on purpose. Second, the interviewer's response, a cue for a similar (though much vaguer) attribution included into Netanyahu, this time addressed to both Peres and Netanyahu ('the two candidates responded in the level of specificity they chose to') seems to imply that the interviewer considers the flouting of the Quantity Maxim as intentional, both candidates having provided less information than required. On this interpretation, then, it is rather clear that the interviewer does not work on the assumption that the apparent unrelatedness of Netanyahu's answer to his preceding question is attributable to misunderstanding.

Negotiated misunderstandings: D-events and double articulation

We have seen so far that whereas in cases where in ordinary talk ambivalent messages allow for the attributions of misunderstandings by participants and analysts, in political talk these attributions are replaced by assumptions of deliberate flouting of the maxims of conversation. Thus, when the journalist on the panel does not get an answer to his question from the politician, he and the audience at home will notice the apparent lack of coherence, but would normally assume that it was done on purpose and will not attribute it to a misunderstanding. Yet journalists can and do demand a certain degree of pragmatic accountability from politicians, rephrasing questions and making metapragmatic comments that show that politicians, like other speakers, are bound by communication obligations and theoretically at least might even misunderstand a question. Thus evidence for the operating of conversational constraints in the genre comes from instances of metacommunication concerning breaches. Requests for repair or attempts of self-repair of breaches show, in Goffman's terms (1981, p. 287), that the speaker is 'alive to', 'mindful of' his or her communication obligations. This brings us to cases of ostensibly negotiated misunderstandings in political discourse.

Two of the above-mentioned features of the speech event come to the fore in negotiated misunderstanding in this genre:

1. The fact that political discourse by definition concerns disputable events (what Labov and Fanshel, 1977, call D-events, to be differentiated from B-events concerning the other's biography, which are typical of non-political talk-show interviews. The discussion of disputable events is inherently argumentative (Blondheim *et al.*, 1999) and constantly invites challenges and counter-challenges, especially to claims of sincerity (in Scannell's, 1996, p. 67 terms, oriented to both that speakers say what they mean and that they mean what they say).

2. Meyrowitz (1985, p. 6) calls this feature 'the geography of the situation'. As pointed out by several students of the media (e.g. Meyrowitz, 1985; Montgomery, 1991; Scannell, 1996) all mediated discourse is publicly double-articulated, in that communication in the media operates simultaneously in two spaces: that from which it speaks and that within which it is heard. Talk is directed outwards from the studio into the imagined space within which it is heard (Montgomery, 1991). As Scannell notes, in discussing the notion of 'identity' in broadcasting, 'to enter a studio is to cross a threshold . . . to assume for the duration, a role and identity appropriate to the particular communicative event' and 'participants display an orientation to the character of the event by sustaining the part they are called upon to play' (Scannell, 1986, p. 140). The structure of the event orients all participants to the roles and performances they are expected to produce for absent viewers and listeners.

Double articulation has at least two consequences for the processes of communication, and hence for misunderstanding: it problematises the notion of accountability and relatedly, it calls for shifts in footing that mark shifts of orientation from one space to another. We mean 'accountability' in the sense of responsibility taken or denied for abiding by the conversational maxims. On the final account it is the audience at home who are the targetted recipients of the messages heard. But the audience is prevented structurally in most cases (unless calls to the studio are a built-in feature of the programme) from holding the speakers accountable in real time. This role is assigned to the journalist in the studio, who acts as the people's spokesperson in at least two ways: by presumably asking the politician the most pertinent questions at any given moment on the public agenda; and by holding the politician accountable for providing coherent and relevant answers.

Shifts in footing are related to accountability because they mark the targetted audience to whom the speaker orients himself in 'being accountable'. They are played out against a complex participant framework, in which all participants act out a variety of roles. Participation frameworks, as we know from Goffman (1981), are dynamic, complex networks of various speakership and listenership roles in a given interaction that can be constantly shifted by changes in footing. Changes in footing can affect the degree of accountability for intended meaning assumed by the speaker (whether he is talking as animator or as principal) as well as the degree of accountability for interpretation required of the listener (as ratified participant or eavesdropper). The issue of accountability is further complicated by the nature of the power relations between the participants. For exploring the notion of (mis)understanding in media discourse, the question is: who in this discourse at any given moment are the principals, namely the parties socially accountable for the meanings conveyed, and who are the targeted recipients, namely the parties who are supposed to process the message and can hold the principals accountable for purported misunderstandings?

In everyday discourse, social accountability for meaning can vary with power: from reciprocal in presumably symmetrical encounters, to resting with the powerful in asymmetrical encounters. Thus, between student and teacher, though both parties act as principals socially accountable for meanings conveyed, in practice the onus of interpretation lies heavily with the student and it is the teacher who can hold the student accountable and even penalise him or her for misunderstanding.

There are several consequences from this account for the treatment of the notion of misunderstandings in political interviews. First, from the politician's point of view, the politician can always exploit the ambiguous nature of his own pronouncements and use his or her studio appearances as public occasions for attempting repair of a claimed misunderstanding that presumably occurred in between his last public appearance and the current one. Note that since neither the evidence (namely the original quote) nor probably the original interpreter are available in real time, such claims are basically non-negotiable within the framework of the programme. The claim

'I have been misunderstood' underlies arguments for having been misquoted (consider the frequent comment 'my words have been taken out of context') and might also find its expression in metapragmatic comments directly concerning talk. In both cases, the unique feature of this discourse is its *double articulation*: the repair might be ostensibly addressed to the interviewer in the studio, but in effect it is targetted at the overhearing audience of viewers at home. This means that the issue foremost foregrounded in such cases is accountability in the public sphere. Extract 5.4 illustrates a case of repair through the use of a disclaimer.

Extract 5.4: Political talkshow discussion on the forthcoming redeployment of Hebron. Members of Tzomet, a right-wing party included in Netanyahu's coalition, have threatened to dissolve the coalition if an agreement is reached with the Palestinian authorities on this issue

Journalist on the panel:	Okay, so first of all I address you, Deputy Minister Moshe Peled from tzomet, **why do you think** this Coalition needs to be dissolved (.), why this government needs to be dissolved. Explain to us.	okay, az kodem kol ani pone elexa, sgan ha-sar Moshe Peled me-comet, **lama ata xoshev** she-carix lefarek et ha-koalicya ha-zot lefarek et ha-memshala ha-zot (.), tasbir lanu.
Peled:	**I did not say** dissolve the coalition. **I said** if [. . .]	**ani lo amarti** lefarek et ha-koalicya. **ani amarti** im [. . . .]

Source: Israeli Television, Channel 1, Popolitika, 13.1.97

Note that the journalist's question 'why do you think x' packages the presupposition that by saying x the politician has committed himself to x (i.e. that he abides by the requirement of sincerity and means what he says). The politician sidesteps the issue of sincerity by referring to the words only: 'I did not say' (not 'I do not think'), allowing for the inference that he might still think that the coalition should be dissolved, but wishes to go on record saying otherwise.

Second, politicians signal a need to repair suspected misunderstandings as well as to ward off potential future ones. Being accountable here means communicating *the need to go on record as sincere; as being seen and heard as saying what one means.* This display of sincerity can be framed as if occurring in intimate dyadic communication such as Extract 5.5.

Extract 5.5: News interview with Shlomo Lahat, at the time mayor of Tel-Aviv, on winter fbods in Tel-Aviv

Interviewer:	There is a problem if we focus for a moment on Hadar Yosef neighborhoods, for which a solution hasn't been found. Is this < corre:ct>?	yesh ba'aya im nitmaked lerega be-Hadar Yosef, she-exshehu lo maclixim liftor. ze nax<on>?
Lahat:	**<Let me> explain this to you** (.). *Yes. Certainly.* First of all it's not the neighborhood that was flooded (.) uh so far ten apartments were flooded [. . .]	**<ani> asbir lexa** *(.) ken. be-hexlet.* reshit lo ha-shxuna hucfa (.) e:: rak eser dirot hucfu [. . .]

Source: Israeli Television, Channel 2, 16.12.92. Interviewer: Rafi Reshef

In Lahat's response, 'let *me* explain this to *you*' (our emphasis), the two pronouns mark reciprocity, yet can be easily interpreted as condescending. This metacomment appeals to solidarity and tries to establish common ground, while at the same time it counter-challenges the interviewer's challenge that 'Hadar Yosef is a problem for which a solution has not been yet found'. Note that we have here an explicit comment signalling potential misunderstanding on the part of the hearer, which in ordinary talk might imply the speaker's genuine belief that he or she had been misunderstood. Depending on relationships and context, such a comment might or might not have the perlocutionary effect of a face threat. In the context of the discussion of a disputable event, keeping in mind the double articulated nature of the discourse and importantly the interviewee's powerful social role as the mayor of the city, the comment's main function is to act as a counter-challenge to the interviewer for failing to grasp in this case not so much the words but the true nature of the situation. The comment suggests to the overhearing audience that only those in a position of responsibility, like Lahat, can really understand what is going on and they should be allowed to explain this to the public.

In other cases, as in Extract 5.6, we have clear indications of how the politician orients himself to the imagined space where the audience is.

Extract 5.6: News interview with Binyamin Netanyahu, at the time Deputy Minister to David Levy, Minister of Foreign Affairs in Shamir's right wing government

1 Interviewer:	Yes (.) before that I just wanted to know, [. . .]	ken (.) ani od lifney ze rak raciti lehavin, [. . .]
2 Netanyahu:	Look (.) there is no ultimatum here [. . .]	tir'e (.) eyn kan ultimatum [. . .]
3 Interviewer:	Yes (.) but excuse <me for stopping> you uh at this point uh	ken (.) aval <slax> li she-ba-nekuda ha-zu ani e: kotea otxa e:
4 Netanyahu:	<I . . .>	<ani>
5 Interviewer:	for a moment (1.0) **You are in fact saying** [. . .]	le-rega (1.0) **ata be-ecem omer** [. . .]
6 Netanyahu:	yes Rafi I want you to know something [. . .]	ken Rafi ani roce she-teda mashehu, tir'e [. . .]
7 Interviewer:	Yes <but uh>	ken <aval e::>
8 Netanyahu:	<Now (.) the fact is> (.) let me finish because it is important for understanding this line of reasoning. [. . .]	<ken axshav (.) ha-uv>da hi (.) ten li lehashlim ki ze xashuv lehavin ma ha-higayon po [. . .]

Source: Israeli Television, Channel 2, 26.11.91. Interviewer: Rafi Reshef

Note that in turn 6 Netanyahu addresses the interviewer by his first name and uses the second person pronoun, signalling a 'within studio, between friends' intimate framing ('Rafi I want you to know'), but in turn 8 there is a clear shift in footing through the use of the impersonal construction 'it is important for understanding this line of reasoning', which now orients to the audience at home. The shift, which is also a shift in register, signals a transition from the discourse role of the politician–interviewee in dyadic dialogue with the interviewer, to the social role of the politician as Deputy Minister. The Deputy Minister speaks in the diplomatic impersonal language of politics, where it is 'important to understand lines of reasoning'.

Except for the way in which it implies that the audience did not understand, the function of the explicit comment here differs from ordinary talk as in the last extract. Metacomments on the part of the interviewers further support our claim that negotiated misunderstandings in political discourse

are inherently different from their parallel in ordinary talk. Consider first
the interviewer's comment in Extract 5.6, turn 5 'You are in fact saying that'.
By signalling the need to reformulate, the interviewer is implicating a failure
on the part of the politician to abide by the maxim of informativeness and
clarity, thereby inviting misunderstanding. The comment thus frames him as
accountable for his communication obligations. But note that assuming the
right to reformulate for the public at large foregrounds the social role of the
interviewer as the appointed mediator; the journalist professionally in charge
of interpreting politicians for the public. Clearly the reformulation here
does not function as it would in day-to-day conversations, where it would be
taken again to imply potential misunderstanding on the part of the hearer.

*Extract 5.7: News interview with Uzi Bar'am and Shlomo Hillel, at
the time Labour MPs were in opposition*

1 Interviewer:	**I must understand what you are saying.** You are saying that the fact that the PLO was not mentioned means that maybe <somehow>	**ani carix lehavin et ma she-ata omer. ata omer** ha-uvda she-lo hizkiru et Ashaf omeret she-ulay <be-eyzeshehi>
2 Bar'am:	<No it> does not. **It means clearly** that the Labor Party is in negotiations with the Palestinians and it does not mention the PLO.	<lo hi lo> omeret **hi omeret be-cura brura** she-mifleget ha-avoda be-ad nihul masa u-matan im Palestinaim ve-hi lo meazkeret et Ashaf.
3 Interviewer:	**Meaning** it does not <deny the PLO>	**klomar** hi lo <sholelet et ashaf>
4 Bar'am:	<yes yes **this may imply**> that the PLO is not banned [...]	<ken ken **mi-ze yaxol**> **lehishtamea** hainyan she-ashaf lo *pasul* [...]

Source: Israeli Television, Channel 2, 17.11.91. Interviewer: Dan Margalit

In Extract 5.7, the interviewer's reformulation ('what you are saying') is
preceded by an explicit comment concerning understanding. What is interesting about this example is that the negotiation that follows over the meaning of the Labour Party's recent resolution with regard to negotiations with
the Palestinians is explicitly about implicatures. Note that in turn 2 Bar'am

negates an unsaid implication that Labour is not acknowledging the PLO (an implication attributed to the interviewer's unfinished sentence), and then proceeds with a clarification. When further pressed in turn 3, Bar'am responds with spelling out the implicature the journalist is waiting for: 'The PLO is not banned'. This a rare case of truly collaborative, supportive discourse between the journalist and the politician, where instead of challenges and counter-challenges, the two collaborate in resolving a potential misunderstanding. It seems that Bar'am's wish to go on record with a dovish interpretation of his party's decision matches the journalist's goal to have the politician commit himself to a specific interpretation. Indeed, the interviewer's inference here seems based on little evidence yet proves correct.

Our last example (Extract 5.8) concerns a case where the geography of the situation becomes the focal point for the potential misunderstanding. As Scannell notes: 'to be physically present in the studio, whether as program host, participant or audience member, is to be inescapably aware of the broadcast character of the event, for the technology and personnel of broadcasting – cameras, microphones, lights, production stuff – are pervasively evident' (1996, p. 140). It is the design of setting which plays a crucial role here. There are three participants present in the studio: the host, Rafi Reshef; the interviewee, Binyamin Netanyahu; and a second journalist, Akiba Eldar. Eldar is the political correspondent of Channel 2 and he is to be interviewed later in the programme. The camera frame includes only Reshef and Netanyahu; we as audience do not see Eldar when the exchange takes place. Uncharacteristically for broadcast practices, we hear his voice without seeing him:

Extract 5.8: News interview with Binyamin Netanyahu, at the time Deputy Minister to the Minister of Foreign Affairs in Shamir's right-wing government. The interviewer is Rafi Reshef. Present also in the studio is the political correspondent, Akiba Eldar, who is the next interviewee. The audience knows he is there because he is heard addressing a comment to Netanyahu, but he is not seen.

| 1 Interviewer: | Yes, we will hear the details shortly from Akiba Eldar, but as far as I know Yitzhak Shamir came in today with much tougher, more resolute opinions, and somehow a number of cabinet ministers managed to soften him [. . .] | ken, texef nishma pratim me-mi-Akiva Eldar ba-inyan ha-ze, aval ad kama she shamati me-menu Yicxak Shamir higia hayom im deot, harbe yoter e:: kashot, |

		nexushot ve-eyxshehu mispar sarim ba-kabinet hiclixu lerakex oto [...]
Comment:	There is a long pause of 3.5 seconds, during which Netanyahu gazes only at the audience.	
2 Eldar:	The question is for you to answer	ha-she'ela hi elexa
3 Netanyahu:	**The question <is for me?>** I thought you were asking *Akiba Eldar*	**ha-she'ela hi <elay?>** xashavti she-hifneta ota le-A*kiva Eldar*
4 Interviewer:	<of course> **but perhaps your silence was <also> an answer of sorts.**	<kamuvan> **aval ulay ba-shtika <gam> hayta kvar tshuva.**
5 Netanyahu:	No I [//] my silence simply resulted from the fact you turned to *someone else* But the answer Rafi is that [...]	lo ani [//] ha-shtika sheli hayta e:: pashut havana she-hifneta et ha-she'ela le-*mishehu axer* aval ha-tshuva la-she'ela shelxa Rafi she [...]

This is a case of acknowledged, negotiated misunderstanding which concerns the specifics of space and floor allocation in this programme (i.e. its geography) as related to participation frameworks. Its source, which is Netanyahu's long silence following the interviewer's question, is interpreted by the journalists on two levels: first, as a failure to fulfil the communication obligations posed by being asked a question. Eldar states this failure in turn 2. Netanyahu rejects this accusation in turn 3 on the grounds of having worked with a different participation framework in mind (a different geography) from the one posited by the two journalists. From his point of view he has not been nominated as addressee. Turn 4 brings up a second level of interpretation: in his first words 'of course' the host of the programme here acknowledges the incongruity in assumed participation frameworks claimed by Netanyahu, thereby seemingly aligning with the politician and resolving the misunderstanding. But then a second, contradictory orientation follows, this time in a challenging mode rather than the supportive mode of 'of course'. Netanyahu's silence is opened up again for interpretation, thereby framing the misunderstanding as unresolved. Following the protest in turn 5 we as audience are left with a choice: should we believe Netanyahu that this is a case of negotiated and resolved misunderstanding, or should we believe the journalist who conveys to us his strong disbelief in the possibility of misunderstandings on the part of politicians.

Thus, when Akiba Eldar turns to Netanyahu and says, 'The question is for you to answer', he is indicating indirectly that a misunderstanding has occurred and is inviting a repair on the part of the politician. But when Netanyahu claims misunderstanding he is intercepted by the host's 'of course your silence is also a sort of an answer'. By this metacomment the journalist has shifted footing. Though ostensibly talking to the politician as a co-participant, he is actually talking to us, the audience, in effect contesting Netanyahu's claim that a misunderstanding has occurred. The comment foreshadows Netanyahu's subsequent protests, implying that his so-claimed misunderstanding is in effect strategic. This is the general claim that seems to underlie reformulations of questions by interviewers in news interviews. If a politician fails to answer a question to the journalist in a way that leads the journalist to reformulate it in more specific terms, in this speech event, the reformulation is not motivated by an assumption of misunderstanding (as it would in other contexts) but by an assumption of strategic non-understanding. Because of the on-stage nature of the interaction, it is the audience that is invited to interpret if a misunderstanding has occurred. The journalist, as in Extract 5.3, often takes on the role of implying to the audience more or less directly that this is not the case. The analysis of negotiations so far shows that what counts as a misunderstanding in other types of speech event does not count as such in political interviews.

Concluding comments

We began this chapter by asking whether misunderstandings in broadcast political interviews are inherently different from misunderstandings in ordinary talk. Our answer is that indeed they are, but that the differences are played out against a set of assumptions and expectations about the processes of communication shared by ordinary talk and institutionalised discourse. These assumptions include, as Shakespeare noted, the possible gaps between what is said and what is meant, and the role played by verbal and non-verbal cues as well as contextual constraints, including role relations, in the process of interpretation. Within the pragmatic theory of communication to which we ascribe, this means that communicators across different speech events need to engage constantly in processes of pragmatic reasoning, guided by a given set of pragmatic principles like cooperativeness, to arrive at what Gardiner (1932, p. 81, quoted in Taylor, 1992, p. 127) called 'the essential lines' of what is meant. Political discourse operates within the same system, but by giving prominence to certain assumptions over others transforms considerably the notion of misunderstanding. Thus in the pragmatic reasoning employed for bridging the gap between what is said and what is meant, preference is given to expectations of deliberate maxim exploitations over misunderstanding. The result is that when no verbal indications of misunderstanding are displayed, the possibility of misunderstanding is greatly diminished, if not completely cancelled. A parallel process of transformation affects the fate of verbal and non-verbal cues used in the process of interpretation. Such cues emerge in the metapragmatic talk surrounding instances framed as misunderstandings. Whereas in ordinary talk such metapragmatic discourse stands a high chance to function as a genuine indicator of misunderstandings, in political interviews in the media it stands a much higher chance to function, when employed by politicians, in the service of 'doing sincerity', or when employed in negotiation between politicians and journalists, as challenges and counter-challenges in conflicting talk. This functional transformation in the processes of negotiated misunderstandings is in large part motivated by the geography of the media situation, namely by the targetting of the discourse to an imagined audience in an imagined space. Considering these findings against the background of previous accounts of misunderstandings in ordinary talk supports a context sensitive, speech event specific account of misunderstanding and strengthens the claim for the need for context sensitive theories of communication in general.

Appendix

(.)	a noticeable pause of 0.5 to 0.8; longer pauses are timed
< >	overlapped talk
[//]	self-correction
[...]	deleted talk
italics	speaker emphasis
bold	our emphasis
.	falling intonation
?	rising intonation
(.) (?)	mixed intonation
(!)	exclamation
:	elongated vowel

Acknowledgements

An earlier version of this chapter has been presented at the Ross Priori Seminar on Broadcast Talk in September 1997. We thank our co-members of the Ross Priori Broadcast Talk Group for useful comments.

Note

1 For former work on broadcasted political interviews, see, for example, Blum-Kulka, 1983; Bull *et al.*, 1996; Clayman, 1992; Greatbach, 1992; Jucker, 1986; Weizman, 1998, 2001, in press.

References

Bavelas, J. B., Black, A., Chovil, N. and Mullett, J. (1990). *Equivocal communication*. London: Sage.

Blondheim, M., Blum-Kulka, S. and Hacohen, G. (1999). Traditions of dispute: From negotiations of Talmudic texts to the arena of political discourse in the media. Paper delivered at the Israeli Pragma99 Conference, Tel-Aviv and Jerusalem, June.

Blum-Kulka, S. (1983). The dynamics of political interviews. In *Text*, 3, 131–153.

Blum-Kulka, S. and Liebes, T. (1999). Peres versus Netanyahu: Television wins the debate. In S. Coleman (ed.), *Televised election debates*. London: Macmillan.

Blum-Kulka, S. and Weizman, E. (1988). The inevitability of misunderstandings: Discourse ambiguities. In *Text*, 8, 219–243.

Bull, P., Elliott, J., Palmer, D. and Walker, L. (1996). Why politicians are three-faced: the face model of political interviews. In *British Journal of Social Psychology*, 35, 267–284.

Clayman, S. A. (1992). Footing in the achievement of neutrality: The case of news interview discourse. In P. Drew and J. Heritage (eds), *Talk at work*. Cambridge: Cambridge University Press, 268–302.

Dascal, M. (1983). *Pragmatics and the philosophy of mind I: Thought in language*. Amsterdam: John Benjamins.

Dascal, M. (1992). On the pragmatic structure of conversation. In H. Parret and J. Verschueren (eds), *(On) Searle on conversation*. Amsterdam: John Benjamins, 35–56.

Dascal, M. and Berenstein, I. (1987). Two modes of understanding: Comprehending and grasping. In *Language and Communication*, 7, 139–151.

Dascal, M. and Idan, A. (1989). From individual to collective action. In F. Vandamme and R. Pinxten (eds), *The philosophy of Leo Apostel – descriptive and critical essays*. Ghent: Communication and Cognition, 133–148.

Dascal, M. and Weizman, E. (1987). Contextual exploitation of interpretation clues in text understanding: An integrated approach. In M. J. Verschueren and

M. Bertucceli-Papi (eds), *The pragmatic perspective*. Amsterdam: John Benjamins, 31–46.

Gardiner, A. (1932). *The theory of speech and language*. Oxford: Clarendon Press.

Goffman, E. (1981). *Forms of talk*. Philadelphia: University of Pennsylvania Press.

Greatbach, D. (1992). On the management of disagreement between news interviewees. In P. Drew and J. Heritage (eds), *Talk at work*. Cambridge: Cambridge University Press, 268–302

Grice, P. H. (1968). Utterer's meaning, speaker's meaning and word meaning. In *Foundations of Language*, 4, 1–18.

Grice, P. H. (1975). Logic and conversation. In P. Cole and J. L. Morgan (eds), *Syntax and semantics. Vol. III: Speech acts*. New York: Academic Press, 41–58.

Jucker, A. (1986). *News interviews: A pragmalinguistic analysis*. Amsterdam: John Benjamins.

Labov, W. and Fanshel, D. (1977). *Therapeutic discourse*. London: Academic Press.

Meyrowitz, J. (1985). *No sense of place*. Oxford: Oxford University Press.

Montgomery, M. (1991). Our tune: A study of a discourse genre. In P. Scannell (ed.), *Broadcast talk*. London: Sage, 138–178.

Scannell, P. (1996). *Radio, television and modern life*. Oxford: Blackwell.

Searle, J. R. (1992). Conversation. In H. Parret and J. Verschueren (eds), *(On) Searle on conversation*. Amsterdam: John Benjamins, 7–29.

Shakespeare, W. (1597ff/1970). *King Richard II* (ed.), P. Ure. London: Methuen.

Taylor, T. J. (1992). *Mutual misunderstanding*. Durham: Duke University Press.

Weizman, E. (1998). Individual intentions and collective purpose: the case of news interviews. In S. Čmejrková, J. Hoffmanová, O. Müllerová and J. Světlá (eds), *Dialogue analysis VI*. Tübingen: Max Niemeyer Verlag, 269–280.

Weizman, E. (1999). Building true understanding via apparent miscommunication: A case study. In *Journal of Pragmatics*, 31, 837–846.

Weizman, E. (2001). Addresser, addressee and target: negotiating roles through ironic criticism. In E. Weigand and M. Dascal (eds), *Negotiation: The dialogic question*. Amsterdam: John Benjamins, 125–137.

Weizman, E. (in press). News interviews on Israeli television: normative expectations and discourse norms. In S. Stati and M. Bondi (eds), *Dialogue analysis VIII*. Tübingen: Max Niemeyer Verlag.

Weizman, E. and Blum-Kulka, S. (1991). Ordinary misunderstanding. In M. Stamenov (ed.), *Current advances in semantic theory*. Amsterdam: John Benjamins, 419–434.

Weizman, E. and Dascal, M. (1991). On clues and cues: Strategies of text understanding. In *Journal of Literary Semantics*, 20(1), 18–30.

6

Identity, role and voice in cross-cultural (mis)communication

Claire Kramsch

Introduction

Instances of miscommunication among people who speak different languages and belong to different social groups are usually attributed to linguistic or cultural factors that are believed to pre-exist the verbal exchanges in which miscommunication occurs, thus determining in advance the failed outcome of these exchanges (e.g. Hofstede, 1983; Triandis, 1995). Furthermore, the institutions that regulate people's lives as organisations of power and control are believed to impose their ideology on the discourse of individual speakers, thus creating yet another obstacle to cross-cultural communication (Gee, 1990; Scollon and Scollon, 1995, p. 115). This tendency to essentialise cultural group characteristics and to equate one individual with one culture or one institution has been countered by work done in anthropology, sociology and psychology within an interactionist (Bateson, 1972; Garfinkel, 1967; Goffman, 1974) and a constructionist view of social reality (Berger and Luckmann, 1966; Gergen, 1985; Harre, 1986; Shotter, 1993a). These scholars see culture and cross-cultural understanding as constructed and negotiated on the microlevel of everyday transactions. In a similar vein, anthropological linguists and sociolinguists show that it is on the level of discourse that choice of language, topic management and the presentation of self are carried out simultaneously, thus creating, recreating or subverting the very identities that their discourse puts forth (Gumperz, 1982b; Hanks, 1996; Meeuwis, 1994; Ochs, 1993; Scollon, 1996; Scollon and Scollon, 1981). But what exactly gets constructed in these cross-cultural encounters? And how does such a construction take place?

Anthropological linguists like Ochs (1996) and Hanks (1996) have shown the importance of indexicality in discourse in linking the individual utterance to the larger social context. Ochs in particular identified an 'indexicality principle' that undergirds all communicative practice. Members of a social community understand one another along two situational dimensions that are indexed or cued by the language itself: the social identities of the participants (e.g. roles, relationships, group membership, rank)[1] and their epistemic stances (e.g. sources of knowledge, truth of proposition, certainty of knowledge) (Ochs, 1996, p. 410). When the participants belong to different social and historical communities, speak different linguistic codes and even 'animate' (Goffman, 1981, p. 144) different social and institutional discourses, it is of course much more difficult to reach an agreement on who speaks, on behalf of whom, with which recipient in mind. It is equally difficult to know for sure what is meant by what is said, what is alluded to and where the speaker stands vis-à-vis his or her own words. What seems to be needed is the ability temporarily to read one's interlocutor's cues as someone else's cues without losing the sense of one's own reading. This double movement – 'reading' and 'reading as', or 'seeing' and 'seeing as' – has its roots in the fundamentally metaphorical or 'tropological' nature of discourse, that moves between the known and the foreign objects of knowledge according to a metaphorical process that I discuss below (Gibbs, 1994; White, 1978).

Several strands of linguistic research have examined the relationship of discourse and sociocultural identity, as well as the construction of knowledge in encounters where the participants do not share the same discourse conventions and assumptions. One strand can be found in work done in sociolinguistics (Johnstone, 1996; LePage and Tabouret-Keller, 1985; Linde, 1993; Ochs and Capps, 1996; Rampton, 1995; Sarangi, 1994; Scollon and Scollon, 1981, 1995), pragmatics (Blommaert and Verschueren, 1991; Gumperz and Roberts, 1991), and second language acquisition within a sociocultural framework (Kramsch, 2000; Kramsch and Lam, 1999; Lantolf, 2000; Peirce, 1995). Sociolinguists have invoked the notions of Self (Johnstone, 1996; Kramsch, 2000; Linde, 1993; Ochs and Capps, 1996), cultural identity (LePage and Tabouret-Keller, 1985), ethnic (Rampton, 1995) or social identity (Ochs, 1993; Peirce, 1995), textual identity (Kramsch and Lam, 1999), discourse identity (Scollon, 1996) and role (Rampton, 1995). These echo terms used in cultural studies, like self-identity (Giddens, 1991), enunciating subject (Bhabha, 1994) and voice (Bakhtin, 1981; Kristeva, 1986; Wertsch, 1991). They all attempt to capture the negotiation of the individual, the social and the cultural when people try to understand each other across linguistic, social, gender and/or ethnic boundaries. I discuss some of these concepts in section one of this chapter.

Another strand is to be found in the general field of discourse analysis, which has been useful in revealing interlocutors' attitudes and values underlying their choice of linguistic code (e.g. Gumperz, 1982a; Milroy and Muysken, 1995), as well as the ideological biases revealed by their choice of lexical and grammatical structures (e.g. Fairclough, 1992; Scollon and Scollon, 1995). However, discourse analysis is often used to uncover the power differential imposed a priori by institutional settings such as courts of law or police stations (Atkinson and Drew, 1979; Candlin, 1987), job interviews (Gumperz, 1992) or medical examinations (Drew, 1998; Mehan, 1990), rather than to explore how the institutionalisation of identity and knowledge gets constructed by the participants at the microlevel of their interactions. In this chapter I adopt the view of *institution as practice or process*, and consider how institutionalised routines are constitutive of both the success and failure of cross-cultural communication.

In the first section, I discuss the terms identity, role and voice and associated concepts, as well as tropological processes in the construction of voice. I then show in the concrete case study of a multiparty international encounter how these notions get played out on the conversational grid of turns at talk. Finally, I suggest that cross-cultural miscommunication is not the result of a failure at the discrete linguistic or propositional level, but is the outcome of the interaction of identity, role and voice within a general attempt both to see reality as what it is and also as something else. In this complex dynamic, institutional discourse emerges as both the enabling and the disabling power of history to generate trust in the creation of a joint present.

Identity, role and voice

To appreciate the work that participants have to do in encounters across different social groups, it is necessary first to review the way social reality is constructed among people who belong to the same social group. For this, I would like to re-examine the notion of 'identity' from the social constructionist perspective adopted in this chapter and contrast it with the closely related notions of role and voice.

The sociologists Berger and Luckmann (1966) trace back the origin of the notion of *identity* to the process by which the child identifies with one, then with many significant others during his/her primary socialisation. 'He now has not only an identity vis-à-vis this or that significant other, but an identity in general, which is subjectively apprehended as remaining the same no matter what others, significant or not, are encountered' (p. 133). This identity is experienced as possessing a reality of its own: 'Society, identity *and* reality are subjectively crystallized in the same process of internalization.' One could add that these three factors, the social, the historical and the reality coefficient, together constitute someone's 'culture' (Kramsch, 1995, 1998).

Specific historical social structures engender *identity types*, which are recognisable in the individual cases. In this sense one may assert that an American has a different identity from a French person, a New Yorker from a Midwesterner, a teacher from a corporate executive. Orientation and conduct in everyday life depend upon such typifications (Berger and Luckmann,

1966, p. 174) or, as Bourdieu would call them, durable dispositions that together constitute a 'habitus' (Bourdieu, 1991).

It is this process of typification that, according to Berger and Luckmann, forms the basis for the institutionalisation of human activity: 'Institutionalization occurs whenever there is a reciprocal typification of habitualized actions by types of actors' (p. 54). In other words, when verbal and non-verbal actions of type X get repeated enough in time by actors of type X, these actions 'congeal in recollection as recognizable and memorable entities' (p. 54). This phenomenon, which Berger and Luckmann call 'sedimentation', enables members of a social group to incorporate their experiences into a common stock of knowledge, a large aggregate of collective memory (p. 67), and a common definition of what is good and just (Taylor, 1989). For example, for a French person raised in the French school system, the expression 'abolition of privileges' is the depository of the collective sedimented memory of a well-known event that happened during the French Revolution of 1789. Through the acquisition of historicity, institutions like the French nation-state, together with institutional identities like the French nationality, appear as 'given, unalterable and self-evident' (Berger and Luckmann, 1966, p. 59) for members of the group, which is why they are perceived as natural and why they often exercise such strong social control over the group.

Institutions are embodied and get enacted in individual experience by means of *roles* (Berger and Luckmann, 1966, p. 74). The institution, with its assemblage of 'programmed' actions, is like the script of a drama whose realisation depends upon the reiterated performance of its prescribed roles by living actors. Roles are types of actors (e.g. teacher, seminar participant, seminar leader, student, colleague, French, German, American) (Berger and Luckmann, 1966, p. 75), or social performances (Vygotsky, 1989). For example, X and Y begin to play roles vis-à-vis each other, based on the memory of past actions by the same actors. In so doing, they are able to predict each other's actions, and to construct a discursive background that serves to stabilise both their separate actions and their interaction (Gumperz, 1996). Thus are sown the seeds of an expanding institutional order (Berger and Luckmann, 1966, p. 57), of which the most important gain is that it allows people to trust one another and to predict each other's actions. But, as we shall see in the case study presented here, people can play multiple institutional roles that are likely to change over time and are consonant with or clash with others' roles (Peirce, 1995).

Both identity and role index historicity and collectivity, two of the main features of the institutionalisation process that controls our social reality and makes us 'see' it in such a way that it appears natural, objective and self-evident (Kramsch, 1998). The characteristics of social identity and role – continuity and objectivity – find their counterparts on the rhetorical plane where, as Charlotte Linde suggests, the Self is characterised by the discursive construction of its own biographical coherence and by reflexivity, i.e. the ability to see itself as an object or as an other (Linde, 1993, Ch. 4). In cross-cultural encounters, reflexivity includes the attempts of the Self to see itself through the eyes of others, which might create a challenge to its sense of coherence.

But as Berger and Luckmann (1966, p. 77) remark: 'To learn a role it is not enough to acquire the routine immediately necessary for its "outward" performance. One must also be initiated into the various cognitive and even affective layers of the body of knowledge that is directly *and* indirectly appropriate to this role.' How do identity and role intersect with the construction of this 'body of knowledge' through discourse? This is where we need the concept of *voice*, taken from literary studies but adopted by linguists to capture the idea that utterances reproduce, subvert or create institutional roles and identities through the discursive choices they make (see Wertsch, 1991, p. 12, for a discussion of voice vs. role in Bakhtin, Vygotsky, Habermas).

Unlike the concepts of *identity* and *role* that come from sociology and psychology respectively, *voice* comes from literary studies (Bakhtin, 1981) and rhetoric or stylistics (Sebeok, 1960). It includes all dimensions of style, such as point of view and modality in written narratives (e.g. Simpson, 1993) and stance and subjectivity in spoken exchanges (Ochs, 1996). Sociolinguists like Barbara Johnstone (1996) equate voice with the expressive style that distinguishes one speaker or writer from another in adaptation to the situation at hand. Others like John Shotter, working within a social constructionist perspective, view it as the manifestation of 'the continuously creative or formative process in which we construct the situation or context of our communication *as we communicate*' (1993b, p. 100). Voice, then, is the act of meaning making itself (Bruner, 1990, Ch. 4), the choice of which role we will play, which identity we will put forth in our interaction with others. If identity and role stress the historically and socially constructed nature of institutions, the concept of voice underscores the fact that institutions are created, maintained and changed by the individual utterance in discourse. For Bakhtin 'voice is the speaking personality, the speaking consciousness' of the enunciating subject (Holquist and Emerson, 1981, p. 434).

Identity, role and voice find their realisation in the way speakers present and represent themselves and others through their discourse, defined by Lemke as 'the social activity of making meanings with language and other symbolic systems in some particular kind of situation or setting' (1995, p. 6). Because voice, like language, can 'make' different meanings within the same utterance – what Scollon calls 'polyvocality' (personal communication) – and can echo many prior utterances of self and others – what Bakhtin calls 'heteroglossia' (Holquist and Emerson, 1981, p. 428) – it lends itself to a high degree of reflexivity, both on the part of the speaker and the analyst. For example, someone's voice can animate other people's utterances, distance itself from its own saying, indirectly borrow someone else's voice, counterpose registers, modes, tones against one another, thrive on polysemy and intertextuality, and potentially insert change in institutionalised systems. In fact, as Wortham (2000) showed, if, as Bakhtin argues, the self exists only on the boundary between self and other, it can only develop a voice by positioning itself with respect to other voices and stances that others have taken. Personal voice must be 'wrought' from the institutionalised discourses in the environment.

Identity, role and voice may be seen in terms of Goffman's three interactional footings or 'production formats' in an individual's utterances: principal, animator, author (1981). Here, I reinterpret Goffman's famous distinction as three different ways of looking at a speaker. From the perspective of his or her institutional status, an individual may be seen as a principal, i.e. as someone 'whose position is established by the words that are spoken'; not so much 'a body or mind', but 'a person active in some particular social identity or role, some special capacity as a member of a group, office, category, relationship, association, or whatever, some socially based source of self-identification' (Goffman, 1981, p. 145). This perspective highlights the speaker's institutional identity.

Seen from the perspective of the origin of the words uttered, if indeed our mouths are filled with the words of others, then we are most of the time animating other people's discourses without necessarily subscribing to them. Thus a speaker may also be seen as an animator, as 'someone who openly speaks for someone else and in someone else's words, as we do, say, in reading a deposition or providing a simultaneous translation of a speech, without taking the position to which these words attest' (pp. 145–146). This perspective highlights the speaker's social role.

From the perspective of the linguistic selections made, a speaker may also be seen as an author: as 'someone who has selected the sentiments that are being expressed and the words in which they are encoded' (p. 144). This notion highlights a speaker's rhetorical choices or voice. Voice (like choice) does not refer to an unsocialised, uninstitutionalised self – which would be impossible – but to the selection, exercised by any speaker, as to which historicity and which collectivity he or she wishes to uphold and construct. As mentioned above, someone may be both the author of his or her words (by selecting to say this or that rather than something else) and reproduce to varying degrees prior utterances of self and others. The acquisition of a personal voice is a difficult achievement. It is not the natural correlate of someone's institutional identity and social role.

At the intersection of the diachronic and synchronic dimensions of language, personal voice is achieved by mediating between different, often conflicting, historicities and collectivities. Through a process that Hayden White (1978) calls 'tropological', i.e. metaphorical operations by which cultural praxis comes to terms with conflictual domains of experience, speakers attempt to see one reality in terms of another, to pass from 'seeing' to 'seeing as'. Metaphor is a cognitive process by which we project patterns from one domain of experience in order to structure another domain of a different kind (see Cameron and Low, 1999; Lakoff, 1987; Lakoff and Johnson, 1980; Turner, 1996). Lakoff and Johnson view understanding as 'intimately connected to forms of imaginative structuring of experience' (1980, p. xiv). In *The Body in the Mind*, Johnson writes: 'Metaphor is not merely a linguistic mode of expression; rather, it is one of the chief cognitive structures by which we are able to have coherent, ordered experiences that we can reason about and make sense of' (1987, p. xv). In cross-cultural communication, the term metaphor refers to a cognitive and linguistic act of 'carrying over', a 'translation', in which we strive to preserve an appropriate regard to two or several cultures while bringing them into meaningful and creative relation with one another. A metaphorical stance is the attempt to 'see' our experience 'as' it is seen by others, or temporarily seeing X as Y, or temporarily performing the role of the other (Turner, 1996, Ch. 1).

This is done through four basic cognitive operations that White considers to be the 'archetypal plot of discursive formations' (1978, p. 5) and that characterise 'all efforts of human beings to endow their world with meaning': metaphor, metonymy, synecdoche and irony. The narrative 'I' of the discourse moves from an original metaphorical characterisation of a domain of experience, (e.g. *America is a land of equal opportunity*), through metonymic deconstructions of its elements (e.g. *one aspect of equal opportunity is that privileges are earned through personal merit*), to synecdochic representations of the relations between its superficial attributes and its presumed essence' (e.g. *what Bill Clinton, a movie star and Bill Gates have in common is that they have all earned their success*) (p. 5). The fourth move is an 'ironic reflection on the inadequacy of the characterization', a 'self-reflexivity on the constructivist nature of the ordering principle itself' (e.g. *come to think of it, the notion of personal merit is problematic in a country that has so many racial inequalities*) (p. 6).

Table 6.1 summarises the various aspects of identity, role and voice as they have been discussed up to now.

Table 6.1   Identity, role and voice in cross-cultural communication

Identity Historical continuity	Role Social variability	Voice Rhetorical style
Group member, type, institutional category, cultural affiliation and recognition *principal*	Ethnographic individual, social agent, interactant, creator of biographical coherence, social performance *animator*	Ling. individual, mediated Self, stance, subjectivity, narrative point of view, polyvocality, heteroglossia, tropological processes of meaning construction *author*
Berger and Luckmann (1966), Bourdieu (1991), Taylor (1989), Goffman (1981)	Goffman (1981), Gumperz (1996), Linde (1993), Peirce (1995), Vygotsky (1989)	Bakhtin (1981), Goffman (1981), Johnstone (1996), Ochs (1996), Scollon (1996), Sebeok (1960), Wertsch (1991)

Voice, or, one could say, linguistic identity, partakes of the historical (diachronic) and the social (synchronic). At the boundary of self and other, voice positions itself at every utterance between the historical and the social, between the constant and the variable, through tropological processes of meaning making.

A case study

The discussion above can help us make sense of the way in which interlocutors from three different countries using three different languages, English, French and German, negotiate identity, role and voice through tropological processes of discourse in their attempt to understand one another. The data are taken from a trilingual, tricultural Goethe Institute seminar for language teachers conducted in Leipzig in summer 1993, four years after the fall of the Berlin Wall. Twelve teachers from the United States, France, East and West Germany respectively, teaching each other's languages in their respective countries, discuss two documents that are presented by the French teachers to their colleagues and which they propose for teaching French in the United States and Germany.[2] One is a publicity advertisement for the Parisian department store Le Bon Marché on the Left Bank of the Seine, featuring a regal looking woman holding up a credit card offering a reduction of '–10 pour cent avec la carte rive gauche' on all articles in the catalogue. Above her head, a caption reads: 'Rive gauche, il existe encore des privilèges que nul ne souhaite abolir' (On the Left Bank, there still exist privileges no one wishes to abolish) – a clear allusion to the night of 4 August 1789 when the nobility abolished its own privileges on the altar of the revolution. The other is a one-franc coin with the motto of the French revolution: 'liberté, égalité, fraternité' (freedom, equality, brotherhood). The participants could choose which language they wanted to use in the discussions.[3] When one of the participants did not understand the language currently in use, informal simultaneous translations took place around the large seminar table where the group was seated. As the participants seek to comprehend the topic under discussion, it quickly becomes clear that their lack of understanding stems less from their lexical deficiencies than from their inability to visualise the topography of identity, role and voice in the ongoing discourse (Extract 6.1). See Appendix at end of Chapter for transcription conventions.

Extract 6.1

M and J are French teachers of German. P is a French teacher of English. T is an American teacher of French.

1 M: pour faire l'équilibre je vais parler français (0.5) chacun à son tour,
      hein?
2   ici (0.2) vous avez avez devant vous deux documents qui doivent
      être présenté::s (0.2)
3   simultanément? c'est pas ce qu'on a dit?
4 J: non pas simultanément
5 M: ah bon d'accord
6   alors voilà (0.2)
7   le premier c'est un agrandissement (0.2) fait par la photocopieuse
      ici=
8 P: =d'une *authentique* pièce de un franc=
9 J: = UN FRANC (0.5)
10 M: et est-ce que vous savez c'qui est écrit (-) là d'ssus? (0.3)
11 T: république française
12   ( )
13 M: oui (0.4) république française (0.5)
14   Et la devise de la France >liberté, égalité fraternité<(.)
15   <premier temps de la démarche> euh (0.3)
16   voilà (0.2)
17   on fait prendre connaissance aux apprenants (0.2) de::: ça ((points
      to the coin))

1 M: to establish a balance, I will speak French (0.5) everyone his turn, eh?
2   here (0.2) you have before you two documents that should be
      presented (0.2)
3   simultaneously? Isn't it what we said?
4 J: no, not simultaneously
5 M: ah OK
6   so here (0.2)
7   the first is an enlargement (0.2) done by the xerox machine here =
8 P: = of an *authentic* one franc coin
9 J: = ONE FRANC
10 M: and do you know what is written on it? (0.3)
11 T: French republic
12   ( )
13 M: yes (0.4) French republic (0.5)
14   and the motto of France > freedom, equality, brotherhood< (.)
15   <first step> eh (0.3)
16   there (0.2)
17   you have the learners examine (0.2) this ((points to the coin))

M, as the spokesperson for the 'French' group (cf. 'we' in line 3), decides
to present the group's documents in French. Note that, although English is
a language M understands, she might not feel comfortable enough in it to

present in English, but she could have equally well used German, since she teaches German at a French lycée. Her deliberate use of French, which she explicitly justifies by invoking her concern for linguistic fairness among the seminar participants (line 1), 'performs' a national identity that subliminally imposes itself onto the teacher identity that her discourse constructs in this excerpt. The interactive nature of her discourse (line 10), its slow enunciation (line 15), its initiation-response-feedback style (lines 10–13) give her an unmistakable teacher's voice. That voice is amplified by the overlapping utterances of her fellow compatriots P and J who turn M's monologic didactic voice addressed to learners (lines 5–8) into a patriotic polylogue (lines 8–9) addressed to 'foreigners' unfamiliar with things French. In the process of constructing for herself an identity as foreign language teacher and native speaker by adopting a teacher and a French native speaker voice, M constructs her listeners primarily as learners and non-native speakers. The quickened pace of M's utterance 'liberté, égalité fraternité' in line 14 indexes her belief that her audience is familiar with this routine motto of the French revolution, and that its significance in this context need not be further explained. Hence, the apodictic falling intonation (.) at the end of line 14. M treats the motto on the French coin as a fact, not as the textual voice of the French state. This allows her to present herself as a disengaged teacher, in the business of merely transmitting institutional facts without herself being imbricated in their institutional reproduction. One participant is quick to ask what this motto means for present-day French persons like M. The French participants M, J, and P rally around a joint response as can be seen below (Extract 6.2).

Extract 6.2

M and J are French teachers of German. P is a French teacher of English.

1 J: [la devise] c'est l'IMAGE que les Français veulent donn-
2   enfin qu' la FRANCE veut donner d'elle-même (.)
3   c'est le pays d'la *révolution*
4   c'est l'pays des *libertés*
5   c'est l'pays d'l'*accueil*
6   et c'est l'pays de l'*égalité* (.)
7 P: ((whispered to J)) c'est la devise
8 J: ((loud to all)) c'est la DEVISE
          ((distributes documents)) ( )
9 M: bon alors bien entendu (0.2)
10   la confrontation de la devise et puis ça ((points to poster))
11   a pour but de faire prendre conscience (0.2) euh (0.2)
12   du décalage entre le discours officiel (0.2) et (0.2)
13   ce que les Français souhaitent (0.2) vraiment

14   au fond d'eux mêmes >puisque visiblement<
15   c'est à c'est à cela qu'on fait appel
16   lorsqu'on fait (0.2) d' la publicité (0.2) pour un grand magasin
17   qui n'est pas un magasin d' luxe, il faut l' savoir.

1 J: it's the image that the French wish to gi-
2   I mean that France wishes to give of itself (.)
2   It's the land of the revolution
4   It's the land of liberty
5   It's the land of hospitality
6   It's the land of equality (.)
7 P: ((whispered to J)) that's the motto
8 J: ((loud to all))it's the [national] MOTTO
        ((M distributes documents))
9 M: so of course (0.2)
10   the confrontation of the motto and then that ((points to poster))
11   is meant to make the students aware (0.2) eh (0.2)
12   of the discrepancy between the official discourse (0.2) and (0.2)
13   what the French really wish (0.2)
14   deep down >since obviously<
15   this is what is being appealed to
16   when one designs (0.2) publicity (0.2) for a department store
17   which, you should know, is not a luxury store.

What the French participants have to do to explain the value of the motto is switch identities from foreign language teachers to French nationals. J first takes on a teacher's voice in lines 1–2, but then, in lines 3–6, performs a typified French national ideology, complete with the institutional voice of the nation-state reciting its national credo. The dichotomy made between France and the French in line 2 is echoed in line 13 by M who seems to attribute more 'deep down' authenticity to the consumerism than to the patriotism of her French compatriots. The ardour of J's tone of voice and his rhapsodic eloquence in lines 3–6 suggest that at that moment he is not only animating but authoring the voice of a mythical France rather than that of the 'real' French (line 13) who buy at the Bon Marché. P seems to have sensed this possibility. His utterance in line 7 reminds the group that J might not have intended to author these patriotic words, but only animate the national ideological motto. J resignifies P's cautionary remark in line 7 into a didactic remark in line 8, addressed to the non-native speakers – thus maintaining the ambiguity of the voice he is assuming.

Immediately following Extract 6.2, M remarks: 'Je pense que tout le monde ayant traduit, vous avez bien compris' [I believe that since everyone has finished translating, you have well understood], referring to the informal simultaneous translations taking place around the table. She obviously underestimates the multiple and possibly conflicting interpretations that her two documents might elicit because of the multiple identities her discourse has constructed for her fellow teachers – as teachers, learners, native speakers, non-native speakers.

What the Bon Marché advertisement presents is the triple contradiction ('décalage') between three types of French identity: a French pre-national and pre-revolutionary identity as symbolised by the advertisement's royalist reference to birth privileges ('les privilèges'); a French national, republican identity symbolised by the post-revolutionary national motto ('la devise'), and a French commercial identity symbolised by the publicity advertisement and the credit card. When used pedagogically, the combination of the poster and the coin presents the French teacher with three potentially conflicting voices:

1. A national republican voice, linked to the French revolutionary ideal of 'liberté' that always implies a freedom from royal arbitrary, birth privileges, social inequalities; this voice seems contradicted by the advertisement's praise of and fascination with royalty.
2. A consumer voice, linked to the idea that one can now buy the privileges of the aristocracy with a credit card; this consumer voice sounds like a return to pre-revolutionary times, when one could buy birth privileges.
3. An educational voice, linked to the use of an authentic text for the teaching of French; this voice has to deal with the inherent contradiction between the money-related, commercial practices suggested by the advertisement and the traditional values of the French educational system, born out of the revolutionary republican ideal.

In addition, the confrontation of the advertisement and the coin juxtaposes two contradictory metaphors: France IS the land of equality – France IS the land of inequality, which forces viewers into an untenable epistemic dilemma.

What M is proposing is a third metaphor that could read as follows: France IS a land of contradiction ('décalage'), that requires of her fellow seminar participants that they see this contradiction the way she does.

In order to get a grasp on this complex interplay of the contradictory voices of three institutions: nation-state, corporate state, school, and their epistemic stances, the non-French participants use tropological projections and extensions that attempt to go from 'seeing' to understanding or 'seeing as'. The first go-betweens in this process are the US teachers of French (R and T) and German (A), who attempt to deconstruct M's 'décalage' metaphor into its constituents – an essentially metonymic move.

Extract 6.3

A is an American teacher of German. R and T are American teachers of French.

```
1 A:  much like we are with our movie stars
2 R:  ((sighs, under her breath)) yes we have movie stars (.)
3 T:  ze ri::ch and femous=
4 A:                              =right!
```

A, a US-born American citizen, has no difficulty finding a parallel between the French fascination with royalty and the American fascination with movie stars. Her choice of English to take the floor and the use of *we* in line 1 clearly index not only her American identity, but also her membership in the American group that includes R and T. The ironic sigh that precedes R's rejoinder in line 2 shows that R, although a naturalised American, implicitly resignifies A's *we* into a *they*, as if she were ventriloquating some American voice that she would rather distance herself from. T expands on A's attempts at metonymic deconstruction by using the voice of Hollywood despite her French accent. Her exclamation, made tongue in cheek and with the irony afforded by her status as a French immigrant to the United States, is endorsed without irony by A in line 4 who thus seems satisfied with the extension of meaning afforded by the metaphor: French aristocracy IS LIKE American movie stars.

The metonymic extension offered by A in English in Extract 6.3 is supplemented in Extract 6.4 by a relational extension of M's metaphor, a synecdochic move that A makes this time in German, addressing M directly.

Extract 6.4

A is an American teacher of German.

```
1 A:  ((tentative tone)) ich dachte gerade daran, M.
2     bei uns steht 'e pluribus unum' drauf
3     aber 'e pluribus unum' passt irgendwie nicht
4     da gibts unter Freiheit natürlich verschiedene
5     ich meine in Einem gibt's Viele . . .
6     ((loud and with conviction)) aber ja!, ich find das GANZ toll!
```

```
1 A:  ((tentative tone)) I was just thinking, M.
2     in our case it says 'e pluribus unum' on it
3     but 'e pluribus unum' somehow doesn't fit
4     there are of course many different types of freedom
5     I mean in one there are many
6     ((loud and with conviction)) but yeah, I find this REALLY great!
```

Because A doesn't speak French, but could have used English as she did in Extract 6.3 and will do again in Extract 6.5, her use of German, the language she teaches in the United States, must be seen as significantly reaching out to meet M halfway, as a sign of solidarity from one teacher of German to another. Her tentative tone of voice in lines 1–5 seems to want to mitigate the potential threat to M's face as she acknowledges the negative evaluation given by M of her own country and validates it by finding a synecdochic equivalence with the motto on US coins. The noticeable change in tone in line 6 initiated by 'aber' and her praise of M's two documents for pedagogical purposes suggest that their common identity as teachers and moreover teachers of the same foreign language may indeed bridge their differences as two nationals with different national ideologies. A tries to seek not only lexical equivalencies but also conceptual relations between the contradictions expressed by the French advertisement – in other words, she attempts to see 'unity versus pluralism' in the same way as M sees 'privilège versus égalité'. According to A, American unity is to American pluralism what French 'privilège' is to French 'égalité', namely a 'décalage' or discrepancy. Her mention of 'bei uns', meaning 'we Americans' as in Extract 6.3 but this time said in German, enables her to distance herself and objectify American group identity in order to examine it more critically.

However, as Berger and Luckmann (1966) warned, it is one thing outwardly to objectify oneself, but it is another to adopt for oneself someone else's metaphors. Shortly thereafter, A puts in question the very institutional basis for M's original metaphor – the perceived French 'décalage' (Extract 6.5).

Extract 6.5

A is an American teacher of German. JP is a French teacher of English.

1 A: do you see it as a contradiction M. (0.2) the ad and the franc? (0.2)
2   liberty and =
3 JP: =equality (.) equality and privilege (0.4)
4 A: do you see that as any contradiction?
5   how about the perspective that we all have the equ- equal opportunity
6   to achieve what we want to achieve within society? =
7 JP: =the word privilege impl*ies* that it's something that is *due* to *you*
8   it's not something that you earned (0.2) by your merits
9   you're a category apart (0.2)
10   to the French people it refers to nobility
11   before the French revolution
12   because nobility had certain privileges
13   by right you know
14   not because they are they WERE better but by birth (0.2) right

A addresses M this time in English, thus performing an American identity clearly demarcated from the French. What appears to be problematic is not the mapping of one aspect of the 'décalage' onto another, in a metonymic or synecdochic sense, but the metaphor of 'décalage' itself between a societal myth and its reality. A is taking a distinct ironic stance here, which puts into question M's ordering principle per se. What started out as a simple pedagogic problem requiring teachers to enter into their expected professional roles, then turned into a linguistic or cultural problem eliciting the performance of national roles, has now become a larger problem of differing historical and political continuities whose performances clash.

In Extract 6.5, A proposed an alternate metaphor to M's, namely, instead of the French left-wing metaphor: 'France IS a land of contradiction', the American liberal metaphor: 'France IS a land of equal opportunity'. The challenge is once again to see one institutional discourse in terms of another.

Extract 6.6

C and A are American teachers of German. R is an American teacher of French.

```
 1 C:  in the States privilege means something that could be
 2      earned (0.2) in a sense
 3      there is something called perks
 4      that you would get (0.2)
 5      that they would give you to woo you away
 6      maybe from another company
 7      and those are privileges that the other people who work there may
        not have
 8      but since they WANTED you to come (3)
 9      it's something else then ( )
10 R:  privilege is earned (0.2) it's a matter of merit
11      and since you earned it
12 A:  take Clinton for example
13      he's a young man who was the typical (xxx)
14      comes from a lower middle class family
15      and he EARNED his privilege to become president of the United
        States
16      it's not (0.2) you are not BORN into something
```

Extract 6.7

```
 1 R:  we have another word in English now called entitlement (0.4)
 2      in a sense entitlement carries with it the idea of a privilege that you
        are born with
 3      but an entitlement in America means that you are entitled to welfare
```

4   if you are handicapped you are entitled to (0.5) access to equal access
5   so we use entitlement in a totally different way from a privilege.
6 A: it's a freedom (0.2) it's almost a freedom that we have

Both C in Extract 6.6 and R in Extract 6.7 begin by giving formal definitions for the American English words 'privilege' and 'entitlement' respectively, thus positioning themselves as native speakers vis-à-vis the non-native
speakers of English. However, in both excerpts the participants quickly adopt
national identities marked by *we* and an impersonal *you* that, in its frequency,
takes on a personal flavour. The combination of these two pronouns in each
excerpt has the effect of constructing a 'we–you' community of personal
relationships among equals, that is emblematic of the ideology of 'equal
opportunity' proposed by the American participants. The many examples
given in both excerpts reinforce the personal, suasive tone of these excerpts,
as if rather than understand, the parties were intent on trying to persuade
each other of the validity of their arguments. The tropological move here is
once again a synecdoche of the alternate metaphor proposed by A in Extract
6.5: 'France IS a land of equal opportunity', the two examples chosen by the
American participants – commercial perks and career politics – attempting
to map the French institutional ideology onto the American.

Throughout the first 20 minutes of this 30-minute exchange, the German
colleagues have remained relatively silent, especially the East Germans. Then
suddenly, in Extract 6.8, G takes the floor. Her discourse, as well as that
of U and F in Extract 6.9, reveal the difficulty that the Germans around the
table had in negotiating identity, role and voice in the united Germany of
1993.

Extract 6.8

G is a West German teacher of French.

1 G: ich überlege mir die ganze Zeit
2   es ist ganz klar
3   es geht hier nicht um Freiheit sondern um *égalité*
4   es geht darum ob wir *égalité* in einem sozialistischen Sinn meinen (0.4)
5   oder ob wir bei uns nicht eher Gleichheit vor dem Gesetz haben
6   oder auch Chancengleichheit
          ( )
7   Gleichheit (0.5) schließt glaube ich (0.2) für einen Deutschen
8   so wie es bei uns gebraucht wird
9   auch gewisse Privilegien, die man durch Arbeit
10   durch Leistung erwirbt, nicht aus
11   wir gehen bei uns immer von dem Begriff der Leistungsgesellschaft
      aus

12   das andere, das ist schon lange vorbei, nicht?
13   Vorrechte durch Geburt gibt es nicht mehr, ((loud general laughter))
14   wir haben keine Adligen mehr, die (0.5)
15   il y a des nobles oui mais il y a une noblesse pauvre egalement
       ((laughter))
16   il n'y a pas seulement des nobles riches, hein?
17   also (0.5) ich würde wirklich sagen
18   diese Leistungsgesellschaft kann dann auch eben für sich in Anspruch
       nehmen
19   dass sie eine Kreditkarte hat
20   und damit eben alles kaufen kann

1 G: I've been thinking the whole time
2   it is quite clear it
3   is not a question of freedom but of equality
4   the question is whether we mean equality in a socialist sense (0.4)
5   or whether we mean rather equality before the law
6   or equality of opportunity.
7   Equality (0.5) for a German doesn't exclude (0.2)
8   – in the way we use the word –
9   certain privileges that are
10   earned through work, through performance
11   we [in Germany] always go from the notion of merit society
12   the other, it's long past, isn't it?
13   we have no more birth privileges ((loud general laughter))
14   we have no longer a nobility, that (0.5)
15   there is some nobility yes but there is also a poor nobility ((laughter))
16   there is not only a rich nobility, eh?
17   so (0.5) I would really say
18   that this merit society can claim for itself
19   the right to have credit cards
20   with which one can buy anything

G, a West German teacher of French, who first takes the floor in Extract
6.8, aligns herself at this point less with her East German colleagues, who
might not feel included in her use of 'bei uns', despite her use of German,
than with the Americans, with whom she seems to share the idea of *merit*
through performance ('Leistung'), although she might not mean the same
thing by the verb 'erwerben' (to earn, line 10) as the Americans C and A
meant by *earn* in Extract 6.6 (lines 2, 10). But her position is certainly closer
to the Americans than to the French, as evidenced by the general laughter in
line 13 when she openly contradicts the French, and then tries to win them
over to her argument by switching to French in line 15, thus showing solidarity despite differences in worldviews. The laughter itself in line 13 is

worthy of special note. It definitely breaks the mounting tension one senses among the German participants. It is the manifestation of a sense of trust that has been accumulating since the beginning of this debate. As a language in itself, laughter welds the group together at that particular moment, beyond ideological differences and historical discontinuities. More than anything else, this general laughter indexes the ironical stance that every participant is taking at that moment vis-à-vis the 'décalage' that they perceive between myth and reality in their own respective countries.

This is the moment that the two East Germans, U and F, choose to enter the discussion. On the face of it, G's reference to privileges earned through performance or merit and hard work would seem to apply also to the East Germans. Yet the word performance itself covers too many different historicities and collectivities. The East German colleagues contest G's West German definition of equal opportunity ('Chancengleichheit') and align themselves explicitly with the French, as we see in Extract 6.9.

Extract 6.9

U and F are East German teachers of English and French respectively.

1 U: das heißt für die Französischlehrer, die Begriffe sind mit Sicherheit im Osten anzusetzen
2 G: klar natürlich!
3 U: Gleichheit bei uns wird *nicht* gleich mit Leistungsgesellschaft gesetzt (0.4)
4   als Beispiel in der Gesellschaft, in der wir groß geworden sind
5   waren die Gehaltsunterschiede zwischen Facharbeiter und Professor lächerlich
6 F: ja (0.4) Gleichheit ist schwer zu formulieren ( )
7   Gleichheit (0.3) das ist eine Wirkungsgelegenheit

1 U: that means that for the French teachers these notions clearly come from the East
2 G: absolutely!
3 U: We [in East Germany] do not equate equality with a performance-oriented society
4   for example in the society in which we grew up
5   the differences in salary between a specialized worker and a professor were minimal
6 F: yes (0.4) equality is a difficult notion to formulate ( )
7   equality (0.3) that's an opportunity for action

In an attempt to bring the East German voice into the debate, U and F try to resignify the concepts used in G's discourse, by linking them metonymically to different political institutional discourses: the West German concept of equal opportunity of access to material goods ('Chancengleichheit') is mapped onto an East German concept of equal opportunity for societal action ('Wirkungsgelegenheit'). But the general silence of the East German colleagues in this particular debate, and the difficulty they have in 'formulating the notion of equality' (line 6) is emblematic of the difficulty that former citizens of the GDR had in 1993 in formulating for themselves an identity that is linked to an institution that no longer exists – namely the GDR and its socialist discourse. Even the word 'Wirkungsgelegenheit', an improvised coinage, is a brave attempt at explaining in German to non-East Germans, what the ideology of equality might have meant in their country before 1989, and why they feel closer to J's French revolutionary ideal (equality IS equal access) than to C or A's American ideal (equality IS equal opportunity) or G's West German ideal (equality IS equal reward). The reason they did not enter the debate around M's original metaphor 'France IS a land of contradiction' 20 minutes earlier may have to do with their own difficult position between two identities: one linked to an institution that is no longer theirs; the other to an institution that they have not yet made theirs; and their uncertain voice between the two.[4] How the French materials should be taught in Leipzig schools? U's response reveals a willingness to explore a new discourse, as we can see in Extract 6.10.

Extract 6.10

U is an East German teacher of English.

1 u: ich fände es wahrscheinlich eine interessante und spannende Sache
2   weil man hier das Thema an Begriffen (0.3) an Einzelgruppen (0.5)
3   die Welt aufmachen kann
4   ich könnte mir das gut vorstellen
5   unabhängig vom Fach

1 u: I think it could be an interesting and exciting approach
2   because one can open up the topic with [such] concepts (0.3)
3   in individual groups (0.5) one can open up the world [for the students]
4   I can imagine that very well
5   independent from language teaching

In this statement, terms like 'Begriffe' (concepts), 'Einzelgruppen' (individual groups), 'die Welt aufmachen' (to open up the world), 'unabhängig vom Fach' (independent from language teaching) which remain rather vague precisely because they are not linked to any identifiable institutional discourse, might be seen as an attempt to imagine a new way of seeing within an East German teacher's discourse.

Conclusion

This 30-minute interaction between language teachers from three different countries teaching three different languages has shown a dizzying and often quite sophisticated manoeuvering between choices of languages, identities and epistemic stances in order to understand one another. These choices reflect those which the participants had to make when positioning themselves as speakers vis-à-vis themselves and others and vis-à-vis the linguistic, cultural and pedagogic challenge posited by the French group at the outset – the theme of a 'décalage' between institutional myth and institutional reality.

Across national languages and national cultures the participants were confronted with the need to negotiate synchronic and diachronic institutional identities. The synchronic identities were of a linguistic, professional, national, political/ideological nature, as participants could choose to play the roles of native speakers, teachers, citizens of their respective nation-states, or adherents to a specific political ideology. Each of their choices entailed a corresponding construction of the other participants' identity, which these in turn could accept or contest. The diachronic identities were similarly diverse as participants had to position themselves vis-à-vis historically contradictory ideologies, such as French pre-revolutionary, republican or consumerist, and German pre- or post-1989.

The multiple voices that populate this short exchange can be viewed as attempts by the participants to deal with conflict and ambiguity. Whether they animated an official national ideology, ventriloquated the official pedagogical voice of a national standard language, or were authors or principals of other's recontextualised discourses, they all had to choose for themselves a voice in response to the voice of others. These voices could hardly be expected to position themselves outside the institutional context in which they were allowed to emerge, namely an international, carefully structured seminar for language teachers conceived just after the Cold War as part of the world peace mission of the Goethe Institute. But through various epistemic stances based on tropological variations of the theme 'myth versus reality', the participants' voices tried to resignify traditional national, professional, historical identities within a 'third place' (Kramsch, 1993) that favours irony and critical distance towards institutional discourses of all kinds.[5]

The way this group managed (mis)communication shows that the process of interdiscursive communication is not a question of finding the right words to fit what you want to say, but of trying to see things as others see them. It is a tropological process that attempts to embrace two or several incompatible historicities and socialities under one metaphor in order to grasp them in their contradiction, such as, in this case, the metaphor of the 'décalage'. In this process, voices can get ignored, or be led astray through metonymic or synecdochic extensions that explore one pole or the other of the contradiction without really examining the contradiction itself. Irony plays an important role in these explorations as the critical moment when the contradiction itself is put into question and challenged by alternative contradictions and further tropological explorations. Paradoxically, the institutional discourses that through their diverging historical memories may lead to miscommunication ultimately provided the necessary historical continuity or trust to engage in irony, even in the face of seeming communication breakdowns. An ironical stance – sometimes expressed by laughter as in Extract 6.8 – reveals that there are multiple historicities and multiple institutionalities to draw from, as the historical process of institutionalisation gets enacted at each encounter on the grid of turns at talk.

Appendix

Transcription conventions

(.)	falling intonation
> . . . <	speech faster than normal cadence
< . . . >	slower than normal cadence
italics	sounds pronounced with emphasis
CAPITALS	louder speech
(0.2)	time elapsed in tenths of seconds
:	elongated sound
=	overlapping speech
((double parentheses))	non-verbal behaviour
( )	skipped over portion of the conversation
(xxx)	incomprehensible speech

Notes

1 The distinction is often made between individual and social identity. In fact these are two different ways of looking at the same phenomenon. One can either consider the autonomous individual as the primary entity, in which case social identity is but the various incarnations of that individual in various social contexts; or, like Berger and Luckmann, one can take the social individual to be primary – in which case a person's identity consists of the style in which that person makes use of the social resources available to him/her. I take this latter view here, following Buffon's

famous dictum: *Le style c'est l'homme même*. Because style is inextricably linked to an individual's ways with words, I use the term *voice* here instead of identity to refer to individual style in discourse. Voice, in its historical, social and rhetorical dimensions, encompasses such stylistic features of discourse as ideological alignment, narrative point of view, epistemic stance, etc.

2 This seminar followed the same format as that conducted the year before and described in Kramsch (1993). The participants had been asked to bring to the seminar some authentic materials they used to teach the foreign language in their respective countries, as well as some materials they would recommend to teachers of their own native language in other countries. The first day of the seminar was devoted to the former, the second day to the latter, from which this case study was taken. The participants worked in small groups before they presented their materials to the larger international group.

3 It is possible that, because of the frequent private simultaneous translations going on around the table and not captured by the tape recorder, the choice of language addressed to the whole group might have been conditioned by the language used in private directly prior to taking the floor in public. However, because of the relatively large group of 15 persons sitting around the table, and thus the relative pressure imposed on 'public' speaking, the participants were quite conscious of which language they chose to address the group in.

4 One could argue that it also had to do with the dynamics of the interplay of identity, role, and voice where roles generate counter-roles, and voice counter-voice, so that it was only because the French teachers foregrounded their institutional identity as French nationals that the East German teachers were forced to do the same. One could argue that, had the discourse remained on the pedagogic ground common to all language teachers, the East German participants might not have had to deal with issues of national identity. Such arguments are plausible. However, they ignore the fact that all teaching, and foreign language teaching in particular, is done within an institutional context that is historically, socially and politically motivated. In fact, the materials that the German group presented were as politically and ideologically marked as those of the French, with an equal restraint on the part of the East German colleagues to participate, at least in the larger group.

5 The slightly utopian character of this third place is a common feature of many educational endeavours to 'change the world'.

References

Atkinson, J. M. and Drew, P. (1979). *Order in court: The organization of verbal interaction in judicial settings*. London: Macmillan.

Bakhtin, M. (1981). *The dialogic imagination*. ed. by M. Holquist. Transl. by C. Emerson and M. Holquist. Austin: University of Texas Press.

Bateson, G. (1972). *Steps to an ecology of mind*. New York: Ballantine.

Berger, P. L. and Luckmann, T. (1966). *The social construction of reality*. New York: Doubleday.

Bhabha, H. (1994). *The location of culture*. London: Routledge.

Blommaert, J. and Verschueren, J. (eds) (1991). *The pragmatics of intercultural and international communication*. Amsterdam: John Benjamins.

Bourdieu, P. (1991). *Language and symbolic power*. Cambridge: Cambridge University Press.

Bruner, J. (1990). *Acts of meaning*. Cambridge, MA: Harvard University Press.

Cameron, L. and Low, G. (eds) (1999). *Researching and applying metaphor*. Cambridge: Cambridge University Press.

Candlin, C. N. (1987). Explaining moments of conflict in discourse. In R. Steele and T. Threadgold (eds), *Language topics: Essays in honour of Michael Halliday*. Amsterdam: John Benjamins, 413–429.

Drew, P. (1998). Misalignments in 'out-of-hours' calls to the doctor. Plenary talk at the 6th IprA conference in Reims, France.

Fairclough, N. (1992). *Discourse and social change*. Cambridge: Polity Press.

Garfinkel, H. (1967). *Studies in ethnomethodology*. Englewood Cliffs, NJ: Prentice Hall.

Gee, J. P. (1990). *Social linguistics and literacies. Ideology in discourses*. London: Falmer Press.

Gergen, K. (1985). The social constructionist movement in modern psychology. In *American Psychologist*, 40, 266–275.

Gibbs, R. W. Jr. (1994). *The poetics of mind. Figurative thought, language, and understanding*. Cambridge: Cambridge University Press.

Giddens, A. (1991). *Modernity and self-identity. Self and society in the late modern age*. Stanford: Stanford University Press.

Goffman, E. (1974). *Frame analysis*. New York: Harper & Row.

Goffman, E. (1981). *Forms of talk*. Philadelphia: University of Pennsylvania Press.

Gumperz, J. J. (1982a). *Discourse strategies*. Cambridge: Cambridge University Press.

Gumperz, J. J. (ed.) (1982b). *Language and social identity*. Cambridge: Cambridge University Press.

Gumperz, J. J. (1992). Interviewing in intercultural situations. In P. Drew and J. Heritage (eds), *Talk at work. Interaction in institutional settings*. Cambridge: Cambridge University Press, 302–327.

Gumperz, J. J. (1996). The linguistic and cultural relativity of inference. In J. J. Gumperz and S. C. Levinson (eds), *Rethinking linguistic relativity*. Cambridge: Cambridge University Press, 374–406.

Gumperz, J. J. and Roberts, C. (1991). Understanding in intercultural encounters. In J. Blommaert and J. Verschueren (eds), *The pragmatics of international and intercultural communication*. Amsterdam: John Benjamins, 51–90.

Hanks, W. (1996). *Language and communicative practices*. Boulder, CO: Westview Press.

Harre, R. (1986). An outline of the social constructionist viewpoint. In R. Harre (ed.), *The social construction of emotions*. Oxford: Blackwell, 2–14.

Hofstede, G. (1983). Dimension of national cultures in 50 countries and three regions. In J. B. Deregowski, S. Dziurawiec and R. C. Annis (eds), *Explications in cross-cultural psychology*. Lisse: Swets and Zeitlinger, 335–555.

Holquist, M. and Emerson, C. (1981). Glossary for *The dialogic imagination: Four essays by M. M. Bakhtin*, ed. by M. Holquist. Transl. by M. Holquist and C. Emerson. Austin: University of Texas Press.

Johnson, M. (1987). *The body in the mind. The bodily basis of meaning, imagination, and reason*. Chicago: University of Chicago Press.

Johnstone, B. (1996). *The linguistic individual. Self-expression in language and linguistics.* Oxford: Oxford University Press.

Kramsch, C. (1993). Language study as border study: Experiencing difference. In *European Journal of Education*, 28 (3), 349–358.

Kramsch, C. (1995). The cultural component of language teaching. In *Language, Culture and Curriculum*, 8 (2), 83–92.

Kramsch, C. (1998). *Language and culture.* Oxford: Oxford University Press.

Kramsch, C. (2000). Social discursive construction of self in L2 learning. In J. Lantolf (ed.), *Sociocultural theory and second language learning.* Oxford: Oxford University Press, 133–154.

Kramsch, C. and Lam, E. (1999). Textual identities: The importance of being non-native. In G. Braine (ed.), *Non-native educators in English language teaching.* Mahwah, NJ: Lawrence Erlbaum, 57–72.

Kristeva, J. (1986). *The Kristeva reader.* ed. by Toril Moi. New York: Columbia University Press.

Lakoff, G. (1987). *Fire, women, and dangerous things. What categories reveal about the mind.* Chicago: University of Chicago Press.

Lakoff, G. and Johnson, M. (1980). *Metaphors we live by.* Chicago: University of Chicago Press.

Lantolf, J. (ed.) (2000). *Sociocultural theory and second language learning.* Oxford: Oxford University Press.

Lemke, J. L. (1995). *Textual politics. Discourse and social dynamics.* London: Taylor and Francis.

LePage, R. and Tabouret-Keller, A. (1985). *Acts of identity. Creole-based approaches to language and ethnicity.* Cambridge: Cambridge University Press.

Linde, C. (1993). *Life stories. The creation of coherence.* Oxford: Oxford University Press.

Meeuwis, M. (ed.) (1994). *Critical perspectives on intercultural communication.* Special issue of *Pragmatics*, 4 (3).

Mehan, H. (1990). Oracular reasoning in a psychiatric exam: The resolution of conflict in language. In A. D. Grimshaw (ed.), *Conflict talk. Sociolinguistic investigations of arguments in conversations.* Cambridge: Cambridge University Press, 160–177.

Milroy, L. and Muysken, P. (eds) (1995). *One speaker, two languages.* Cambridge: Cambridge University Press.

Ochs, E. (1993). Constructing social identity: A language socialization perspective. In *Research in Language as Social Interaction*, 26, 287–306.

Ochs, E. (1996). Linguistic resources for socializing humanity. In J. J. Gumperz and S. C. Levinson (eds), *Rethinking linguistic relativity.* Cambridge: Cambridge University Press, 438–469.

Ochs, E. and Capps, L. (1996). Narrating the self. In *Annual Review of Anthropology*, 25, 19–43.

Peirce, B. N. (1995). Social identity, investment, and language learning. In *TESOL Quarterly*, 29 (1), 9–32.

Rampton, B. (1995). *Crossing. Language and ethnicity among adolescents.* London: Longman.

Sarangi, S. (1994). Intercultural or not? Beyond celebration of cultural differences in miscommunication analysis. In *Pragmatics*, 4 (3), 409–427.

Scollon, R. (1996). Discourse identity, social identity, and confusion in intercultural communication. In *Intercultural Communication Studies*, 6 (1), 1–18.

Scollon, R. and Scollon, S. (1981). *Narrative, literacy, and face in interethnic communication*. Norwood, NJ: Ablex.

Scollon, R. and Scollon, S. (1995). *Intercultural communication*. Oxford: Blackwell.

Sebeok, T. (ed.) (1960). *Style in language*. Cambridge, MA: MIT Press.

Shotter, J. (1993a). *Cultural politics of everyday life: Social constructionism, rhetoric, and knowing of the third kind*. Milton Keynes: Open University Press.

Shotter, J. (1993b). *Conversational realities. Constructing life through language*. London: Sage.

Simpson, P. (1993). *Language, ideology and point of view*. London: Routledge.

Taylor, C. (1989). *Sources of the self. The making of the modern identity*. Cambridge, MA: Harvard University Press.

Triandis, H. (1995). *Individualism and collectivism*. Boulder, CO: Westview Press.

Turner, M. (1996). *The literary mind. The origins of thought and language*. Oxford: Oxford University Press.

Vygotsky, L. (1989). Concrete human psychology. In *Soviet Psychology*, 27 (2), 53–77.

Wertsch, J. V. (1991). *Voices of the mind. A sociocultural approach to mediated action*. London: Harvester Wheatsheaf.

White, H. (1978). *Tropics of discourse. Essays in cultural criticism*. Baltimore: Johns Hopkins University Press.

Wortham, S. (2000). Self on the margin: Positioning the moral self in classroom literature discussions. Paper presented at the Annual Conference of the American Association for Applied Linguistics, Vancouver, Canada, March.

7

Misunderstanding teaching and learning

Joan Turner and Masako Hiraga

Introduction

As market values permeate higher education globally and students from widely varying educational systems and cultures study in a different one, the context of higher education has become a site of cultural flux and tension. This is the case whether it is a matter of traditional academic values confronting the market-place, e.g. academic freedom being pitted against the need to generate income, or whether it is students from one distinctive culture meeting another, e.g. students from Japan studying in Britain. Within any culture, traditional educational values will also be the subject of competing tensions, at a range of levels.

In higher education across the world, therefore, issues of power, finance, epistemology, language and cultural history interact in a prototypically post-modern melée. In such circumstances, misunderstandings abound, whether they are realised as such or not, in varying permutations at different levels of analysis.

Against this backdrop, we look at misunderstandings emanating from the level of deeply embedded ideologies regarding teaching and learning when two very different linguistic and cultural backgrounds, namely those of Japan and Britain, interact in higher education. Our perspective is that given such circumstances, misunderstandings at the pragmatic level are always latent, but do not necessarily occur in fixed ways. Examples of misunderstanding are then analysed as effects of ideological issues rather than as problems of real-time communication. These ideological issues include cultural value systems informing the roles of tutors and students, the effects on tutor–student interaction of epistemological values and the effects on language use of cultural conceptualisations of communication.

We use the term ideology in the broad-based, interdisciplinary way advocated by van Dijk (1998). Although he is concerned to develop a theory of ideology, as opposed to defining it, he gives a fairly loose definition which we accept as a heuristic in our own work: 'an ideology is something like a shared framework of social beliefs that organise and coordinate the social interpretations and practices of groups and their members, and in particular also power and other relations between groups' (van Dijk, 1998, p. 8).

In this chapter, we are not emphasising relations of power, more the power of embedded belief systems to inform actions in a very specific context, namely that of interaction between the institutional roles of tutor and student.

Cultural value systems and educational ideologies

One traditional manifestation of cultural value systems is proverbs. They are particularly valued as a source of cultural understanding by social historians. Obelkevich (1987, p. 67), for example, states: 'When people habitually use proverbs and similar expressions they will tend to think in terms of them and act in accordance with them. If social life can be interpreted like a text, then as often as not it is the proverb or the stock phrase that provides the clue.'

However, in eighteenth-century British culture, as Obelkevich also documents, proverbs became the victim of social snobbery. He quotes from Lord Chesterfield's advice to his son: 'A man of fashion never has recourse to proverbs or vulgar aphorisms' (Obelkevich, 1987, p. 57).

Although occasionally revived and restored to social dignity, the proverb has effectively been removed from educated discourse and discourse about education, in English. However, this is not the case in Japanese (see Mori and Komiyama, 1984; Shouji, 1987) or in Chinese (see Scollon, 1997). The respect in which proverbs are held is manifested in the more than one hundred books of Japanese proverbs that exist. A few of these source books are mentioned at the end of this chapter.

In acknowledgement therefore of the relevance of proverbs to underlying value systems, and the esteem in which they are held in Japan, we would like to look at some Japanese proverbs for learning and teaching and explore how they both outline traditional structures of understanding and explain continuing patterns of contemporary behaviour. (For the abbreviations of function words, see Appendix at the end of this chapter.)

The first three proverbs we want to look at are:

1. Nanashaku sat-te shi no kage o fuma-zu
    Seven.feet leave-GER teacher of shadow ACC step.on-NEG
    'Follow your master seven feet behind so that you don't step on his shadow.'

2. Shi ni wa shitaga-e
    teacher DAT TOP follow-IMP
    'It is the teacher that you should follow.'
3. Shi wa hari no gotoku, deshi wa ito no gotoshi
    teacher TOP needle GEN look.like, disciples TOP thread GEN look.like
    'The teacher is a needle, and the disciples are a thread which goes with
    the needle.'

These proverbs emphasise the importance and separate distinction of the
'master' or 'shi' in Japanese. They indicate the authoritative presence of
the teacher, the respect in which he/she is held in Japanese culture and the
concomitant deferential attitude which is incurred.

In her discussion of professor–student interaction in Japan, from the point
of view of non-native speaker (NNS) students, Siegal (1996, p. 364) implies
the specific cultural importance of deference when she states: 'It is not
reductionist to say that in Japan, students should be deferential to their
professors and should use the appropriate language to show deference.'
Pre-empting the argument of reductionism moves the discussion away
from what Sakamoto and Naotsuka (1982) term 'polite fictions', namely the
polarisation of cultural differences in communicative style, one which
says 'you and I are equal' and another which is concerned to observe the
reciprocal superiority and inferiority of the interlocutors. In a culture where
'vertical' relationships (Nakane, 1970) and an 'asymmetrical' (Lebra, 1992,
1993) communication style are the norm, strategies of deference in both
verbal and non-verbal communication are to be expected. Matsumoto (1988)
has also demonstrated that deferential language use is pervasive in the linguistic system of Japanese. The point to be made here is that while the
pragmatic variables of power and distance may be universal, the semantic,
indeed semiotic, concept of deference is culturally variable. This in turn
makes the relevance of the pragmatic variables relative at another level of
analysis. So, for example, whereas negative politeness strategies in English
may be the major basis for deferential language use, deferential language use
in Japanese is germane to speaking Japanese. This makes deference not only
a pragmatic parameter, but also an ideological one.

Following a path

In the Japanese educational context, the social ideology of deference is
strengthened by the educational ideology of 'following the master', which is
also embedded semantically in vocabulary relating to teaching and learning.

In her study of Japanese metaphors for learning, Hiraga (1998) linked
the etymological origins in the Chinese characters of vocabulary relating
to study and learning to the conceptual metaphor, LEARNING IS A

JOURNEY. The phrase, 'manabi-no michi' (learning-GEN road, 'path of learning'), which literally means 'study, learning, etc.', manifests this metaphor most overtly. The verbs involved are 'michibiku' ('to lead') and 'shitagau' ('to follow'), both of which have an etymological trace in the JOURNEY metaphor. 'Michibiku' etymologically means 'to let someone pass through by holding or pulling his/her hands'; and 'shitagau' 'to follow after someone or to obey'. In modern usage, 'sensei ni tsuku' (teacher DAT attach, 'to take lessons from a teacher'), 'sensei ni tsui-te-iku' (teacher DAT attach-GER-go, 'to follow the teacher') or 'sensei ni tsui-te-ike-nai' (teacher DAT attach-GER-go-NEG, 'not be able to follow the teacher') also imply that learning involves an act of following the teacher, which is represented metaphorically as 'going with the teacher'. The most common Japanese word for a teacher is 'sensei'. 'Sen' in 'sensei' originally means 'one's feet going before others', or 'to make an advance before others'. On the other hand, the Japanese word for a pupil, 'seito', and for a student, 'gakuto', both have the Chinese character, 'to', which etymologically means 'to step and walk along a path'. Hence, both the teacher and the pupil/student are represented metaphorically as people leading or walking along a path. The nouns for study and research in Japanese both imply JOURNEY and PATH. 'Gakumon' ('study') etymologically means 'to study, to listen, to ask, and to visit', and 'kenkyuu' ('research') means 'to polish and to reach the extreme end of the dwelling'.

A significant part of learning in this metaphorical conceptualisation is to follow the master loyally and faithfully. This conceptualisation of learning transfers also to spoken interaction, as Extract 7.1 between a Japanese professor of sociolinguistics and her student demonstrates:

Extract 7.1

JAPANESE STUDENT:	Could you tell me, for example, which book I should read?
JAPANESE TUTOR:	Well, people like X and Y write individualism and collectivism. If you read them and relate them to what you argue about 'losing face,' I think your claim would sound more comprehensive.
JS:	Would it be strange if I wrote about the contrast between individualism and collectivism in here?
JT:	I don't think you should really need to write about the contrast, because you're writing about Japanese apology only.
	. . .
	As this paper concerns only Japanese apology, you can introduce collectivism in order to explain why Japanese people behave the way they do when they want to save their face.

. . .
It is said that the Japanese tend to behave collectively.
If you wanted to refer to this tendency, you can try to
look for the books on inter-cultural communication
and then quote or paraphrase some passages that would
explain collectivism.

JS: (silent for 7 secs.)

JT: You can consult some dictionaries of communication.
There would be a concise explanation and definition
of technical terms such as collectivism.

JS: Oh . . .

JT: And then you can also find further references in such
dictionaries.

JS: I see.

[English gloss of authentic data in Japanese]

The student is asking for advice, an educational situation that might occur anywhere in the world. However, the manner of advice-giving by the professor is distinctive, in that she provides it extensively. First of all, she makes a specific suggestion for a specific topic, providing also a rationale for the suggestion. She then rebuts the student's interpretation of her advice, making more concrete the task that the student should be engaged in. After several utterances of digression (deleted in the extract) she further elaborates on her suggestion and its significance for the student's task. After another digression, the teacher fully elaborates reasons and mentions other reference texts, even telling the student how she can use those textbooks. The student is then silent for seven seconds, (which would be inappropriately long in the British context) when the teacher continues the turn with further clarification. The student now must have a very clear idea of a step-by-step procedure (the tutor has literally mapped out the steps for her) and she expresses her understanding.

As well as exemplifying particularly well the expectation invested in the teacher to show the way, this extract also points up the extent to which it is incumbent upon the teacher to elaborate, an expectation at odds with the interactional dynamic expected in British tutorials in the creative and performing arts (see Hiraga and Turner, 1995; Turner and Hiraga, 1996), where this was a function expected rather of students.

Drawing students out

In data drawn from one-to-one tutorials between Japanese students and British tutors in disciplines related to the creative and performing arts, namely, fine art, drama, music, media studies and dance, the teaching/learning dynamic was not so much one of the tutor leading the student along the path, but more one of the tutor eliciting certain kinds of information from the students. In eliciting comment on their work or their understanding of the discipline from the student, the most frequently occurring speech acts used by the British tutors were:

- requests for more general evaluations by the student such as: 'Who is your favourite composer?' 'Was there any play that you have seen that you were particularly impressed by?' 'Why do you want to study dance?'
- more focused requests for evaluation relating to the student's own work: 'Does it work, do you think?' 'Are you more interested in space or the material?'
- implicit suggestions: 'You might want to try it from a different angle'
- implicit recommendations: 'Are you familiar with the work of X?'
- implicit criticisms: 'It seems to me you need to do a lot of drawing.'

The student role in the exchanges was to describe what they had done or were doing or had tried to do, in the appropriate disciplinary terminology, to evaluate the extent to which their intentions were or were not successful, to show evidence of understanding the criteria on which a work may succeed or fail, and to express possible future directions for the work. The developmental dynamic of the tutorials is explained more fully in Turner (1996). Extract 7.2 from a music tutorial shows the conflicting dynamic of tutor–student interaction, as the tutor attempts to elicit more from the student while the student's responses remain minimal.

Extract 7.2

BRITISH TUTOR:	What sort of twentieth-century music do you like best?
JAPANESE STUDENT:	Berg.
BT:	Why do you like it?
JS:	(pause)
BT:	Do you think he uses the violin well?

In terms of cross-cultural pragmatic failure (Thomas, 1983), the student has 'failed' to respond appropriately by not justifying her preference for Berg. The expectation of such a justification is embodied in the tutor's subsequent elicitation. The tutor's third attempt at an elicitation of the required information is a guess at what might constitute her reasons, as the student was herself a violinist. Evaluating the tutor in Japanese terms, he has 'failed' (although the code of honour pertaining to the 'sensei' would not allow conceptualisation in those terms) to signpost clearly enough for the student what she was expected to tell him. As the Japanese students were on bridging courses, that is combining work in English language, specifically EAP (English for Academic Purposes), with work in the disciplines of fine art, music, media studies, drama and dance, preparatory to going on to degree courses at undergraduate or post-graduate level, the recurrent pattern of 'too few words' could have been put down to insufficient language proficiency. While in some cases, the students' language proficiency was not very good, 'too few words' was also in the academic context a case of pragmatic failure, one at the opposite end of the spectrum from that identified by Blum-Kulka and Olshtain (1986) of 'too many words'. In Extract 7.2 the student's language proficiency was not the drawback to the smooth flow of interaction. She was linguistically capable of elaborating, but did not. We submit that the pragmatic failure is in turn an effect of a deeper ideological misunderstanding of the roles of tutors and students and epistemological understanding of the significance of elaboration.

Ideological misunderstandings of elaboration

We initially investigated the apparent reluctance of the Japanese students to talk about their work as a pragmatic problem of elaboration (Hiraga and Turner, 1995; Turner and Hiraga, 1996) and devised a discourse completion task (DCT) to investigate strategies of elaboration among Japanese and British students. Using the kinds of British tutor utterances found in the authentic data such as requests for evaluation, implicit recommendations, implicit criticisms and hedged suggestions, we applied them to more general tutorial situations between lecturer and student. The situations were made as general as possible to be recognisable to students in both countries. Although the tutorial is not prevalent in Japan, students of English and linguistics, for example, commonly receive one-to-one consultations on their thesis writing in English, and the situations and content of the elicitations aimed to reflect this. The choice of 'term paper' over 'essay' which would be more common in Britain, was to facilitate recognition of the situation in Japan, while not being incomprehensible to British students. The form of the prompts was based on commonly occurring prompts in authentic data derived from tutorial interaction in Britain. For example, 'You haven't done a lot of work, have you?' addressed to a fine art student transfers to a more generalisable situation as: 'You haven't written very much, have you?' (Situation A). 'If you were able to do the production all over again, what would you change?' addressed to a student who had been involved in a TV drama production becomes: 'I think you're doing good work, what would you say if I suggested you made the concluding section a bit shorter?' (Situation B)

Discourse completion task (DCT) samples

- **Situation A:** *You're reaching the end of your course and are discussing the final term paper with your tutor.*

     Tutor: You haven't written very much have you?
     Student:

- **Situation B:** *You're having a discussion with your tutor about your recent work.*

     Tutor: I think you're doing good work. What would you say if I
               suggested you made the concluding section a bit shorter?
     Student:

- **Situation C:** *In the middle of a tutorial on your work, the tutor asks about the work of a contemporary scholar.*

     Tutor: Are you familiar with the work of [any scholar you know]?
     Student:

Extract 7.3 demonstrates examples of fairly extensive elaboration in the British DCT (Situation C) data from students in a range of disciplines and gives a flavour of 'British' elaboration strategies, analysed more fully in Hiraga and Turner (1995) and Turner and Hiraga (1996).

Extract 7.3

BS 1: Yes, at least I've read one or two of her recent papers on contourite drifts in the North Atlantic . . . but she doesn't seem to relate the structures to paleoclimate, and that's what I'm really looking for. Do you know of any papers that address this issue?

BS 2: Not extensively, no. I've, of course read her 'international politics'. It was one of the set texts for a seminar last term, but I thought that her very heavy reliance on macro-economic determinism discounted the role of, often irrational, perceived national interests in shaping policy decisions.

BS 3: Yes, I've read his works on immunisation and his latest research on AIDS, where he questions its significance as a new syndrome, postulating many of its manifestations could in fact be symptoms of syphilis.

Extracts 7.4 and 7.5 demonstrate a selection of the responses from the Japanese EFL students and give a sense of their difference.

Extract 7.4

JS 1: No, I'm not, tutor.

JS 2: Yes, I am. (If I know the work of X very much.) I read and study the work of X so much.

JS 3: No. (shaking my head).
JS 4: Ah, . . . I read his paper, but I don't think I understood exactly.
JS 5: Yes, a little.

Retrospective interviews with some of the Japanese students at a Japanese university gave further insight into how students were evaluating this situation. Extract 7.5 is an example (actually from JS 5 above, speaking in English).

Extract 7.5

INTERVIEWER:	So you think the tutor is making a suggestion rather than testing your knowledge. What would you do?
JAPANESE STUDENT:	I would find X's book after the class, I always do that.
I:	Your actual response is very short. A little. Is there a reason for that?
JS:	It depends on the X, but maybe I want more or some brief information from my teacher even if I know more [than] a little.
I:	Right. Yeh. So, it's . . . Is that because you don't want to take too long a turn before the tutor. Why don't you give the information that you know already, now.
JS:	Maybe I think my understanding . . . the way of understanding is not so good or is not so . . . in the right way . . . not right but in a good way, so maybe I want to hear my teacher's suggestion first. It sometimes happens for example in the music class, I have played the flute since I was six years old and my teacher always asks me how long did you practise this piece, and I practise every day, I practise six hours every day but I said I played a little or I tried my best . . . but. . . . That kind of thing this means . . . a little means.
I:	So you're being kind of . . . deliberately modest.
JS:	Yeh.

From a British perspective, the student's DCT response takes the form of not elaborating, that is, not saying the kinds of things that one might expect in the British educational context. As shown in the examples from the British DCT responses (Extract 7.3), these include making clear how they interpret the rationale behind the elicitation by, for example, giving a view to the tutor of what the student's perspective of author X was and in general taking the elicitation further than what was immediately required at face value.

However, what the retrospective interview makes clear is that the Japanese student was more concerned to act modestly in interaction with the tutor, which meant waiting for her/him to lead the conversational way, as it were. Such a relatively greater concern for the interpersonal mode of communication could be an explanation for the perceived lack of elaboration, of taking things further, in intercultural tutorials in the British context. The Japanese semiotician Ikegami, acknowledging the Hallidayan terminology, asserts that 'the Western languages relatively focus on the ideational function, while Japanese relatively focuses on the interpersonal function' (Ikegami, 1991, p. 6). The expectation of elaboration in the British tutorial context then may be seen as serving a particular ideational function for that context, which the role of the student in a Japanese context is in conflict with. In other words, the non-elaborative, or differently elaborative behaviour of Japanese students in intercultural tutorials and DCT responses may be an effect of attending to the culturally different priority of respect and silence before the teacher.

This particular tutor–student ethos has a long cultural pedigree, as Scollon and Scollon (1994, p. 145) show in their discussion of the historical context of conversational interaction in Asia. They quote some recommendations from the *Li Chi*, which dates from before Confucius. They include:

(1) 'When the elder asks a question, to reply without acknowledging one's incompetency and [trying to] decline answering, is contrary to propriety.'

(2) 'When he is following his teacher, he should not quit the road to speak with another person. When he meets his teacher on the road, he should hasten forward to him, and stand with his hands joined across his breast. If the teacher speaks to him, he will answer; if he does not, he will retire with hasty steps.'

These rules of social etiquette appear to have some traces in the contemporary behaviour of Chinese and Japanese students, which perhaps are more apparent when the behaviour occurs in a western educational setting. From a western perspective, such an embedded ideology appears to slap an injunction on student elaboration, which the western system by contrast is attempting to encourage. This suggests that the issue of elaboration is not only one of pragmatics but one of ideology. In the British context, it is ideologically important for the student to elaborate, but in the Japanese context this militates against due respect to the teacher.

Embodying wisdom

A further strand of ideological assumptions invested in the role of the teacher can be seen in the following proverb and saying.

4. Shi wa sanze no chigiri, oya wa isse no mutsubi
    teacher TOP three worlds GEN bond, parent TOP one world GEN care
    'The bond between the teacher and the student lasts from the former world to another world through this world; but, the caring between the parent and the child lasts only in this world.'
5. Shi no notamawaku, furuki o atatame-te atarashiki o shiru, motte shi to naru beshi
    teacher NOM say, old ACC animate new ACC know, by which master become should
    'The Master said, He who by reanimating the Old can gain knowledge of the New is fit to be a teacher.'

Both of these proverbs suggest a reverence for what is old and worthy of transmission. The task of transmission is embodied in the teacher, whose role in this respect is more important than that of the parent. The saying listed in (5) is from the Confucian analects and signals both respect for the old and the importance of the teacher having the ability to reanimate it.

In their discussion of western and Chinese conceptions of language and the significance of writing in the Chinese conceptualisation, Scollon and Scollon (1994, p. 141) refer to the role that writing plays in communicating the wisdom of the ancients. The earliest uses of writing in China were based on communication with the ancestors to whom were ascribed: 'the knowledge and power to direct the lives and fortunes of living descendants'. In the context of tutor–student interaction that we are looking at here, it is not writing itself that is important but the value *inscribed* in the role of the tutor, as it were the mediator of esteemed knowledge, which goes beyond the merely institutional role. The tutor in Japan is not just the higher status interlocutor but the embodiment of an ideology to do with wisdom and the cultural value of education. This ideological underpinning is evident also in the use of and in the etymology of the term 'sensei'. It is used not only in the address of a schoolteacher or professor, but also of such professionals as medical doctors, politicians, lawyers, architects and masters in various fields of arts and crafts, sports and board games. As mentioned in the etymological examples above relating to the JOURNEY metaphor, 'sen' in 'sensei' etymologically means 'one's feet going before others', or 'to make an advance before others', but now it means simply 'before', while 'sei' in 'sensei' means 'to be born'. Therefore, 'sensei' literally means someone born before you.

Diverging paths and contrasting epistemologies

Whereas the role of the tutor mapping out the way for the student to follow, as in Extract 7.1, chimes both with the value system embodied in the three proverbs cited in (1) to (3) and with the Chinese character etymologies of words for students and teachers, learning and teaching, the importance of student elaboration in the creative and performing arts disciplines is linked not only to the relevant pedagogies, but also epistemologically to creative performance. In this project, students themselves are pivotal. Especially in fine art, they are the source of ideas. In order to receive guidance from their tutors, they have to explain what they are trying to do, how they are hoping to do it and why they want to do it. This ultimately puts the onus on the student if not exactly to lead the tutorial interaction, to determine its subject matter and therefore in effect to lay out the path that the tutorial is going to take. That is, the subject matter is the student's work, both its physical presence in visual terms and the verbal discussion on issues surrounding the work. The following exchange between a British tutor and a Japanese student (Extract 7.6) is symptomatic of the student being the engine of forward movement.

Extract 7.6

> BT: Is there anything that you want to tell me?
> JS: No.
> BT: Are you sure?
> JS: Yes.

The apparent reluctance of students to move the discussion forward was not just a problem of pragmatic failure but also a problem at the epistemological level of engaging with the subject of study. They were in the position of finding out the next step, not having it pointed out for them. In Extract 7.7 from a tutorial with a British student, although the student is unsure about 'where he is going', he knows that he is the one who has to find a means of determining this.

Extract 7.7

> BT: You seem not to be using the circular device any more.
> BS: Yeah, that kinda stems from when I was trying to work with the image of the pebble dropping in the water, and the kind of rhythm that ensued . . . but that wasn't getting me anywhere, I'm not really sure where I'm going. . . .

The need for the students to determine the next step is evident in the following utterance from a British fine art lecturer, in the context of a tutorial with a Japanese student (Extract 7.8).

Extract 7.8

> BT: I want to know from you now, the kinds of areas that YOU (stressed)
> think you want to go into \<pause\> because I need to begin to get an
> idea of you – you the artist, if you like, – of what are the different
> elements of your practice.

The tutor now waits for five seconds, looking for a reaction from the student, who is respectfully signalling attention by nodding and 'Uh-huh'-ing, and 'mmm-mmm'-ing in the manner of Japanese 'aizuchi' (see LoCastro, 1987) then goes on: 'So at the moment you appear to be offering a range from something which is illustration through to ceramics with a kind of thematic connection.'

The tutor's utterance is explicit about the requirements placed on the student. He attempts to help her voice the direction in which she wants her work to develop by reformulating what he has understood from what she has done and said previously. In contrast to the PATH metaphor operating in the Japanese context, he is attempting to push her forward along a path of her own choosing, rather than follow him.

An epistemological contrast with fine arts practice in Japan is embodied in the traditional maxim of 'shu ha ri' (see Maruno, 1993, p. 70) which translates as 'keep', 'break' and 'leave' in English. Japanese arts students must first follow ('keep') the style of their master by imitation, repetition and practice. When the student has finished the long process of imitative learning and passed the test to become a junior master, then he/she is allowed to transform ('break') the style by introducing modifications. Only a few students can succeed in reaching the last stage in which he/she is allowed to 'leave' the former master to create a style of his/her own. The epistemological framework for this classical Japanese fine arts practice is encapsulated in the following saying:

6. Kata kara hait-te, kata o deru
    model from enter-GER, model ACC exit
    'To enter by imitating the model, and exit out of the model.'

The traditional arts, namely, 'sadoo' ('tea ceremony'), 'kadoo' ('flower arrangement'), 'budoo' ('martial arts') and 'shodoo' ('calligraphy') in which the disciples must diligently observe and imitate their master from a distance (see Ikuta, 1987) all share the suffix 'doo' in Japanese, which, as in the perhaps more familiar to a western audience as 'tao' in Chinese, means 'the way'. The philosophical ring of the concept 'tao' has epistemological significance in the 'doo' of the classical Japanese disciplines, in parallel with the western suffix '-logy' in scientific disciplines. The ramifications of this epistemological contrast are crystallised in the metaphorical concepts on which they are based. On the one hand, it is the spatial metaphor of the way or path and on the other hand it is the verbal metaphor of speech derived from the ancient Greek 'logos' meaning speech. It is the epistemological significance of speech or verbalisation per se, as opposed to what or how much is actually said that we would like to look at a little more closely now, as we suggest that it is subject to culturally contrasting ideologies.

Ideological perspectives on the verbal

One of the main reasons why Japanese students were attracted to the creative and performing arts disciplines in the British university where this study took place was their desire to work in the 'freer' (as they put it) tradition of Britain. The post-graduate students often expressed some dismay with the restricted ways in which they had been instructed in fine art in Japan. However, they were not prepared for the ideological underpinnings of what such 'freedom' meant in the fine art educational context. It meant that not only were the students themselves the source of ideas, but also they were expected to verbalise those ideas. They were required to describe what they were trying to do, explain the criteria on which they thought the work succeeded or failed and express possible future directions for the work.

In a focus group recording made by a group of four Japanese fine art students in Britain who were asked to speak (in Japanese) about what they thought of the kinds of prompts made by their tutors and why they thought they were making them, the students were quite vociferous in their condemnation of what they saw as constant verbalisation. They did not want talk, they wanted techniques. They also found it strange that they never saw any of their tutors' work. Despite the fact then that strictly guided instruction was what they were avoiding, it appears that ideological remnants of the 'shu ha ri' or 'the master as model' educational ethos remained in their expectations of the teaching and learning situation.

The significance of verbalisation in the western tradition is considerable. It can be traced back to Socrates and his search for clear definitions of the virtues. Similarities were rejected and distinctions made because what could be *said* of one thing, for example, could not be said of another. Tarnas (1991, p. 36) describes Socrates's arrival at his dialectical method as follows: 'After having investigated every current system of thought from the scientific philosophies of nature to the subtle arguments of the Sophists, Socrates had concluded that all of them lacked sound critical method. To clarify his own approach, he decided to concern himself not with facts but with *statements about facts* [italics added].'

The importance of language for the representation of knowledge and communication recurs in various forms throughout the western philosophical tradition (see e.g. Baker and Hacker, 1984). One concern, particularly manifest in the British empiricist tradition, was to remedy the imperfections of language. This concern reached its apogee in Russell, who aspired to a logically perfect language where 'there will be one word and no more for every simple object . . . A language of that sort . . . will show at a glance the logical structure of the facts asserted or denied' (quoted in Crowley, 1988). This concern is intricately linked with judging the truth or falsehood of assertions, as evidenced in different ways in both quotes above, so truth itself cannot be distinct from its assertion in language. Steiner (1961, p. 30) imputes the 'essentially verbal character' of western civilisation to its 'Graeco-Judaic inheritance' and compares the difficulty of speech conveying 'the shape and vitality of silence' by reference to the metaphysics of the orient, where in Buddhism and Taoism 'the highest, purest reach of the contemplative act is that which has learned to leave language behind it'. The roles of language in these two cultural traditions are therefore diametrically opposed. In the one context, it is of inordinate importance, whilst in the other, it is in a subordinate position. The cultural embeddedness of such a value system for language can manifest itself in different ways. There is a far greater number of proverbs portraying the value of silence in Japanese than there is in English, for example. Here are a few examples of proverbs of silence:

7. Iwa-nu ga hana
    say-NEG NOM flower
    ' "Not to say" is better [profitable].'
8. Chinmoku wa kin
    silence TOP gold
    'Silence is golden.'
9. Kougen reishoku sukunasi jin
    effective(clever) words amiable colours small virtue
    'There is little virtue in clever words or flattering manners.'
10. Kuchi wa wazawai no moto
    mouth TOP fight GEN cause
    'What you say is a cause of fight.'

While proverb (8) also exists in English, it is likely to be used differently, for example, as a welcome contrast to noise, rather than a positive virtue in its own right. Loveday (1986) analyses a number of different ways in which silence is important in Japanese communicative patterns. In making cross-cultural contrasts of expectations in classroom interaction, Cortazzi (1990) also draws attention to the culturally weighted importance of verbalisation in the western (British and North American) context. While we are not suggesting that culturally embedded attitudes are consciously drawn upon by individuals in different contexts, it is possible that the dismissive attitude to words displayed by the Japanese focus group students is a symptom of entrenched ideological focus.

A further strand of culturally embedded thinking relating to the role of language in communication in Japan is the concept of 'ishin denshin' or 'direct transmission'. According to Scollon and Scollon (1995, p. 139), this dominant value in Zen Buddhism originated in China in the early Tang Period (AD 618–907) and has had a major impact on Chinese, Korean and Japanese cultures. In this tradition, it is believed that the most important things cannot be communicated in language; that language is only useful for somewhat secondary or trivial messages.

Hiraga (1998, p. 14) refers to 'learning without clear instructions, or learning by environmental stimulus and habituation' as characteristic of Japanese learning, particularly before the Meiji restoration (1868). Remnants of this value system can still be found in primary education, where teachers avoid giving instructions in words and instead attempt to be themselves an exemplary model for the pupils (Miyake, 1995, p. 85). What might be termed an osmosis model in educational psychology is also the basis for ways in which mothers discipline their children (Azuma *et al.*, 1981).

From the perspective of a westerner teaching English in Japan, Bowers (1988) points to the Japanese values of 'sasshi' or 'the perceptive understanding of messages from a minimum number of explicit clues' and 'enryo' or 'self-restraint vis-à-vis explicit verbal responses out of consideration for the source and/or presence of other receivers' as a source of difficulty in classroom communication. As a further interlinking of the suspicion of the verbal and the importance of observation, it is interesting to note that while the verb 'sassuru' currently means to guess, its Chinese character etymology is 'to observe'. Similarly pointing up the value of observation is the verb 'mi-narau'. It means 'to learn' but it is etymologically compounded with observing and imitating.

Thus observing and imitating does not just have prominence where it might practically be expected, namely in the teaching of fine art, but is germane to the conceptualisation of learning in Japanese culture.

Teaching and learning ideologies

We have looked at underlying cultural values in educational ideologies as a source of explanation for socio-pragmatic misunderstanding in an intercultural tutorial context. We see the dynamics of tutor–student interaction as motivated by the ideologically embedded roles of tutors and students in each culture. The understanding of one's role in such an interaction is likely to influence what kinds of things are said or not said by each of the participants. While socio-pragmatic 'failure' has largely been seen as a problem at the level of the individual speech act, caused, for example, by the introduction of a 'taboo' topic into a discourse, or from an underestimation of the 'size of imposition' or the status difference between participants, we have stressed the importance of ideological factors motivating participants' understanding (albeit not consciously) of the situation they are in. Such factors dictate the particular assumptions and expectations regarding the participant roles in a particular 'genre' or 'activity type' (Levinson, 1979) and stress their relatedness within a deeper cultural matrix.

Frameworks of understanding are ideologically entwined and teaching and learning is always to some extent teaching and learning ideologies. Misunderstanding teaching and learning is therefore always, at some level, to be expected.

Appendix

Abbreviations for function words

- ACC(usative)
- COMP(limentiser)
- DAT(ive)
- GEN(itive)
- GER(undive)
- IMP(erative)
- NEG(ative)
- NOM(inative)
- PASS(ive)
- PAST
- POL(ite)
- PL(ural)
- Q(uestion)
- TOP(ic).

When a string of words in English corresponds to one word in Japanese, dots are used instead of spaces to show word boundaries.

References

Azuma, H. *et al.* (1981). *Hahaoya no taido, koodoo to kodomo no chiteki hattatsu* [Attitudes and behaviours of mothers and cognitive development of children]. Tokyo: University of Tokyo Press.

Baker, G. P. and Hacker, P. M. S. (1984). *Language, sense and nonsense*. Oxford: Blackwell.

Blum-Kulka, S. and Olshtain, E. (1986). Too many words: Length of utterance and pragmatic failure. In *Studies in Second Language Acquisition*, 8, 165–180.

Bowers, J. R. (1988). Japan–US relationships from an intercultural communication point of view. In *The Language Teacher*, 12 (5), 17–20.

Cortazzi, M. (1990). Cultural and educational expectations in the language classroom. In B. Harrison (ed.), *Culture and the language classroom ELT documents*. Modern English Publications in Association and British Council, no. 132, 54–65.

Crowley, T. (1988). *The politics of discourse: The standard language question in British cultural debates*. London: Macmillan.

Hiraga, M. K. (1998). Japanese metaphors for learning. In *Intercultural Communication Studies*, 7 (2), 7–22.

Hiraga, M. K. and Turner, J. M. (1995). What to say next? The sociopragmatic problem of elaboration for Japanese students of English in academic contexts. In *JACET Bulletin*, 26, 13–30.

Ikegami, Y. (ed.) (1991). *The empire of signs: Semiotic essays on Japanese culture*. Amsterdam: John Benjamins.

Ikuta, K. (1987). *Waza kara shiru* [Knowing from skills]. Tokyo: University of Tokyo Press.

Lebra, T. S. (1992). Self in Japanese culture. In N. Rosenberger (ed.), *Japanese sense of self*. Cambridge: Cambridge University Press.

Lebra, T. S. (1993). Culture, self and communication in Japan and the United States. In W. B. Gudykunst (ed.), *Communication in Japan and the United States*. Albany, NY: State University of New York.

Levinson, S. (1979). Activity types and language. In *Linguistics*, 17, 365–399.

LoCastro, V. (1987). Aizuchi: A Japanese conversational routine. In L. E. Smith (ed.), *Discourse across cultures: Strategies in world Englishes*. London: Prentice Hall, 101–113.

Loveday, L. (1986). *Explorations in Japanese sociolinguistics*. Amsterdam: John Benjamins.

Maruno, S. (1993). *Gakushuu-kyooju katei* [Process of learning and teaching]. In K. Haraoka (ed.), *Kyooiku sinrigaku* [Educational psychology]. Tokyo: University of the Air Press, 66–76.

Matsumoto, Y. (1988). Reexamination of the universality of face. In *Journal of Pragmatics*, 12, 403–426.

Miyake, K. (1995). *Kodomo no hattatsu to shakai bunnka* [Child development, society and culture]. Tokyo: University of the Air Press.

Mori, T. and Komiyama, K. (1984). *Kotowaza kyooikugaku* [Pedagogy through proverbs]. Tokyo: Child sha.

Nakane, C. (1970). *Japanese society*. Berkeley, CA: University of California Press.

Obelkevich, J. (1987). Proverbs and social history. In P. Burke and R. Porter (eds), *The social history of language*. Cambridge: Cambridge University Press, 43–72.

Sakamoto, N. and Naotsuka, R. (1982). *Polite fictions*. Tokyo: Kinseidoo.

Scollon, S. W. (1997). Metaphors of self and communication. In *Multilingua*, 16 (1), 1–38.

Scollon, R. and Scollon, S. W. (1994). Face parameters in east–west discourse. In S. Ting-Toomey (ed.), *The challenge of facework: Crosscultural and interpersonal issues*. New York: State University of New York Press, 133–157.

Scollon, R. and Scollon, S. W. (1995). *Intercultural communication: A discourse approach*. Oxford: Blackwell.

Shouji, K. (1987). *Kotowaza kyooiku no susume: Mirai no kyooikugaku no tame no bunka-kenkyuu* [Promotion of proverb education: A cultural study for pedagogy in the future]. Tokyo: Meiji Tosho Shuppan.

Siegal, M. (1996). The role of learner subjectivity in second language sociolinguistic competency: Western women learning Japanese. In *Applied Linguistics*, 17 (3), 356–382.

Steiner, G. (1961). *Language and silence*. London: Faber & Faber.

Tarnas, R. (1991). *The passion of the western mind*. New York: Ballantine Books.

Thomas, J. (1983). Cross-cultural pragmatic failure. In *Applied Linguistics*, 4, 91–112.

Turner, J. (1996). Cultural values in genre skills: The case of the fine art tutorial. In M. Hewings and T. Dudley-Evans (eds), *Evaluation and course design in EAP*. London: Macmillan in association with The British Council, 121–130.

Turner, J. M. and Hiraga, M. K. (1996). Elaborating elaboration in academic tutorials: Changing cultural assumptions. In H. Coleman and L. Cameron (eds), *Change and language*. Clevedon: British Association for Applied Linguistics in association with Multilingual Matters Ltd, 131–140.

van Dijk, T. (1998). *Ideology: A multidisciplinary approach*. London: Sage.

Sources of etymologies and proverbs

Kaizuka, S. *et al.* (eds) (1959). *Kanwa chuu jiten* [Chinese characters dictionary in Japanese]. Tokyo: Kadokawa Shoten.

Shibata, T. *et al.* (eds) (1995). *Sekai kotowaza daijiten* [Dictionary of the proverbs of the world]. Tokyo: Taishuukan.

Shoogaku tosho henshuu. (1982). *Koji, zokushin, kotowaza daijiten* [Dictionary of proverbs and sayings]. Tokyo: Shoogakkan.

8

'I couldn't follow her story...'
Ethnic differences in New Zealand narratives

Janet Holmes

Introduction

> I could hear them speaking English but I didn't understand what they were saying ... and they were using language that while I understood the individual words or spurts of sentences I couldn't understand the the concepts that they were talking about.

This is a quotation from a conversation between two young, well-educated Maori men. It identifies a communication problem which has nothing to do with understanding the meaning of individual words, but rather with comprehending the global meaning that the speaker is trying to convey. There are many different levels at which people can miscommunicate (Coupland *et al.*, 1991). Some reflect differences in the linguistic resources which participants bring to an encounter, such as different ranges of vocabulary. Others are more difficult to identify because they arise from different socialisation and acculturation processes, resulting in different sociolinguistic and pragmatic rules of which participants may be unaware.

So, for example, different social and ethnic groups may use different rules for encoding and interpreting speech acts, or different rules for interaction, including turn-taking. At an overt and conscious level, such differences often go unnoticed, but they can nevertheless have an effect on intergroup relations at a less conscious level. Participants may leave an encounter feeling dissatisfied, bemused or uneasy, though they are not able to identify the source of these reactions. Others may feel angry, frustrated and resentful because they have failed to communicate their message to what appear unreceptive ears. Still others may feel exhausted after the effort involved in constantly adapting their style to that of the dominant group whose members remain oblivious of any 'communication problems'.[1] This chapter explores some features of spontaneous conversational narratives, one area where the ways of communicating appropriate to particular cultural groups may be a source of misunderstandings.

Narrative characteristics

Storytelling appears to be a universal function of speech, but there is ample scope for sociocultural variation in the ways stories are told, as well as the functions they serve and the values they express in different speech communities. So, while certain elements may be considered essential to the structure of any narrative, there is considerable potential for cultural and social variation in the management of the optional components, as I will illustrate below. Indeed, even the issue of what is considered an obligatory versus an optional component of a story may differ between groups.

Stories may also function differently in different groups. In some they may be considered a crucial means of conveying cultural knowledge to the next generation, for example; in others, they may be regarded as primarily a source of entertainment. Stories typically express social and cultural values and provide insights into the social and cultural concerns of the storytellers. Hence the stories told by members of particular groups tend to reflect the preoccupations, values, beliefs and attitudes of group members. Analysing narratives can thus provide interesting insights into the cultural and social concerns of a community at a particular point in time. This chapter explores potential areas of miscommunication between Maori and Pakeha New Zealanders, exemplifying with features of their conversational narratives.

Maori and Pakeha in New Zealand

The indigenous Maori people constitute about 14 per cent of the New Zealand population, which is predominantly made up of people of European (mainly British) ancestry, widely referred to by the Maori term 'Pakeha'. A recent survey puts the number of relatively fluent adult speakers of the Maori language at about 22,000, a very small proportion (0.6 per cent) of the total population (*National Maori Language Survey*, 1998). English is now the first language of most Maori people and the language used in most domains in New Zealand society. As Metge (1986, p. 139) says:

All the main institutions of public life in New Zealand are grounded in Pakeha culture and dominated by Pakeha in positions of power. By law, Maori must participate in these institutions whether they want to or not, and their participation is judged by standards and values of Pakeha origin.

Nevertheless, the Maori language can still be heard in New Zealand. Where fluent speakers are available, Maori is used on the 'marae', the traditional meeting place of Maori tribes, for formal, ceremonial speech-making, particularly by men. (In most tribal areas, men have more extensive formal speaking roles than women.) Maori is used for some religious ceremonies and in some homes for informal conversation between those older Maori who still speak the language. It can sometimes be heard in pubs in the very few remaining Maori-speaking areas. It can also be heard on radio for reasonably extensive periods in some regions, though television coverage is minimal. This is likely to change soon with the establishment of a Maori TV channel. Maori can be heard occasionally in court and parliament when a Maori speaker chooses to exercise their rights in this respect (Benton, 1991, p. 188).

In addition, Maori people in New Zealand generally maintain some Maori cultural traditions, even when they live in Pakeha-dominated urban environments (Metge, 1976, 1995). Crucially, this means celebrating important rites of passage in traditional Maori ways: births, marriages and especially deaths are occasions when Maori people from the same tribe gather together at an appropriate 'marae' to mark the occasion and pay their respects to the families involved. Since the 1950s most Maori people (like most Pakeha) live in the cities and so such occasions frequently involve a return to a rural and often distant marae. In such cases, the tribal group is likely to include some elderly Maori who may be relatively fluent, if not native, speakers of Maori. More recently, however, Maori people from urban areas sometimes gather at one of the increasing number of urban marae. Regardless of where the marae is located, the Maori language is used on such occasions, wherever possible, but particularly for the formal ceremonial aspects of such speech events. These occasions also provide a social context in which Maori is 'licensed' and appropriate for informal conversations among those who know the language.

So, although English tends to dominate, especially in the cities, these cultural traditions mean that a surprising number of even urban Maori people are exposed to the Maori language reasonably regularly. Consequently, passive knowledge of Maori is more widespread than might be expected (*National Maori Language Survey*, 1998). Importantly in relation to the topic of this chapter, Maori people have many opportunities to absorb both the distinctive rhetorical patterns of Maori discourse, whether expressed in Maori or in English, and the values, beliefs and attitudes which distinguish Maori and Pakeha culture (see Metge, 1976, 1986, 1995).

With this brief background, I turn to a discussion of some evidence from our Wellington Corpus of New Zealand English of contrasting patterns in features of the conversational narratives of Maori and Pakeha New Zealanders, focusing in particular on the potential for miscommunication raised by such differences. First, I provide a brief description of the database.

Narrative database

The database for this analysis consists of 96 narratives from spontaneous conversations between 60 friends. The data is taken from the one million word Wellington Corpus of Spoken New Zealand English (WCSNZE).[2] Each conversation was a relaxed chat between two friends of the same age, gender, social class and ethnicity: 24 of the conversationalists were people who self-identified as Maori and 36 were Pakeha; half were women and half men. Most of the conversations were collected in the home of one of the participants; only the participants were present and they recorded themselves. (For more details of the database see Holmes et al., 1998; for more details of the narratives see Holmes, 1998a, 1998b, 1998c.)

Maori and Pakeha culture: potential sources of miscommunication

Though Maori and Pakeha people interact freely in all social spheres in New Zealand with apparently few difficulties at a superficial level, there is evidence that cultural differences between the two groups often result in miscommunication at a more fundamental level (see Metge, 1986, 1995; Metge and Kinloch, 1984). Coupland et al. (1991, pp. 13–15) present a model integrating different levels of analysis of miscommunication. In terms of their model, the analysis in this chapter deals with issues at a relatively 'deep' level of analysis, identifying potential problems with a certain level of 'weightiness' and social significance (1991, p. 12). At this level 'miscommunication resides in group and cultural phenomena' and explanations draw on 'cultural differences in behaviors, beliefs or construals' (1991, p. 15).

Many of the differences between Maori and Pakeha ways of communicating are subtle. Maori people emphasise non-verbal signals more and verbalisation less than Pakeha, while many Pakeha define communication primarily in terms of verbal expression. In Maori culture, silence in face-to-face interaction is generally not negatively evaluated as it tends to be in most western cultures (Metge and Kinloch, 1984). Rather, silence functions for Maori in many contexts as a negative politeness device; it avoids imposing on others and indicates a willingness to keep listening until the speaker has said all s/he wishes to say. Often, expressive non-verbal signals substitute for words and context is crucial in interpreting meaning (Stubbe, 1998; Stubbe and Holmes, 2000). Indeed, in general, Maori tend to understate rather than overstate their messages. Meanings are often left inexplicit, to be inferred by the listener. This point is well exemplified in some features of the narratives produced by the Maori conversationalists.

Narrative structure: some distinctive ethnic features

The narrator's role

A narrative is 'one method of recapitulating past experience by matching a verbal sequence of clauses to the sequence of events which (it is inferred) actually occurred' (Labov, 1972, pp. 359–360; Labov and Waletzky, 1967, p. 20). Less formally, a story is an account of an event, structured in a particular way, which in western culture basically entails having a beginning, a middle and an end. Most narrative analysis over the last 30 years has adopted Labov's analytical framework (Holmes, 1997a). This identifies six components: abstract, orientation, complicating action, evaluation, resolution, coda, some of which are optional and some obligatory (see Bell, 1991; Labov, 1972; Toolan, 1988). The relative importance of different components is thus one area of potential difference between different social and cultural groups.

Many of the stories told both by Maori and Pakeha in the New Zealand sample conform to Labov's suggested structure in broad outline. Extract 8.1 is a very brief example from a young Pakeha woman. (See Appendix for transcription conventions.)[3]

Extract 8.1: Driving test

1	ANN:	mm + I went for my driving test	
2		last week	**Abstract/Orientation**
3	BEV:	oh did you?	
4	ANN:	yeah?	
5	BEV:	how did that go?	
6	ANN:	oh I was good	**Evaluation**
7		apart from I forgot to um [laughs]	
8		stop at the red light	**Action/Evaluation**
9		and so I went straight through it	**Action/Evaluation**
10	BEV:	really	
11	ANN:	so I have to resit it	**Resolution**
12		but I'll get it next time	**Coda**

As is often the case, the evaluation extends throughout the action, since the statement in line 5, 'I was good' (implying she drove well) is said ironically, and influences the interpretation of the following two clauses.

Extract 8.2 is a story told by a young Maori woman which similarly includes the six components in Labov's analytical framework.

Extract 8.2: Set-ups

1	talking about set-ups	**Abstract**
2	oh I'm getting sick of it man	**Evaluation**
3	um Fay said to me after the lecture today	**Action/Orientation**
4	oh so Mere who're you going to the ball with	**Action**
5	and I said um why [laughs]	**Action**
6	she said because I've got someone for you to	
7	go with	**Action**
8	I said I'm going with Jonathan Davis [laughs]	**Action**
9	she said oh I've got this really gorgeous	
10	nephew	**Action**
11	and I want him to meet you [laughs]	**Resolution**
12	I said well bring him along anyway [laughs]	**Coda**

As these examples suggest, there were many similarities in the structure of the stories told by members of each ethnic group, but there were also some interesting differences. In particular, Maori storytellers were more likely: (a) to omit narrative components such as the resolution and coda; (b) to reduce lexicalised support for the complicating action. I will briefly illustrate each of these patterns.[4]

Reduced narrative structure

While many of the stories told by Maori and Pakeha are structurally complete, there are a number of Maori stories which have no explicit resolution or coda, and as a result, from a Pakeha perspective, the story seems to have been left unfinished.[5] A typical story will end with an overt resolution clause, as in Extracts 8.1 and 8.2. Extract 8.3 provides further examples, many introduced quite explicitly with the discourse marker 'so'.

Extract 8.3: So

1. *Tom, a middle-aged Pakeha, tells the story of how he got his video machine to work*

    but the whole point about this is I solved the technology problem
2. *Story of visit to father told by middle-aged Pakeha woman*

    so Annie stayed there and made him some lunch

3. *Story of why he hadn't been in his office all day told by middle-aged Pakeha man*

> so you see this is why I haven't been in my office

4. *Story of a series of phone calls which disrupted his evening told by young Pakeha man*

> so that was four phone calls

In some of the Maori stories, however, the evaluation is lexically inexplicit and the resolution and coda may be omitted entirely. Listeners are left to draw their own conclusions or, more accurately from the Maori participants' viewpoint, the narrator considers the point of the story requires no elaboration. When there is no explicit evaluation, resolution clause or coda, the effect from a Pakeha point of view is that the story seems incomplete.

Extract 8.4, narrated by an older Maori woman, is a story where the resolution and evaluation are nowhere expressed by the narrator in explicit lexicalised form.

Extract 8.4: Setting the bed on fire

1	NINA:	yep see I used to smoke f- first thing in the	
2		morning	**Orientation**
3	HANA:	yeah	
4	NINA:	and one famous morning	**Orientation**
5		I nearly set fire to my bedding	**Abstract**
6	HANA:	[laughs] I know it's not funny but [laughs]	
7	NINA:	I reached over and grabbed a fag and lit up	**Action**
8	HANA:	mm	

Line 8 is the end of the story and Nina moves on to reflect on the habit of smoking. This might be regarded as a very embryonic story, but it progresses beyond an abstract to a clause that is clearly classifiable as constituting complicating action (line 7). The narrator provides no explicit evaluation, resolution or coda. However, the point of the story, as well as its resolution, is apparently adequately indicated as far as the listener, Hana, is concerned. Hana herself provides a potential evaluation by indicating that she finds the story amusing, but the narrator nowhere states the 'point' of the story explicitly. In context, the implicit signal provided in the abstract is perfectly adequate from the point of view of both conversationalists. So, although this story seems incomplete from a Pakeha perspective, the Maori narrator assumes the point does not need to be made lexically explicit in a resolution clause; the discourse context provided is sufficient.

Extract 8.5 involves a much longer story, but once again it appears to finish very abruptly from a Pakeha perspective. Kay recounts with considerable descriptive detail the story of how her son, Sam, wooed his wife, Lynnette.

Kay tells, for example, how she advised Sam on effective courtship strategies. Her story ends with an account of how Sam would turn up at Lynnette's workplace in his navy officer's uniform.

Extract 8.5: Courting

1 with a bunch of flowers
2 and take [laughs] Lynnette out to lunch
3 she goes it was [drawls] lovely
4 I said that's the way to do it [laughs]
5 and he said and I listened to you Mum [laughs]
6 yeah which is good

This last section is clearly a closing evaluation but there is no explicit state-ment spelling out the resolution: for example, 'and so he won her' or 'and so that's how they got together'. The story grew out of a discussion of Lynnette's vow that she would never marry a navy man because her two sisters had done so and she knew the costs. In this context, and especially given its length and the level of detail with which the complicating action is elabor-ated, a Pakeha listener expects an ending conveying the message 'so despite her vow Lynnette ended up marrying a navy man after all'. But the narrator assumes this point is quite clear on the basis of the earlier contextualisation of the story and, indeed, it is a comment from her addressee, Hine, 'and then she ended up marrying a navy man', which encourages her to elaborate and develop the story at such length. The narrator clearly assumes the point does not need to be made lexically explicit in a resolution clause; the dis-course context already provided is sufficient.

This tendency to leave the story 'unfinished' or open-ended is typical of many Maori narratives, myths or 'life stories' told in Maori contexts. One never finishes a story because the narrative continues and is continually updated. On the next appropriate occasion, speakers may pick up and con-tinue the ongoing narrative. It seems possible that the tendency to avoid closing off a story in English reflects this practice in Maori cultural contexts. Pakeha listeners tend to feel puzzled, confused and unsure of whether they have got the point. They may wonder whether they have missed some vital element. Reduced lexical scaffolding – discussed in the next section – is also a feature which illustrates the Maori narrator's tendency to be less rather than more explicit in telling a story.

Reduced lexical scaffolding

When Pakeha people recount a story which involves reported speech, they typically provide the listener with considerable guidance about who is speak-ing. The following example, taken from a conversation between two young

Pakeha men, illustrates extensive explicit lexical attributions of speakerhood, using forms of the verbs *say* and *go*.

Extract 8.6: Leaving work

```
 1 CON:  she says oh you're not going to work on the night fills
 2       (and) I go oh no
 3       Wally just only said he'd give me three hours a week
 4       and she goes yeah I know
 5       which means what Wally was telling me about the ten hours
 6       was all bullshit
 7       'cause she goes yeah I know
 8       I've had the productivity through and everything...
 9       and then I rung up Wally on Tuesday
10       and says oh is that okay you know the dates I put down there
11       and everything for leaving
12       and he said oh what's this I see on my desk what's this
13       and I go well I'm leaving you know
14 BEN:  yeah
15 CON:  he said WHY [laughs]
16       I said well you can only offer me three hours a week
17 BEN:  yep
18 CON:  it's hardly worth my while
19       and he goes um what did he say
20       he goes I could've given you anywhere up to ten
21 BEN:  [laughs]
22 CON:  and I go oh
```

In this story, every reported utterance is explicitly attributed to a speaker with a phrase such as 'she says' (line 1), 'she goes' (lines 4, 7) 'I said' (line 16), 'I go' (lines 2–13), or 'he goes', and some are supported by several such devices, for example, lines 19–20. By contrast, in some Maori narratives, these indications of who is speaking tend to be assumed or left implicit. In Extract 8.7, the listener is expected to follow the story with very few explicit lexical signals.

Extract 8.7: Making Maori bread

```
 1 REWI:  well it's like I tried learning off the old um my grandmother
 2        and she was saying like
 3        I thought how how much do you
 4        how do you leave it in
 5        how long do you leave it in the fridge for
 6        oh till you knead (need?) it
```

```
 7 PETER:  yeah [laughs] [laughs]
 8 REWI:   I said how long's that
 9         I don't know
10         how long are you going to knead it
11 PETER:  (yeah)
12 REWI:   next I said well who knows
13 PETER:  yeah
14 REWI:   is it two weeks can you leave it
15         oh I suppose so
16 PETER:  [laughs]
17 REWI:   couldn't get any answers out of her like
18 PETER:  [laughs] yeah
19 REWI:   you know how do you make it-
20         she goes oh well you get a bit of flour
21         you put it in you put a bit of
22         you put a bit of sugar in
23         and then you put a bit of water in
24         how much?
25         oh as much as you need
26 PETER:  [laughs] yeah [laughs]
27 REWI:   sorry Nana I sort of
28         I don't understand those sort of instructions
```

A similar story told by a Pakeha would typically provide more overt lexicalised scaffolding in the form of signals of speakerhood, such as 'she said' and 'I said' throughout. Rewi provides some indications of who is speaking: e.g. 'she was saying' (line 2), 'I said' (lines 8, 12), 'she goes' (line 20). But there are many more places where the identity of the speaker is implicit: e.g. lines 6, 9, 15, 19, 24, 25, 27. The effect of withdrawing the lexical framing is to emphasise and give impact and immediacy to the quoted words, and this can be used to convey evaluative affect (cf. Toolan, 1988, p. 121). Some of the (from a Pakeha perspective) missing information is conveyed by the intonation and prosody, but there remains a considerable amount of work to be done by the listener to follow who is saying what. There are a number of examples in the corpus of Maori speakers using this strategy of presenting direct reported speech without indicating explicitly who produced the quoted utterances.

The features I have described – the omission of an explicit resolution clause and the reduction of lexical scaffolding for reported speech in the complicating action – are more frequent in the Maori than the Pakeha stories, but it is certainly not the case that they characterise only Maori stories or all Maori stories. However, the fact that such features are not typical of all Maori narratives means that they are more likely to account for cross-cultural misunderstandings. Because their stories often resemble those of

Pakeha narrators, Pakeha interlocutors may not realise that Maori conversationalists are sometimes less explicit in their accounts of an event than Pakeha.

One consequence is that Pakeha may misunderstand speaker attributions. This could cause comprehension problems or, more seriously, lead to later accusations that the narrator had misled the listener about who had said what. Another consequence, and a very likely one, is that Pakeha listeners may not recognise these reduced structures as signals of solidarity but will rather consider them problematic. In other words, they will be perceived not as positive politeness signals, reflecting shared knowledge and good rapport, but rather indications of at the least lack of concern for the listener's needs and at worst narrative incompetence.

The features I have identified as characteristic of some Maori stories occur most often in contexts where the conversationalists are well versed in Maori culture. They also typify contexts where the conversationalists know each other well. Hence, the implicit meanings conveyed by narrators may reflect the closeness of the relationship between the conversationalists. However, this was not always the case and, in particular, there was a contrast between the younger and older Maori women where the relationships between the conversationalists were very comparable. While the older Maori women's stories were often characterised by truncated structures of various kinds (e.g. Extract 8.4), suggesting they expected their listeners to follow without needing to spell everything out, the stories of the young Maori women were least characterised by the features I have described in this section (e.g. Extract 8.2).

The listener's role

In western culture, the floor is generally dominated by one speaker during the telling of a story (e.g. Coates, 1996; Labov, 1972). But it is also true that the listener's role may be a relatively active one (e.g. Corston, 1993; Duranti, 1986; Goodwin, 1986; Rymes, 1995). Different patterns of contributions by those listening to stories emerged as another area where Pakeha and Maori patterns did not completely coincide. Once again, there was much in common in the way listeners from both ethnic groups responded to narratives, but there were also two areas where interesting differences were apparent: first, the amount of feedback given by Maori and Pakeha listeners differed; second, there was a contrast in the type of feedback they provided.

Listener feedback

There has been considerable research establishing that cultural groups vary widely in the amount of verbal feedback they consider appropriate or polite in interaction. Polanyi (1989, p. 48), for example, describes how white, middle-class Americans listening to a story are expected to respond with 'nods, minimal responses, laughter, and comments to express interest, sympathy, or surprise'. Japanese listeners are expected to be even more responsive (White, 1989), while at the other end of the spectrum, Lehtonen and Sajavaara (1985, p. 195) report that the use of vocalisations and verbal backchannels is less frequent in Finnish than in many Central European languages, or in British or American English, and that interruptions are generally unacceptable.

A detailed analysis of the verbal feedback provided by listeners in a sub-sample of the narrative corpus made it clear that different norms prevail between Pakeha and Maori too (Stubbe, 1998). There was a striking and statistically significant difference in the overall rates of verbal feedback, with the Maori conversationalists producing, on average, approximately a third less verbal feedback than the Pakeha. Long stretches of narrative went uninterrupted in the Maori conversations, whereas this was not the case in Pakeha interactions. By comparison with Pakeha, Maori conversationalists seem to have a lower baseline for providing verbal feedback.

This finding is consistent with ethnographic observations that verbalisation is of relatively greater importance to Pakeha than it is to Maori (Metge, 1995; Metge and Kinloch, 1984). Whereas Pakeha tend to express their interest explicitly and audibly, Maori do not always do so. This should not be interpreted to mean that the Maori speakers were less involved than the Pakeha speakers in the collaborative production of narrative. An attentive silence is an important way of signalling listener interest in many cultural and social contexts. In fact much of the time Maori listeners demonstrated their attention and involvement in the ongoing discourse by means of verbal feedback in similar ways to the Pakeha speakers, as Extract 8.7 illustrates. Nevertheless, this is potentially another area of cross-cultural misunderstanding. In the absence of audible feedback, Pakeha narrators may mistakenly assume their Maori addressees are not following or, worse, not interested.

Listener questions

Maori and Pakeha narratives also differed in the extent to which the listeners actively asked questions of the storytellers. It was quite common for Pakeha listeners to contribute to the story by asking questions which encouraged the narrator to proceed with the story, to elaborate on particular aspects, or to develop it further. By contrast, there were very few examples of this kind of interactive behaviour among the Maori contributors. Maori listeners tended to listen silently, or to provide instances of minimal feedback or short supportive comments. They rarely actively inserted questions into the course of a narrative.

As Coates (1996, pp. 95–96) comments, narratives are unusual because they are much more solo performances than is typical of conversational interaction. However, in a number of the Pakeha stories particular components

– especially elements of the orientation and evaluation – were elicited by the co-conversationalist's questions, as illustrated in Extracts 8.8 and 8.9. (The relevant questions are italicised.)

Extract 8.8: Jude's marriage

1 VERA: OH and um did I tell you Jude's got married?
2 MEG: JUDE
3 VERA: yeah
4 MEG: *when did that happen?*

Extract 8.9: Giving blood

1 ANN: I gave blood today
2 BEV: *did you whereabouts?*

Questions such as these during the course of a narrative were much rarer in the Maori interactions. The effect they have is by no means clear cut. While they may be supportive, 'licensing' the story and indicating the listener's attention and interest, they may also disrupt the flow of the story. Indeed, there was some evidence of gender difference along these lines among the Pakeha conversationalists (see Holmes, 1998c). The Pakeha women tended to ask questions which furthered the story and which were clearly perceived as facilitative and welcomed by the narrators as evidence of interest, as exemplified in Extract 8.10. Mona is recounting a long story about how a hairdressing salon made a mess of colouring her hair.

Extract 8.10: Hair colour disaster

1 MONA: so I'm going to phone the salon tomorrow and speak to the
2   owner if she's there
3 CAROL: yeah
4 MONA: and um just ask her to do something about it
5 CAROL: *gosh that's pretty poor isn't it*
6 MONA: well I don't have his home phone number or I'd phone him at
7   home
8 CAROL: yeah [tut] *oh so they're trying to avoid you?*

The questions and comments provided by Mona's conversational partner, Carol, are facilitative (e.g. line 5). As Mona appears to be winding up the story, Carol encourages her to elaborate with some interpretive comment (line 8). By asking questions in this way, listeners are expressing positive politeness. Indicating interest in another's topic is clearly a way of signalling positive affect and suggesting that both listener and speaker share similar attitudes and values. Asking questions which elicit further information about the topic is one linguistic strategy for indicating interest in it. The Pakeha men also often asked questions, but they were sometimes questions which, at least from a female perspective, seemed to disrupt the flow of the story and temporarily diverted the narrative from its track. In Extract 8.11, Gary clearly disrupts the flow of Tom's story with his question (line 5).

Extract 8.11: Programming the video

Context: Two Pakeha men, Tom and Gary, in casual conversation. Tom is telling a story about how he set his complex video machine successfully.

```
1 TOM:   I I looked at- looked up where the programme was on in the pap-
2        you know in the paper
3 GARY:  mm
4 TOM:   [drawls] and I picked up the video thingy you know the
5 GARY:  is this the g code?
6 TOM:   /the remote one no no\
7 GARY:  /no\
8 TOM:   no no no just [drawls] the just an ordinary remote
9        and I pushed the appropriate buttons and it ALL worked
```

Maori listeners by contrast generally did not ask such questions at any point in a narrative. Even at the end of a story, there was often no overt comment. When a comment did occur, it was often a very brief evaluative indication of understanding of the narrator's point.

Sometimes the Maori listener responded with a sympathetic mirroring story (cf. Coates, 1996). So, following Rewi's story in Extract 8.7, Peter tells a story which makes a similar point. Sometimes a story was picked up and extended or commented on much later in the conversation, where, from the perspective of a Pakeha listener, it did not obviously seem to 'fit' (another example perhaps of the pervasiveness of implicit contextualisation in Maori exchanges). Overall, however, there seems to be an assumption by Maori conversationalists that the listener is providing an adequate response by simply attending to the story. Being polite in Maori interaction, it seems, does not typically involve initiating further talk or asking questions to extend a person's narrative. Indeed such behaviour may be perceived and experienced as overly intrusive.

To summarise, there are many respects in which Maori and Pakeha responded similarly to the stories of their conversational partners. However, there were also examples where contrasting responses were evident and it seems possible that these reflect different attitudes to the listener's role in conversation. Maori listeners tended to listen relatively silently compared to

Pakeha. They provided less overt verbal feedback of any kind in conversation than Pakeha. Pakeha listeners, by contrast, not only supplied ongoing explicit verbal feedback, but also often asked questions to elicit more information in the course of a narrative and at the end of a narrative. These intra-textual and post-narrative questions occurred much more often in the Pakeha than in the Maori conversations.

Implicit meaning and cross-cultural communication

Acknowledging the danger of over-generalisation, there is evidence from the narrative analyses above that Maori narrators often leave meaning implicit, while Pakeha narrators are more likely to spell out their intended meanings. Maori listeners are more often left to infer the point of a story for themselves. The resolution and the significance of a story tend to be conveyed implicitly by the organisation or juxtaposition of the elements, or through prosodic, paralinguistic or non-verbal signals. Pakeha stories, by contrast, more often include a specific resolution and coda and the speaker's evaluation of the significance of the story is frequently made quite explicit.

These differences suggest the potential for misunderstanding in everyday interaction. Indeed in some of the recorded interactions, the conversationalists comment quite explicitly on the problems of understanding the ways that meanings are encoded by the other group, as suggested in the opening quotation and also in the following comment by a Pakeha woman on her experience at a meeting with a young Maori man:

> he was trying to explain how Maori people see these things you know and he he started to tell a story + I suppose to make his + to illustrate the point I don't know + but anyway I just couldn't follow it I I couldn't see what he was getting at I mean I simply got lost ++ I could understand the words but somehow I missed the point

As suggested in the analysis above, the Maori narrator expects the listener to do a good deal of inferential work. As a result, Pakeha often find Maori contributions to a conversation obscure or opaque, while, from a Maori perspective, Pakeha tend to miss the intended message because they expect meanings to be more explicitly verbalised and even lexically encoded. Consequently, Pakeha often consider Maori unresponsive and difficult to talk to, while to Maori, Pakeha often miss the intended message because 'they are listening with their ears instead of their eyes' (Metge and Kinloch, 1984, p. 10).

These different expectations sometimes result in serious problems. One example involved an agreement between a Maori woman and young Pakeha male about a job of work that he was undertaking for her. The precise scope of the job was never made sufficiently explicit between the two parties and as a result there was a major misunderstanding where each party felt very aggrieved. Another example from a government department entailed a Pakeha woman leaving a meeting where Maori ways of interacting had dominated, feeling that nothing had been resolved, no firm decisions had been reached and the discussion had left all the issues 'up in the air'. This was not the view of the Maori participants who were perfectly satisfied with the outcomes of the meeting.

Maori ways of teaching and learning are often similarly based on the assumption that the most effective educative methods involve the learner doing a good deal of inferential work. At the simplest level, children are expected to learn by observation and repeated experience, as reflected in Extract 8.7. Typically, there is less verbalising of what is going on than in Pakeha interactions. The listener is often led towards a conclusion which is not spelled out (Holmes, 1997b; Metge, 1995).

At another level, learning is conceived of as a gradual and cyclical process. At any point, one takes as much meaning from a narrative or a conversation as one is ready for, or capable of perceiving. Repetition is an important aspect of Maori ways of teaching and learning, thus providing the opportunity for increased understanding over time (Metge, 1995). Consequently, Maori listeners do not expect to understand every aspect of what is said at the time it is said. Maori conversations often revisit issues at a number of points with different aspects of meaning becoming clearer at different points. These ways of talking are unfamiliar to Pakeha conversationalists and, not surprisingly, lead to accusations that Maori are 'woffly', 'vague' or 'imprecise'. Conversely, Maori people often experience Pakeha ways of interacting, teaching and learning as uncomfortably direct, explicit and unsubtle. Making everything explicit can be seen as rather insulting to listeners and as unhelpful to learners. The narrative analyses above provide some suggestions as to how these different perceptions arise.

Ethnic identity signals: cross-cultural differences

One other important area where differences emerged from a comparison of the Maori and Pakeha narratives was in the extent to which ethnic identity was implicitly or explicitly signalled in Maori narratives. Discussing miscommunication which 'resides in group and cultural phenomena', Coupland et al. (1991, p. 15) note that at this level of analysis 'culture is seen as having communicative consequences for participants . . . identity is defined in social rather than personal terms'. This is amply illustrated in the Maori narratives analysed.

The ways in which people use narratives to construct a particular socio-cultural identity has been the focus of a great deal of recent research (e.g. Blum-Kulka, 1993; Bruner, 1990; Chafe, 1994; Gee, 1991; Heath, 1982; Michaels, 1981). We use language in complex ways to express and negotiate our relationships with others. In the process we construct particular kinds of social identities (e.g. Holmes, 1997b; Holmes *et al.*, 1999) including ethnic identities. The stories we tell are an important resource in this process of identity construction in interaction. As Schiffrin says:

> The form of our stories (their textual structure), the content of our stories (what we tell about), and our story-telling behaviour (how we tell our stories) are all sensitive indices not just of our personal selves, but also of our social and cultural identities.
>
> (Schiffrin, 1996, p. 170)

It was clear from our data that Maori and Pakeha narrators used narratives to construct and negotiate rather different ethnic identities.[6]

Most obviously 'being Maori' seemed always a relevant factor in the Maori interactions. Ethnicity, it appears, is omnipresent for Maori conversationalists: it is sometimes foregrounded, the explicit focus of attention, but even when other issues are the ostensible focus of discussion, Maori identity is almost always a relevant background factor contributing to a thorough understanding and in-depth interpretation of what is being expressed.[7] By contrast, the Pakeha narratives do not indicate awareness of ethnicity as an issue; it does not appear to be an ever-present part of the Pakeha narrators' consciousness, as it is for the Maori contributors. Being Pakeha is simply experienced as 'normal' and unmarked.[8]

Aspects of Maori identity are often the explicit focus of narratives. In Extract 8.12, Keti, a middle-aged Maori woman, explains why her sister had not learned Maori from their mother as Keti herself had done.

Extract 8.12: Adopting out my sisters

```
 1  KETI:  oh yes my sister 'cause she was brought up um [tut]
 2         when my dad went to war um my mother was working
 3         she was milking cows on our on our farm
 4         and um she er m- sort of adopted out um two two (in the) family
 5         my older sister Rahera and er my younger one er
 6         until you know my dad was supposed to come back from the war
 7         well she was working at the farm
 8         and so there were only two of us with her
 9         and she used to take us to the cowshed every day
10         I suppose it was a bit much taking four kids [laughs] to the cowshed
```

```
11          every day and doing
12 TIA:     wow that's morning and night
13 KETI:    morning and night
14          so um one auntie had one girl
15          and another auntie who they were Pakeha people er took Rahera
16          well when it came time and my dad was killed
17          um she went back you know (to-) to get these two back
18          but they were you know
19          those two aunties said no they couldn't part with them
20 TIA:     wouldn't give them oh oh
21 KETI:    so she let them have them and
22          they'd just come and have holidays with us
23 TIA:     mm
24 KETI:    it was really quite sad in a way no no
```

The story captures many aspects of Maori life in New Zealand in the 1940s and 1950s. Most Maori lived in the country and worked on farms. Child-sharing or 'atawhai' adoption along the lines described in this story was common. As Metge (1995, p. 140) describes in detail in a book about Maori extended families, *New Growth from Old*, 'children belong, not to their parents exclusively, but to each of the whanau [extended family] to which they have access through their parents'. Informal adoption of children by aunties and grandparents, though very unfamiliar and little understood in Pakeha society, is generally recognised in Maori society and still practised in some Maori communities.[9] The parents are typically regarded as being generous rather than as shirking their responsibilities (Metge, 1995, pp. 212–213). An understanding of normal Maori family relationships is thus an important background component in this story, though its main function in the particular conversation is to account for why Rahera does not know Maori, an important aspect of Maori identity for many Maori of her age, as Keti indicates. Keti's final comment that *it was really quite sad in a way* perhaps reflects current changes in attitudes to such child-rearing practices among educated Maori (see Metge, 1995, p. 254ff).

Another story focuses quite specifically on the importance of the relationship between familiarity with the Maori language and a strong Maori identity. The Maori narrator recounts a struggle with a young boy, Mark, who initially resisted using Maori in school but finally became very fluent in Maori and proud of his Maori identity. Other stories describe the importance of doing things in a Maori way, the difficulties some Maori have in conforming to the Pakeha bureaucratic system, and illustrate differences between a Maori and Pakeha sense of humour (Holmes, 1997b).

Extract 8.13 is an example from a conversation between two young Maori men which draws on a wide variety of background assumptions about what it means to be a Maori living in a Pakeha-dominated society. At this point in their conversation, they are planning a 'haangi', a traditional Maori method of cooking over hot stones in a pit in the ground. For this, they need a fire permit from the city council. Hinemoa is a relative who works for the council, and this interaction constructs an imaginary story involving an exchange with her which first invites her to the meal, and then asks her to provide the fire permit required to cook the food.

Extract 8.13: Hinemoa and the haangi

```
 1  HONE:  cos you might have to get a permit eh from the council eh
 2  MAT:   city council [laughs]
 3  HONE:  yeah hello Hinemoa
 4  MAT:   [funny voice] hello [laughs]
 5  HONE:  knock knock knock [laugh]
 6         yes we've just got this haangi
 7         you want to come around to a haangi
 8  MAT:   yeah yeah yeah
 9  HONE:  want to come round to a haangi
10  MAT:   yeah perfect [laughs]
11  HONE:  two things [laughs]
12         and now here's the application for a fire
13  MAT:   yeah
14  HONE:  sign here
```

This is a fantasy sequence, a humorous piece of discourse built up cooperatively by these two young Maori men for their mutual amusement, in which their Maori identity is fundamental. At a very overt level, the extract presents a contrast between Maori and Pakeha ways of cooking food: a haangi is a very traditional Maori cooking method. Participating in a haangi (as opposed, say, to a barbecue) is a way of asserting or expressing Maori identity, or sympathy for Maori cultural activities. More subtly this excerpt characterises, somewhat satirically, the way some Maori skilfully 'manage' the Pakeha system by means of Maori relatives who have infiltrated it.

Maori people place a very high value on kin relationships, family connections and the mutual obligations these entail (Metge, 1995). Extended family relationships are central to the Maori lifestyle and patterns of interaction. More generally, like other Polynesian cultures, Maori culture is characterised by an emphasis on social relationships, on connection, on the affective functions of discourse and on involvement in interaction (Besnier, 1989; Edwards and Sienkewicz, 1990; Howard, 1974; Ito, 1985). These beliefs, attitudes and values are relevant in interpreting this short exchange which exploits Maori assumptions about the responsibilities of kinship relations, as well as indicating Maori attitudes to the Pakeha bureaucracy. The humour expresses the awareness of these two young men of the ethnic boundaries which divide Pakeha and Maori (Holmes and Hay, 1997). None of this is explicit, of course; indeed it is merely hinted at. Spelling it out as I have done almost certainly gives it more weight and foregrounds it much more than would have been apparent in the context. However, it does suggest how much of the subtext a Pakeha listener might miss.

Pakeha narratives do not focus explicitly on components of Pakeha identity, nor do they discuss ways of doing things which are specifically Pakeha, or contrast them with ways characteristic of other groups. Being Pakcha and doing things in a Pakeha way appears to be a taken-for-granted fact of life. It is rarely a relevant factor in understanding the significance of a narrative. Members of the dominant group appear to take their ethnic identity for granted: while Pakeha attitudes and values are implicit in many of the stories, and relevant to a thorough understanding of the stories, Pakeha identity is not a matter for reflection or an area of conscious awareness.

Ethnic identity and cross-cultural communication

The different preoccupations and assumptions of Maori and Pakeha in inter-action are thus an obvious potential source of misunderstanding. At the very least, such differences result in members of different cultural groups being out of tune, failing to 'get' each other's point and talking past each other. The narratives often reflect important differences in the background experiences of Maori and Pakeha. But more than this, they express different cultural pre-occupations and values. They suggest the extent of Maori people's awareness of their minority group status in the wider society and their awareness that Maori approach many issues from a different position to that of the Pakeha majority. The narratives suggest that Maori New Zealanders are constantly sensitive to differences between Maori and Pakeha norms such as the commit-ment to group rather than individualistic values. If these stories are an accurate indication of the concerns of the contributors, ethnic identity is a much more salient, relevant and ever-present dimension for Maori than for Pakeha.

This preoccupation with ethnic identity in the Maori stories is under-standable in the light of the social position of Maori in New Zealand. As mentioned above, Pakeha values, beliefs, attitudes and behaviours dominate most social contexts. They are simply assumed as the norm by most particip-ants. In the workplace, for example, processes such as staff development, performance evaluation and promotion procedures are predicated on indi-vidualistic, competitive norms. Individuals are expected to compete openly with others, with aggressive self-promotion increasingly the normal way of achieving this. In most New Zealand schools, students are typically required to work as individuals rather than in groups, especially as they grow older. They are expected to compete with each other, to assert their academic strengths and 'blow their own trumpets'. These norms are incompatible with traditional Maori values which promote modesty and humility: you do not speak for yourself, rather, you wait for others to speak for you. Maori culture has a strong prohibition on 'skiting', boasting, arrogance or self-promotion, a concept captured by the Maori word 'whakahiihii'. Individuals are expected to act in a self-abnegating way and to avoid seeking personal glory, recognising that their contributions should always be seen in the context of the group (Metge, 1995, p. 166).[10] Metge comments that Maori disapprove of 'pride which focuses on the self separate from the group' (1995, p. 103). Those who boast 'are quickly cut down to size by other whanau [extended family] members, for they threaten whanau harmony and reflect badly on the group' (1995, p. 103). Hence it is unsurprising that the Maori narratives often indicate awareness of the cognitive dissonance between Maori ethnic identity and the group-oriented traditional values of the old-style rural Maori, and the individualistic values of the modern urban environment, with resulting incompatible demands on ambitious, well-educated modern Maori.

Maori people are, not surprisingly, very aware of the ways in which Pakeha norms are inconsistent with Maori ways of thinking and Maori ways of doing things. The extent to which ethnicity is an issue for Maori but not for Pakeha indicates a deep potential source of misunderstanding. It takes considerable effort for a group to question taken-for-granted ways of talking, listening and learning, and even more effort to realise that the different ways of doing things which characterise another group are not evidence of inferiority. The awareness of ethnic identity apparent in the Maori narratives is just one manifestation of the unavoidable, daily confrontations Maori conversationalists face as they attempt to communicate in a society dominated by Pakeha discourse norms.

Conclusion

Because Pakeha culture is the dominant culture in New Zealand, it is Pakeha ways of doing things, Pakeha norms and Pakeha interpretations which dominate in most social settings, and it is Maori structures, meanings and values which are misunderstood or only partly understood. As Metge notes, it is Maori who are of necessity bicultural; most Pakeha 'are far from knowledgeable about any culture but their own' (Metge, 1976, p. 322). Hence Pakeha interlocutors are often oblivious to potential communication problems.

This analysis of the conversational narratives of Maori and Pakeha conversationalists has identified a number of areas of potential cross-cultural miscommunication. Though much is shared, differences do exist in storytelling, as elsewhere in conversational discourse, and this analysis has focused on contexts where such differences are most likely to emerge – in private social contexts between friends of the same ethnicity. In both cultures it is assumed that one does not need to spell out the obvious. Indeed, to do so in intimate contexts can be insulting. In both cultures, solidarity licenses assumptions about shared values, cultural knowledge and attitudes. One 'does friendship' by assuming common ground. However, the precise areas and ways in which these assumptions become relevant and the interactive strategies through which they are realised sometimes differ.

The areas of difference identified in this chapter suggest that Maori people feel that explicitness is unnecessary more often than Pakeha. The stories told by Maori were sometimes considerably less lexically explicit than the Pakeha. Using Labov's framework, the evaluation component was often conveyed through tone of voice, prosody or paralinguistic strategies; the resolution and coda were sometimes omitted. The Maori narrators assumed more often than the Pakeha that these elements were self-evident. Similarly, there were examples where reported speech was not attributed explicitly to specific characters in a story; the lexical scaffolding typical of reported speech in narrative was omitted. As listeners, Maori conversationalists were also less verbally explicit than Pakeha: they used less overt verbal feedback than Pakeha listeners and, while Pakeha listeners often asked questions in the course of a narrative to elicit further detail, Maori listeners rarely did so.

These differences suggest that behaving as a polite conversationalist may involve different responses from Maori and Pakeha. Pakeha tend to make things clear, spelling out the point of a story for maximum impact. Listening to the stories in the sample, it seems that narrators used this strategy in order to make their stories more entertaining, more of a performance for their listener's benefit. In some of the Maori stories, by contrast, the denouement is low key, underplayed and inexplicit. The narrator seems to assume that the point is self-evident, a climactic ending unnecessary. The emphasis is on the intimacy of the relationship between the two conversationalists – things do not need spelling out.

As listeners, there was a consistent tendency for the Maori informants to produce verbal feedback at a markedly lower overall frequency than the Pakeha informants, suggesting that the two groups operate according to different baseline levels when providing this type of feedback. In conversational contexts, Maori listeners sometimes indicate attention and interest by keeping silent, rather than providing verbal feedback and asking questions as Pakeha do. Silent attentive behaviour is a strategy for signalling interest in both cultures, but it is less common in one-to-one interaction among Pakeha.

Hence, while both groups have experience of the behaviour patterns described, the contexts in which they use them and the extent to which they use them seems to differ. Pakeha tend to use active positively polite behaviour, asserting interest and indicating shared attitudes more overtly. Maori tend to use negatively polite strategies more often than Pakeha in these contexts, avoiding verbal intrusion on the speaker's floor. If these patterns occur in cross-cultural interaction, there is a possibility of misinterpretation. And because it is Maori who are bicultural, it is Pakeha who are most likely to misunderstand.

Turning to the ways in which narratives encode cultural values, the stories told by the Maori contributors consistently involved explicit or implicit reference to Maori identity. Ethnic identity is clearly a central concern for Maori narrators, whereas it does not feature at all in Pakeha stories. The extent of identification with Maori culture of the participants was a relevant factor in understanding and interpreting almost every Maori story. In some stories it was the explicit focus of the story – the story served to emphasise the ethnic boundary between Maori and Pakeha. In others it was an important background assumption, contributing an additional layer of meaning to the narrative. Thus, for Maori the distinctiveness of their culture and its non-normative status appears to be a constant backdrop to everyday interaction, especially with other Maori conversationalists.

The narratives selected for this analysis were told to each other by friends of the same ethnicity. They have thus revealed the shared structural patterns, norms and values which obtain between those who know each other well. The narrators have been doing friendship as much as they have been doing ethnicity. The next phase in this analysis is clearly to investigate the ways in which these patterns are modified when Maori and Pakeha friends talk to each other. In such contexts, it is possible that we may find specific evidence to support Maori people's claims that Maori and Pakeha frequently 'talk past each other'.

Appendix

Transcription conventions

Names have been changed to protect people's identity.

YES	Capitals indicate emphatic stress
[laughs]	Paralinguistic features in square brackets
[drawls]	
+	Pause of up to one second
..../......\...	Simultaneous speech
..../......\...	
(hello)	Transcriber's best guess at an unclear utterance
?	Rising or question intonation
–	Incomplete or cut-off utterance
. . .	Section of transcript omitted

Acknowledgements

I here express appreciation to Mary Boyce, Harima Fraser, Maria Stubbe, Fran Hunia and Peter Keegan who have all contributed to my understanding of the issues covered in this chapter. The chapter draws in parts on material also discussed in Holmes (1998a). I am grateful to Richard Watts, the editor of *Multilingua*, for permission to refer to this material. The research on which it draws was made possible by a grant from the New Zealand Foundation for Research, Science and Technology.

Notes

1 Each of these reactions has been expressed by particular contributors to our workplace corpus in discussion of the communication difficulties encountered in meetings involving colleagues from different cultural or social (including gender) backgrounds.
2 The Wellington Corpus of New Zealand English is available on CD-Rom from the School of Linguistics, Victoria University of Wellington. See Holmes *et al.* (1998) and Bauer (1993) for details of content.
3 For ease of reading, examples have been slightly edited in relation to features which are irrelevant to the discussion in this chapter.
4 See Holmes (1998a) for more detailed discussion.
5 I have discussed my analysis with a number of Maori women and men, but it is unavoidably an analysis undertaken from a female Pakeha perspective. An analysis from a Maori perspective might well identify different features.
6 See Holmes (1998b) for more detailed discussion.
7 The discussion in Metge (1995) supports this viewpoint, and it has been confirmed by the Maori people whom I have consulted.
8 It is possible that this perception simply reflects my Pakeha perspective. However, Maori readers and people with whom I have discussed the material endorse the interpretation offered here. See also King (1985).
9 The Maori term 'whaangai', meaning 'nurture, feed, bring up', captures the concept better than the term 'adoption'.
10 In this context Harima Fraser, one of the Maori women consulted, quotes the Maori proverb 'waiho maa te tangata e mihi', which translates 'Let someone else sing your praises'.

References

Bauer, L. (1993). *Manual of information to accompany the Wellington Corpus of Written New Zealand English*. Wellington: Department of Linguistics, Victoria University of Wellington.

Bell, A. (1991). *The language of news media*. Oxford: Blackwell.

Benton, R. A. (1991). Maori English: a New Zealand myth? In J. Cheshire (ed.), *English around the world*. Cambridge: Cambridge University Press, 187–199.

Besnier, N. (1989). Information withholding as a manipulative and collusive strategy in Nukulaelae gossip. In *Language in Society*, 18, 315–341.

Blum-Kulka, S. (1993). 'You gotta know how to tell a story': Telling, tales, and tellers in American and Israeli narrative events at dinner. In *Language in Society*, 22, 361–402.

Bruner, J. (1990). *Acts of meaning*. Cambridge, MA: Harvard University Press.

Chafe, W. (1994). *Discourse, consciousness and time*. Chicago: University of Chicago Press.

Coates, J. (1996). *Women talk: Conversation between women friends*. Oxford: Blackwell.

Corston, S. (1993). On the interactive nature of spontaneous oral narrative. In *Te Reo*, 36, 69–97.

Coupland, N., Wiemann, J. M. and Giles, H. (1991). Talk as a 'problem' and communication as 'miscommunication': an integrative analysis. In N. Coupland, H. Giles and J. M. Wiemann (eds), *Miscommunication and problematic talk*. London: Sage, 1–17.

Duranti, A. (1986). The audience as co-author. In *Text*, 6, 239–248.

Edwards, V. and Sienkewicz, T. J. (1990). *Oral cultures past and present: Rappin' and Homer*. Oxford: Blackwell.

Gee, J. (1991). A linguistic approach to narrative. In *Journal of Narrative and Life History*, 1, 15–39.

Goodwin, C. (1986). Audience diversity, participation and interpretation. In *Text*, 6, 283–316.

Heath, S. B. (1982). What no bedtime story means. In *Language in Society*, 11, 49–76.

Holmes, J. (1997a). Struggling beyond Labov and Waletzky. In *Journal of Narrative and Life History*, 7 (1–4), 91–96.

Holmes, J. (1997b). Women, language and identity. In *Journal of Sociolinguistics*, 2 (1), 195–223.

Holmes, J. (1998a). Narrative structure: some contrasts between Maori and Pakeha story-telling. In *Multilingua*, 17 (1), 25–57.

Holmes, J. (1998b). Why tell stories? Contrasting themes and identities in the narratives of Maori and Pakeha women and men. In *Journal of Asian Pacific Communication*, 8 (1), 1–29.

Holmes, J. (1998c). Story-telling in New Zealand women's and men's talk. In R. Wodak (ed.), *Gender, discourse and ideology*. London: Sage.

Holmes, J. and Hay, J. (1997). Humour as an ethnic boundary marker in New Zealand interaction. In *Journal of Intercultural Studies*, 18 (2), 127–151.

Holmes, J., Stubbe, M. and Vine, B. (1999). Constructing professional identity: 'doing power' in policy units. In S. Sarangi and C. Roberts (eds), *Talk, work and institutional order: Discourse in medical, mediation and management settings*. Berlin: Mouton de Gruyter, 351–385.

Holmes, J., Vine, B. and Johnson, G. (1998). *Guide to the Wellington Corpus of Spoken New Zealand English*. Wellington: Victoria University of Wellington.

Howard, A. (1974). *Ain't no big thing: Coping strategies in a Hawaiian American community*. Honolulu: University Press of Hawai'i.

Ito, K. L. (1985). Affective bonds: Hawaiian interrelationships of self. In G. M. White and J. Kirkpatrick (eds), *Person, self and experience: Exploring Pacific ethnopsychologies*. Berkeley: University of California Press, 301–327.

King, M. (1985). *Being Pakeha*. Auckland, London: Hodder and Stoughton.

Labov, W. (1972). *Language in the inner city*. Philadelphia: University of Pennsylvania Press. (Ch. 9).

Labov, W. and Waletzky, J. (1967). Narrative analysis: oral versions of personal experience. In J. Helm (ed.), *Essays on the verbal and visual arts*. Seattle: University of Washington Press, 12–44.

Lehtonen, J. and Sajavaara, K. (1985). The silent Finn. In D. Tannen and M. Saville-Troike (eds), *Perspectives on silence*. Norwood, NJ: Ablex, 193–201.

Metge, J. (1976). *The Maoris of New Zealand*, 2nd edn. London: Routledge and Kegan Paul.

Metge, J. (1986). *In and out of touch: Whakamaa in cross-cultural context*. Wellington: Victoria University Press.

Metge, J. (1995). *New growth from old: The Whaanau in the modern world*. Wellington: Victoria University Press.

Metge, J. and Kinloch, P. (1984). *Talking past each other: Problems of cross-cultural communication*. Wellington: Victoria University Press/Price Milburn.

Michaels, S. (1981). 'Sharing time': Children's narrative styles and differential access to literacy. In *Language in Society*, 10, 423–442.

National Maori Language Survey (1998). Wellington: Te Puni Kōkiri/Ministry of Maori Development, Te Taura Whiri i te reo Maori/Maori Language Commission, and Statistics New Zealand.

Polanyi, L. (1989). *Telling the American story: A structural and cultural analysis of conversational storytelling*. Norwood, NJ: Ablex.

Rymes, B. (1995). The construction of moral agency in the narratives of high-school drop-outs. In *Discourse and Society*, 6 (4), 495–516.

Schiffrin, D. (1996). Narrative as self-portrait: Sociolinguistic constructions of identity. In *Language in Society*, 25 (2), 167–204.

Stubbe, M. (1998). Are you listening? Cultural influences on the use of verbal feedback in conversation. In *Journal of Pragmatics*, 29, 257–289.

Stubbe, M. and Holmes, J. (2000). Signalling Maori and Pakeha identity through New Zealand English discourse. In A. Bell and K. Kuiper (eds), *New Zealand English*. Amsterdam and Philadelphia: John Benjamins. Wellington: Victoria University Press, 249–278.

Toolan, M. J. (1988). *Narrative: A critical linguistic introduction*. London: Routledge.

White, S. (1989). Backchannels across cultures: A study of Americans and Japanese. In *Language in Society*, 18 (1), 59–76.

9

The politics of misunderstanding in the legal system
Aboriginal English speakers in Queensland

Diana Eades

Introduction

Over the last two decades John Gumperz and his colleagues have drawn attention to the fact that 'speakers may have similar life styles, speak closely related dialects of the same language, and yet regularly fail to communicate' (Gumperz and Cook-Gumperz, 1982, p. 13). On the basis of interactional sociolinguistic work in the Australian state of Queensland, it has been argued (e.g. Criminal Justice Commission, 1996; Eades, 1994, 1996) that such communication failure is an important factor in the way in which Aboriginal people are disadvantaged by the legal system.

This chapter focuses on the role of misunderstanding of Aboriginal English ways of speaking in this disadvantage, drawing on specific cases. I follow Bremer (1996, p. 40) in saying that misunderstanding occurs when the listener achieves an interpretation which makes sense to him or her, but is not the interpretation meant by the speaker. For the purposes of this chapter, I take misinterpretation to be synonymous with misunderstanding.

In this chapter, I examine how Aboriginal English ways of speaking have been misunderstood in the legal process, highlighted in a brief outline of a particular case, known as the Kina case. I show how the disadvantage which results from this misunderstanding has begun to be addressed. I then turn to another case (the Pinkenba case), which shows how a knowledge of cultural differences in ways of speaking can be used to *achieve* misunderstanding. This leads to a discussion of the politics of misunderstanding in the legal system.

The chapter begins with some background about Aboriginal people in the criminal justice system, and about Aboriginal English, the language variety spoken by most Aboriginal people in their dealings with the law.

Aboriginal people in the criminal justice system in Queensland

The involvement of Aboriginal Australians in the criminal justice system remains one of striking over-representation. Concerns over this situation led to the establishment of the Royal Commission into Aboriginal Deaths in Custody (Royal Commission) between 1987 and 1991, which made over 300 recommendations, concerning issues ranging from conditions in prisons, to far-reaching social, educational and health issues. In 1992, the national government allocated $400 million to federal agencies to support implementation of the recommendations. But still the rate at which Aboriginal people are taken into police custody and imprisoned remains alarmingly high throughout the country. In Queensland specifically, the 1995 statistics indicate that indigenous people[1] are 22 per cent more likely to be in police custody than their non-indigenous counterparts, and 14.8 times more likely to be in prison (ATSIC, 1997). Recent studies of indigenous people in the criminal justice system have concluded:

> Far from providing Indigenous Australians with a just and respected means of social control and protection, appropriate to their needs, the Australian criminal justice system remains an alien and discriminatory instrument of oppression, through which Indigenous people are harassed, subjected to unfair legal procedures, needlessly gaoled and all too often die whilst in legal custody.
>
> (McRae *et al.*, 1997, p. 342)

As attention has been increasingly focused on this situation, linguistic issues have recently been under the spotlight to some extent (although they were scarcely considered by the Royal Commission).[2] For more than a decade I have worked on Aboriginal English in the legal system, as researcher (e.g. Eades, 1994, 2000), expert witness (e.g. Eades, 1993, 1995b, 1996, 1997) and provider of professional development workshops and materials (e.g. Eades, 1992), mainly in the state of Queensland. This work has been primarily carried out within the framework of interactional sociolinguistics and has highlighted the importance of cultural differences in communicative style, as we will see below.

Aboriginal English

While there are still a number of communities in the remote northern and central areas of Australia who speak 'traditional' languages as their first language, for the great majority of Aboriginal people their first language is either Aboriginal English or one of the other English-related varieties, Kriol or Torres Strait Creole.[3] Most Aboriginal people speak a variety of Aboriginal English in their dealings with the law.

Aboriginal English (AE) is the dialect of English spoken by Aboriginal people throughout Australia, which differs from Standard Australian English (SE) in systematic ways. There is considerable variation in the varieties of AE spoken, with the heaviest (or furthest from Standard English) varieties being spoken in more remote areas, and the lightest (or closest to Standard English) being spoken in urban and metropolitan areas. Aboriginal English has 'a complex history of multiple origins' (Kaldor and Malcolm, 1991, p. 68) including depidginisation in some areas, as well as the Aboriginalisation of English and possibly decreolisation in some remote areas.

My work over more than a decade has shown that even where the grammatical differences between SE and AE are not great, there are significant pragmatic differences, which have implications for inter-cultural communication (e.g. Eades, 1984, 1988, 1991, 1993). My academic and applied work has argued that Aboriginal ways of communicating must be taken into account if Aboriginal people are to be treated fairly by the justice system. While this chapter deals with the state of Queensland, where the bulk of my research and applied work has been carried out, there is reason to believe that similar situations exist in other parts of Australia (see e.g. Mildren, 1999).

Aboriginal English 'ways of speaking' in the legal process

One of the most significant theoretical contributions on the topic of misunderstanding has been the work begun by John Gumperz on the way that cultural differences in the use and interpretation of subtle features of linguistic form affect inter-cultural communication. In his ground-breaking work on conversational inference, Gumperz (e.g. 1982b, p. 12) shows the central importance of 'cultural assumptions' (which he also terms 'contextual presuppositions' or 'background knowledge') in inter-cultural understanding. His work has highlighted the fact that even where language forms might be very similar or identical, interpretations may differ because of different cultural assumptions.

Looking at communication between Aboriginal and non-Aboriginal speakers of English in the legal system, we see significant differences in 'cultural assumptions', which have been discussed in Eades (1992, 1994) and will now be briefly summarised.

The widespread western assumption which underlies the whole Anglo legal system is that asking questions is the most effective way to find out information. For this reason, the adversarial legal system, which uses 'getting to/finding out the facts' as the major strategy for the presentation of competing stories, is based on interviews, which use arguably the most restricted form of question–answer discourse structure. But it has been shown that this way of seeking information can greatly disadvantage Aboriginal people, for whom questions are not necessarily the most effective way. In fact, quite a different cultural assumption operates in Aboriginal societies, where indirectness and reciprocity in interpersonal interactions are highly valued (Eades, 1982, 1988). Thus, there are many situations in Aboriginal interactions in which questions are not asked and much more indirect ways of seeking information are used. Therefore many Aboriginal people grow up learning to seek substantial information indirectly as a part of interaction in ongoing reciprocal relationships. Not being socialised into question–answer routines, they are often not skilled at participating in interviews.

So, even where speakers are using a very light variety of Aboriginal English, which differs little from other varieties of Australian English in its forms, the lack of shared cultural assumptions in the use of these forms can result in different situated inferences, with serious consequences for speakers. In this chapter, we will focus on two particular language forms (silence and 'yes' in answer to questions) which are central to the analysis of the regular communication failure between speakers of Aboriginal English and speakers of Standard Australian English in the legal system: silence and gratuitous concurrence. The discussion of each of these forms will first outline how they operate in terms of Aboriginal English speakers' participation in the legal system, and will then be briefly mentioned in relation to the case of Robyn Kina, before being exemplified in the Pinkenba case.

Silence

Silence is an important and positively valued part of many Aboriginal conversations. It is not uncommon for people to sit in silence for lengthy periods of time while thinking about a serious topic of conversation or simply in order to enjoy each other's company.[4] Furthermore, in formal or semi-formal contexts, such as meetings or interviews, Aboriginal people like to use silence as they think through topics of discussion (Ngarritjan-Kessaris, 1997). Thus in many Aboriginal contexts, silence signals that the conversation is working well and that the rights and needs of individuals to think in silence are being respected (see Eades, 1988, 1994).

On the other hand, in western societies silence is often negatively valued in conversations, as well as in formal or semi-formal contexts, such as meetings or interviews. It has been found in many studies of conversation (both formal and informal) in mainstream western English-speaking societies that interlocutors feel uncomfortable with silences which are longer than about one second (Jefferson, 1989). For example, between people who are not close friends or family, silence in conversations or interviews is frequently an indication of some kind of communication breakdown.

To understand silence in any particular interaction requires an understanding of contextual presuppositions which include these culturally different assumptions about the way that relationships are built and the ways in which personal privacy is assured, as well as the relative priority placed on time and the ways in which important issues are thought about.

The difference in the way in which silence works in Aboriginal English and mainstream Australian English contexts has serious implications for police, lawyer and courtroom interviews of Aboriginal people. Aboriginal silence in these settings can easily be interpreted as evasion, ignorance, confusion, insolence, or even guilt. According to Australian law, silence should not be taken as admission of guilt, but it can be difficult for police officers, legal professionals or jurors to set aside strong cultural intuitions about the meaning of silence, especially when they are not aware of cultural differences in the use and interpretation of silence.

Gratuitous concurrence

Just as silence can signal quite different meanings in Aboriginal and mainstream non-Aboriginal Australian interactions, so too can the answer of 'yes' to a question, or 'no' to a negative question. A very common strategy for Aborigines being asked a number of yes–no questions by non-Aborigines is to agree, regardless of either their understanding of the question or their belief about the truth or falsity of the proposition being questioned.

This strategy has been termed 'gratuitous concurrence' and it has been widely reported throughout Aboriginal Australia in anthropological, legal and sociolinguistic literature since as early as 1936 (e.g. Elkin, 1947, p. 176; Lester, 1982; Strehlow, 1936, p. 334). This feature is described by Liberman (from whom the term originated) as:

> a strategy of accommodation [that Aboriginal people have developed] to protect themselves in their interaction with Anglo-Australians. Aborigines have found that the easiest method to deal with White people is to agree with whatever it is that the Anglo-Australians want and then to continue on with their own business. Frequently, one will find Aboriginal people agreeing with Anglo Australians even when they do not comprehend what it is they are agreeing with.

> (Liberman, 1981, p. 248)

This strategy is particularly common where a considerable number of questions are being asked, the situation with both police and courtroom interviews (Eades, 1994; see also Coldrey, 1987, pp. 83–85 for an excellent example). A number of the questions in a police interview lend themselves ideally to this pattern of gratuitous concurrence answers, for example, questions asked at the end of the police interview which start with a phrase such as 'Do you agree that . . . ?'

Furthermore, as a major aim of cross-examination is to get witnesses to agree to damaging propositions, then this is also a situation where Aboriginal people are particularly vulnerable. Once a witness in a court hearing or suspect in a police interview has agreed to a proposition, then this becomes a binding agreement. To renege on such an agreement to a proposition is not just seen as contradictory or contrary, as it might be in ordinary conversation, but it can establish the witness or suspect as a liar, as we will see below.

Thus the simple word 'yes' (or its variants, such as 'yeah' and 'yep') is crucial in legal contexts. From the legal perspective, 'yes' in answer to a question signals agreement to the proposition being questioned. But from the perspective of many Aboriginal witnesses, 'yes' *may* signal something like 'I know I have to cooperate with your lengthy questioning, and I hope that this answer will help bring the questioning to an end'. On the other hand, it *may* signal agreement to a proposition. Certain factors increase the likelihood of such an agreement being gratuitous concurrence, namely repeated and pressured questioning, particularly if over a lengthy period of time; lack of opportunity for the person being questioned to take control of discourse; and shouting by the questioner. These are all factors which can be found in courtroom cross-examination, as we will see below.

In fact the discourse structure of courtroom hearings seems to favour the use of gratuitous concurrence. In addition to the factors mentioned above, studies have amply demonstrated that the 'majority of questions put to witnesses contain already completed propositions' (Harris, 1984), and that 'witnesses can hardly be thought to tell their stories in their own words' (Luchjenbroers, 1997, p. 501). While rules of evidence limit the use of leading questions in examination-in-chief (= direct examination),[5] cross-examination seems to be the ideal communicative context for gratuitous concurrence.

Research on Aboriginal English speaking witnesses has found that silence and gratuitous concurrence are important to an examination of the misunderstanding which is common between Aboriginal and non-Aboriginal speakers of English in many lawyer interviews, police interviews and courtroom hearings (e.g. Eades, 1992, 1994).

Silence and gratuitous concurrence in the Kina case

The consequences of the misunderstanding of silence and gratuitous concurrence are highlighted in the case of Robyn Kina, an Aboriginal woman from southeast Queensland. Kina was found guilty in 1988 of the stabbing murder of her de facto husband in Brisbane (the state capital) and was sentenced to life imprisonment. In her trial, no evidence was given, by Kina or by any other person, of the horrific circumstances which led to her stabbing the victim in self-defence and reaction to provocation. In 1993 Kina successfully appealed against the conviction, on the grounds that her lawyers did not find out the necessary information from her to run her defence (Pringle, 1994). Her conviction was quashed and she was released from prison.

Interactional sociolinguistic evidence about misunderstanding between Kina and her lawyers was part of the evidence in her appeal. This evidence (which is discussed in detail in Eades, 1996) showed how Kina's lawyers, who were not aware of Aboriginal English ways of speaking, lacked sufficient inter-cultural communication ability to find out her story and adequately represent her at her trial. As a result of this, the jury at her trial had convicted her in the absence of important evidence which should have been used in her defence.

The sociolinguistic evidence pointed to the cultural inappropriateness of the lawyer interviews in which there was no chance for Kina to build up a relationship essential to the disclosing of important personal information. Further, it became clear that the lawyers had misunderstood the positive role of silence in Aboriginal English, mistakenly thinking that Kina's silence in their interviews with her meant that she had nothing to say. While we do not have taped or transcript data from her interviews with lawyers, we can deduce from a number of sources[6] that there was also a misunderstanding about the meaning of her 'yes' answers to their questions and suggestions about the way she should proceed. That is, they mistakenly interpreted her answers of gratuitous concurrence as her agreement to their suggestions, for example, that she should not give evidence.

In finding that Kina's trial had involved a miscarriage of justice, the court cited 'cultural, psychological and personal factors' which 'presented exceptional difficulties of communication between her legal representatives and the appellant' (*R v. Kina*, 1993, pp. 35–36).[7] In effect, the court accepted the sociolinguistic argument that Kina and her lawyers had suffered serious misunderstanding, which resulted in her wrongful murder conviction. This misunderstanding, it had been argued, was rooted in cultural differences in their uses of English, as highlighted here in two particular ways of speaking: silence and gratuitous concurrence.

Understanding can promote justice

Gumperz (e.g. 1982a, 1982b) has made a powerful case for the central role of the interactional sociolinguistic analysis of communicative differences in addressing problems of inter-ethnic contact. This position is supported by Kina's case and several direct consequences of it. Indeed the Queensland Attorney-General optimistically said that the Kina judgment would 'mark a turning point in the way that Aboriginal people are treated by the legal system' (King, 1993). Several encouraging signs appeared to indicate that some of the disadvantage and resulting injustices experienced by Aboriginal people in the legal system would be addressed sociolinguistically, starting with the provision of knowledge of cultural differences in ways of speaking which lead to misunderstanding. These efforts (which are discussed in Eades, 1997) include the following:

- a public statement by the Attorney-General, on the day following the decision to quash Kina's conviction, about the need for the legal system to have knowledge of the problem of cross-cultural communication and be sensitive to it, as well as finding 'ways to make special provisions frequently for Aboriginal witnesses' (*7.30 Report*, 30 November 1993).
- the decision by the office of the Legal Aid of Queensland, which had provided Kina's initial (inadequate) legal defence, to learn from Kina's case and thus to institute widespread Cross Cultural Communication in Law Training for staff of its offices in Brisbane and neighbouring offices, as well as Cairns, in the far north of the state.
- widespread interest in and use of a handbook for lawyers about Aboriginal English and the law (Eades, 1992). Following the Kina case, there was renewed interest in the handbook in law journals and newsletters (e.g. Fordham, 1994), as well as judgments (e.g. *R v. Aubrey*, 1994) and hearings (e.g. CJC, 1994).

Analysis of these and other similar developments would support the view that applied interactional sociolinguistics has a significant contribution to make to enhancing inter-cultural communication generally in the Australian legal system, showing how misunderstandings can arise from differences in background assumptions and ways of speaking between speakers of Aboriginal English and Standard English.

In addition, my involvement as workshop facilitator or consultant with a number of legal professionals gave me grounds for optimism that, as Roberts *et al.* (1992, p. 112) claim, 'an understanding of the processes of interaction between people from different cultural and linguistic backgrounds does assist in heightening the perception of those who do not wish to discriminate'. It would seem reasonable to assume that a growing understanding of different ways of speaking, especially as they affect Aboriginal people in interviews, would contribute to greater fairness in the legal system. This is indeed the argument made by Mildren (1999) who is a judge of the Supreme Court of the Northern Territory, which has the largest percentage population of Aboriginal people in the country.

Understanding can impede justice

However, this optimism was powerfully challenged some 15 months later in a case in the same city (Brisbane), known as the Pinkenba case.[8] This case revolved around the committal hearing of six police officers who were charged with the unlawful deprivation of liberty of three Aboriginal boys.

There was no evidence of any criminal conduct by the boys and the police did not have any lawful reason for taking them anywhere without their consent (CJC, 1996, p. 2). The boys had been allegedly taken by the six police officers in three separate vehicles late one night and abandoned in an industrial wasteland some 14 km away (at Pinkenba). The boys, aged 12, 13 and 14 when the event occurred, were witnesses for the prosecution in the committal hearing of the six police officers some ten months later. The case centred on the issue of whether or not the boys had travelled in the police cars against their will. No doubt was ever raised that they were approached and told to get in the police cars and that they were taken to the industrial wasteland and abandoned there. The defence case was that 'the deprivation of liberty was not unlawful' (as quoted by the magistrate in his decision, 24.2.1995).

In their cross-examination (by the two lawyers defending the charged police) these boys became victims of serious miscommunication, as we will see below. Central to this miscommunication were the Aboriginal English ways of speaking which had been raised in Kina's case and addressed by the Attorney-General (see Eades, 1995a). As a result of linguistic and cultural manipulation of their evidence, serious questions were raised as to the boys' credibility and reliability as witnesses and the charges against the police officers were dropped.

While a fuller analysis of this case is still in progress, I will concentrate here on silence and gratuitous concurrence in the cross-examination of these boys, discussing one example of each.

Gratuitous concurrence

We have seen above that the repeated asking of yes–no questions in court can create the communicative environment for gratuitous concurrence. Indeed, gratuitous concurrence can serve a very useful purpose for the lawyer cross-examining a vulnerable Aboriginal witness. One of the main purposes of cross-examination is to show a witness as unreliable, and probably the most frequently used strategy is to use repeated questioning to show inconsistencies in the witness's story. As mentioned above, the legal assumption that repeated questioning is the way to test the consistency of a witness's story is a cultural assumption.

Thus, if an Aboriginal witness is susceptible to gratuitous concurrence, it is not hard for a cross-examining counsel to get the witness to 'agree' to conflicting propositions. There are numerous examples of this in the cross-examination in this case, such as that given in Extract 9.1 below. In this example we see 15-year-old Barry's exposure as an unreliable witness, as a result of his being easily and skilfully pressured into conflicting answers on the central point of the whole hearing.

Extract 9.1

1 DC: And you *knew* (1.4) when you spoke to these six police in the Valley that you didn't have to go anywhere with them if you didn't want to, didn't you?

2 W: (1.3) No.

3 DC: You *knew* that, Mr (1.2) Coley I'd suggest to you, PLEASE DO NOT LIE. YOU KNEW THAT YOU DIDN'T HAVE TO GO ANYWHERE if you didn't want to, didn't you? (2.2) DIDN'T YOU? (2.2) DIDN'T YOU, MR COLEY?

4 W: (1.3) Yeh.

5 DC: WHY DID YOU JUST LIE TO ME? WHY DID YOU JUST SAY 'NO' MR COLEY (4.4)? YOU WANT ME TO SUGGEST A REASON TO YOU MR COLEY? THE REASON WAS THIS, THAT YOU WANTED THIS COURT TO *BELIEVE* (2.1) THAT YOU THOUGHT YOU HAD TO *GO* WITH POLICE, ISN'T THAT SO?

6 W: (1.2) Yeh.

7 DC: AND YOU *LIED* TO THE COURT, TRYING TO, TO (1.2) YOU *LIED* TO THE COURT TRYING TO PUT ONE *OVER* THE COURT, DIDN'T YOU?

8 W: (1.8) (p) No.

9 DC: THAT WAS YOUR REASON, MR COLEY WASN'T IT? (3.1) WASN'T IT? (3.2) WASN'T IT, MR COLEY?

10 W: (1.9) Yeh =

11 DC: = Yes. (2.9) BECAUSE YOU WANTED THE *COURT* TO *THINK* THAT *YOU* DIDN'T KNOW THAT YOU COULD TELL THESE POLICE YOU WEREN'T GOING *ANYWHERE* WITH THEM. THAT WAS THE REASON, WASN'T IT? (1.5) WASN'T IT?

12 W: (0.6) Yes =

13 DC: = Yes.

This excerpt occurs after Barry (who is sarcastically addressed by this defence counsel as 'Mr Coley') has been on the witness stand for over ninety minutes on two consecutive days, most of it being cross-examination. Turn 1 in this example puts the proposition central to the defence argument: that the witness knew he did not have to go in the police car. Barry's answer of 'No' (Turn 2) is not accepted, so he is harassed in Turn 3 until he does agree (in Turn 4). Of course, we cannot know what is in the witness's mind, but we can see the ideal situation for gratuitous concurrence, increased when defence counsel begins shouting angrily in Turn 3. The contradictory answers given by Barry in Turns 2 and 8 on the one hand, and Turns 4, 6, 10 and 12 on the other, are interpreted literally by defence counsel, to provide clear evidence that Barry is a liar (emphasised for the court with the theme of 'Why did you lie?').[9]

However, an understanding of Aboriginal English background assumptions and ways of speaking, might well lead to a situated inference indicating that the answer of 'Yep' in Turns 4 and 10 are answers of gratuitous concurrence – indicating Barry's realisation that he will be harassed until he gives the answer required by his interrogator. The important contribution made by interactional sociolinguistic analysis to the interpretation of such answers is to show that we cannot with confidence assume that the speaker (here Barry) intends to agree with the proposition of the question. Thus, such an analysis would caution against such a literal interpretation, suggesting a strong possibility of gratuitous concurrence.

In this example we see how, when the witness gives an answer which defence counsel does not accept, he is harassed until he agrees. This pattern is frequently repeated in the cross-examination of all three witnesses:

1. Witness disagrees with the proposition, as in Turns 2 and 8.
2. Witness is harassed, through raised voice, at times shouting, and repeated questioning, as in Turns 3 and 9 (Note that defence counsel shouts consistently in this excerpt from Turns 3–11.);
3. Witness gives in and agrees with the proposition (often in a barely audible voice) as in Turns 4 and 10.

It is interesting that the question in Turn 11 contains four clauses embedded in the main clause, a sentence structure which would confuse many witnesses, regardless of age, sociolinguistic background and experience with interviews.

Silence

In some instances defence counsel allowed little time between asking an initial question and following it up with pressured, often shouting, repetition of the verb phrase, as we saw above in Extract 9.1, Turns 3, 9 and 11. In such examples we can see that the witness is given little chance to think about the question, or to use the lengthy silence which characterises many Aboriginal conversations, and particularly interviews with Aboriginal people.

At other times however, there were much longer (uninterrupted) silences. While these could be seen to be accommodating Aboriginal ways of speaking, defence counsel made sure that this is not how these silences would be interpreted, in two ways. First, such silences were invariably followed by some form of harassment. Second, on at least two occasions defence counsel

used gratuitous concurrence to get the witness to agree overtly to the proposition that his silence should be interpreted negatively, as we see in Extract
9.2, excerpted from the cross-examination of Albert by the second (less
aggressive) defence counsel:

Extract 9.2

1 DC: And you told them *lies* to their faces, didn't you? (3.7) Didn't you
   Albert? (3.7) Didn't you Albert? (2.2) You lied in their face, didn't
   you? (3.6) Albert, *an*swer my question, please=
2 W: =I don't wanna.
3 DC: Well I'm sorry, but this isn't one that you can claim privilege on.
4 W: I don't wanna.
5 DC: Pardon?
6 W: I don't wanna.
7 DC: You don't want to answer?=
8 M: =Well, I'm telling you, Albert, you have to answer this question,
   okay? You can't get out of this [one.
9 W: [(Inaudible).
10 DC: Now, Albert (2.7) His Worship's told you to answer the question.
    Will you or won't you? (6.5) We have to take your silence as 'no',
    don't we? (2.5) Albert?
11 W.: (1.2) (p)Yes.

At this point in 13-year-old Albert's cross-examination, he has been on the
witness stand for close to two and a half hours, most of it being cross-
examination. Defence counsel is constructing Albert as a liar, this time in
relation to the way in which he had reported the incident to the lawyers at
Aboriginal Legal Service. Most of the extract is a metapragmatic discussion
of whether or not Albert will answer the question in Turn 1. Albert insists
that he does not want to answer the question asked in Turn 1, and defence
counsel and the magistrate assert that this is not a question that he can
'claim privilege on'. This refers to the ruling (expressed to Albert six times
by this stage) that a witness does not have to answer any question that might
incriminate him in relation to the commission of a criminal offence. Much
was made in the cross-examination of the three boys of their criminal records
(mainly for minor thefts). So, as many of the questions asked about their
'criminal activities' the magistrate was obliged to pronounce the warning
about self-incrimination. The invocation of this right by a witness is a tricky
one and it is hardly surprising that these young boys were unsure of how and
when to use this right. At this stage of his lengthy cross-examination, Albert
appears to be trying to invoke it as a way to get out of answering questions.
   However, he is told that he cannot avoid answering the question (about
whether he lied 'to [the] faces' of the ALS staff). But this is followed with a

ridiculous question in Turn 10 – 'Will you or won't you?' The choice offered by this question seems to contradict the assertion by both defence counsel and the magistrate that Albert does not have this choice. By this stage, it is clear that the cross-examination has moved beyond incrimination and harassment, to control and disciplining which appears to be at the very least confusing and, much more likely, senseless. Having got the witness to this state of confused (and senseless?) subjugation, as well as exhaustion, defence counsel moves in with the powerful assertion 'We have to take your silence as "no".' In this proposition, defence counsel ignores widely available background knowledge which would suggest other (non-incriminating) interpretations of the Aboriginal witness's silence. From here it is very easy to get Albert to agree to the assertion (in Turn 11), in a context which seems highly likely to be an answer of gratuitous concurrence.

The strategies used in relation to silence and gratuitous concurrence were very overt and effective. Given the highly adversarial nature of the hearing and the fact that the two defence counsel were among the top criminal lawyers in the state, it would be safe to assume that these strategies were deliberately used to destroy the credibility of the witnesses (which is, after all, the major aim of cross-examination). It was disturbing to find out that the two defence counsel had at the Bar table a copy of the handbook for lawyers (Eades, 1992). So the handbook which had been written to help lawyers in more effective communication with Aboriginal witnesses appeared to be used to help the cross-examining counsel in this case to have *less* effective communication with the Aboriginal witnesses. And indeed it was very successful in that purpose.

Having maximised the opportunities for gratuitous concurrence in the responses of the three boys, both defence counsel, in their closing submissions, gave literal interpretations to the witnesses' answers of 'yes' to the conflicting and incriminating propositions which had been put to them. Further both defence counsel cited propositions from their own questions as if they were quotes from the boys. Central to the defence argument was their complete ignoring of the fact (as expressed by the prosecutor in his response to the defence closing submissions) that 'all of the [witnesses'] answers on which [defence counsel] rely were brought about as a result of leading questions'.

The tactics and politics of misunderstanding in the legal process

This case shows that knowledge of cultural differences in communication can be just what is needed to promote *mis*understanding. The two defence counsel cleverly used gratuitous concurrence and silence together with non-matching contextual presuppositions to guide the magistrate to a misunderstanding of the evidence of the boys. In coming to his conclusions about the reliability and credibility of these Aboriginal witnesses, the magistrate was well persuaded by the defence arguments, which he appeared to accept completely. It appeared that he did not consider the Aboriginal English ways of speaking relevant to a full understanding of the boys' answers to many of the questions in cross-examination.[10] It seems, in fact, that, relying on 'the universal tendency to interpret in terms of one's own presuppositions' (Gumperz 1996, p. 400), the magistrate gave a literal interpretation to the boys' 'yes' answers (not entertaining the possibility of gratuitous concurrence), and followed defence counsel's interpretations of the boys' silences (as well as the avoidance of eye contact, see Eades, 1995a). The magistrate thus decided that there was thus insufficient evidence for the matter to go to trial. He further concluded that the boys 'had no regard for members of the community, their property or even the justice system'.

The way in which the magistrate was led to misunderstand the boys' evidence raises the question of the extent to which the legal system considers that witnesses in legal hearings should understand and be understood. While the legal right of *accused persons* to understand and be understood are provided for in international conventions, legislation, cases, policy and practices involving interpreters,[11] such rights for *witnesses* appear not to be similarly provided for. The Pinkenba case shows how understanding can be of less importance than the adversarial manipulation of a witness during cross-examination.

Recent sociolinguistic work (e.g. Roberts, 1996) has shown how understanding is an interactive process, involving negotiation by all participants in an encounter. But to what extent does any courtroom interaction actually involve negotiation? While there are many dyadic conversations in courtroom proceedings, the power of the questioner to control so much of the talk of the interlocutor arguably makes interaction so constrained as to leave little room for any kind of negotiation. This is particularly so in cross-examination, which is often typified by overt power struggles between lawyer and witness. These power struggles in cross-examination are well-known, both from popular experience and scholarly analysis (e.g. Matoesian, 1993). Indeed Conley and O'Barr (1998, p. 37) have pointed out that in cross-examination 'the basic linguistic strategies . . . are methods of domination and control'.

Given the way the legal system works, it is hardly surprising then that the two defence counsel in the Pinkenba case would incorporate their knowledge of Aboriginal ways of speaking in asserting their domination and control over the three boys. The Pinkenba committal hearing, like all other committal hearings and trials in the Anglo adversarial criminal justice system, was a contest, a fight in which the defence lawyers exercised considerable skill and cunning in their attempt to develop a winning strategy. Thus it is to be expected that clever lawyers, on either defence or prosecution side, could use an understanding of cultural differences in communication to the advantage of their clients.

So, in analysing what was happening in the cross-examination of the Aboriginal boys in the Pinkenba case, we need to turn attention to another question. Given the widespread publicity and availability of the lawyers' handbook, the public statement of the Attorney-General, the judgments in Kina's case, and the several other developments (such as those outlined above) in taking Aboriginal ways of speaking into account, how could such a strategy succeed unopposed, both by prosecutor and magistrate? Why was this information (about cultural differences in communication) used in such a one-sided manner in this case? And why was there virtually no attempt by the prosecutor to negotiate understanding, particularly on Aboriginal ways of speaking, of which he was well aware (as indicated in his discussions with me throughout the course of the hearing)?

To answer these questions, we need to look more closely at the whole context of this hearing, not limiting our examination to the power in the discourse (that is, in the cross-examination), but considering also the power behind the discourse, both institutionally and societally. As Fairclough (1989, p. 34) has pointed out: 'power relations are always relations of *struggle*'.[12] He further points out (p. 70) that any given piece of discourse may simultaneously be a part of a struggle at each of the three levels of social organisation: a situational struggle, an institutional struggle and a societal struggle.

Situational power struggle

Let us first examine the power struggle being directly enacted in the cross-examination. Issues of personality, experience and relative seniority in the context of the Brisbane Magistrate's Court are undoubtedly relevant to the question of why defence counsel succeeded in using the information about Aboriginal ways of speaking relatively unopposed.

It has been suggested to me that the prosecutor and magistrate were actually afraid of being humiliated by the two defence counsel, who were hired by the Police Officers Union to defend the six police officers, were both Queen's Counsel,[13] and who were each described in media reports as a 'leading barrister'. In contrast, the prosecutor in this case was from the Office of the Director of Public Prosecutions (DPP). He had much less experience than either of the two defence counsel. While it may be thought that the magistrate, as the final judge in this case, had more seniority than the defence counsel, in terms of training, status and income he would certainly be regarded as junior to them.

It is also important to point out that it is rare for members of the police force to be prosecuted; indeed they are typically the prosecutors. The charges in this case arose from the recommendations of an investigation by the

Criminal Justice Commission (CJC), an independent body established in 1989 to investigate complaints about government corruption and malpractice. Their investigation into this incident arose from a complaint lodged by the boys through Aboriginal Legal Services. It is not known whether charges would have been laid at all if these two non-conservative bodies had not been involved. It is also relevant to point out that this case did not start in the same way as most prosecutions. Most charges arise by way either of police arrest or police summons, but this one arose from the Office of the DPP (following the CJC's recommendation).

What about the magistrate's role in this one-sided context? In a disturbing indication that he may have been not entirely impartial, on three different occasions the magistrate addressed one of the boys as 'defendant' (when informing the witness of his right to refrain from self-incrimination), thus suggesting that he accepted, unconsciously at least, the defence construction of the witnesses as lying criminals:[14]

> I warn the defendant that he's not obliged to answer any questions which might incriminate him in relation to the commission of a criminal offence. Do you want to speak with anyone from Aboriginal Legal Aid about this before you answer the question?[15]

Both the prosecutor and the magistrate appeared very reluctant to use their situational power to counter the cross-examination in conventional and expected ways. The prosecution lawyer raised very few objections,[16] expressing to me in private the fear that such action 'would only make them [i.e. defence counsel] worse'. Whereas in other courts I have seen opposing counsel and magistrate/judge take steps to restrain harassing and haranguing tactics in cross-examination, these tactics were allowed without comment in the Pinkenba case. The magistrate had the power to stop questions such as the shouted questions in Extract 9.1, under Sections 20 and 21 of the Evidence Act (1977) (Queensland). For example, 'Section 21(2) provides that a court may disallow a question which in its opinion "is intended only to insult or annoy or is needlessly offensive in form"' (CJC, 1996, p. 55).

Further, in considering the Aboriginal tendency to gratuitous concurrence, Mildren, a judge of the Supreme Court of the Northern Territory, points out (1997, p. 16) that the court has the right to disallow any leading questions 'whenever it appears . . . that the witness is likely not to be protected from suggestibility'. The fact that the magistrate did not use such power was highlighted by the first defence counsel, who said in his closing submission:

> If the cross-examination on my part was not aggressive . . . we wouldn't have obtained the truth of the situation . . . Had I've been out of order Your Worship would have done something about it. Your Worship would

have stopped me. You have the power under the Evidence Act to stop questions if you feel I'm badgering a witness or insulting or am scandalous or browbeating a witness. You have a duty and a power in relation to your running of the court to stop me.

The prosecutor told me however throughout the course of the hearing that he was disturbed by the cross-examination and was aware particularly of the unrelenting gratuitous concurrence elicitation tactics, and the disastrous effect this was having on the boys' testimony. Of course, their evidence had to be tested in cross-examination and the prosecutor's strategy was not to exacerbate the already aggressive cross-examination through objections. His decision was to let the cross-examination run its course and then present evidence to the magistrate to indicate why the boys' answers could not be taken literally. Thus he raised few objections and asked me to study all of the boys' evidence in the hearing and write a report in the form of a statement to be tendered to the court on the last day of evidence. He also asked me to appear as an expert witness.

My report, which analysed cultural and linguistic issues involved in the cross-examination of the boys, was completed and given to the prosecutor early in the morning of the last (fourth) day of evidence. This report, which focused on Aboriginal English ways of speaking in the boys' evidence, advised against literal interpretations of the 'yes' answers and cautioned about misinterpretations of silences (as well as the boys' avoidance of direct eye contact with their questioners). However, the prosecutor's superior officer, the Director of Public Prosecutions, decided that I should not be called as an expert witness, and that my statement was not to be used, because he felt that it was 'arguably inadmissible' (letter to Aboriginal Legal Service 2.3.1995, cited in *Purcell* v. *Quinlan*, 1996, p. 2). The prosecutor did assert briefly in his closing submission that the conflicting answers of the boys could be 'attributed to their being overborne' in cross-examination. However, in comparison to the first defence counsel's discussion of his aggressive cross-examination (partly quoted above), this argument was not made at all forcefully or directly. Further, the prosecutor made no use of the material provided to him in my report.

Institutional power struggle

The consideration of the role of the Director of Public Prosecutions leads to an investigation of power relationships beyond the immediate context of the courtroom, specifically, in Fairclough's (1989) terms, of institutional power struggles which were being enacted in the Pinkenba case.

The Criminal Justice Commission, from whom the charges against the police officers effectively originated, has as a 'key goal' the promotion of 'an effective, fair and accessible criminal justice system' (CJC, 1996, p. i). Its establishment derives from specific recommendations in the much publicised Fitzgerald Inquiry into Police Corruption, held in the late 1980s, which uncovered major scandals and resulted in a number of imprisonments of high profile members of the police force, including the police commissioner himself. Recommending major changes in many aspects of 'police culture', this inquiry and its report (Fitzgerald, 1989), and the Criminal Justice Commission which resulted, have been deeply resented by many police officers.[17]

The fact that this Commission, acting on a complaint from Aboriginal Legal Services, succeeded in having six police officers charged with a sensational and disturbing criminal offence, could be seen as representing a major victory for both of these bodies, whose role and experiences often pitted them against members of the police force. But to understand this struggle at the level of these institutions requires an examination of a much broader struggle, which in Fairclough's (1989) terms would be called the societal struggle.

Societal power struggle

The key power struggle behind the Pinkenba case was that between the Aboriginal community and the police force. Since the early nineteenth century, relationships between Aboriginal people and the police in Queensland have been characterised by bitter conflict. The earliest police presence was in the form of a paramilitary force, fighting a 'bloody frontier war' against Aboriginal people, in which police duties were comparable to that of the US army on the American frontier (Foley, 1984, p. 161). From the early twentieth century, after the end of the frontier war, police officers were often appointed as 'protectors of Aborigines' under legislation which gave them wide discretionary powers over the liberty and property of Aborigines. Since this time there has been continuing hostility and distrust on both sides, as well as documented entrenched anti-Aboriginal racism in the police force and 'consistent and widespread maltreatment of Aboriginal and Islander people by police' (evidence given to Human Rights and Equal Opportunity Commission, 1991, cited in Cunneen, 1996, p. 31).

While Queensland has produced some of the most serious evidence of police maltreatment of Aboriginal people, this is consistent with patterns in other states. Cunneen (1996, p. 29) cites the report of the 1991 National Inquiry into Racist Violence by the Human Rights and Equal Opportunity Commission, which 'found that "Aboriginal–police relations had reached a critical point due to widespread involvement of police in acts of racist violence, intimidation, and harassment"'.

In the 1980s and 1990s, a number of specific incidents heightened the tension in Brisbane between Aboriginal people and police (see Cunneen, 1996). The most serious incident was the death, while in police custody in November 1993, of an 18-year-old Aboriginal man, Daniel Yock. Yock had been arrested for disturbing the peace and there was much criticism of the arrest, especially given recommendations of the Royal Commission about alternatives to arrest in such circumstances. In the unrest following Yock's death, Aboriginal leaders accused the arresting officers of causing his death and a demonstration outside the police headquarters to protest his death led to 'the worst street riot [in Brisbane] in a decade' (Fagan, 1994).

An inquiry by the Criminal Justice Commission found that Yock and his companions had been behaving in a disorderly manner and that Yock's arrest was lawful. Further it could not find sufficient evidence to support allegations of Yock's mistreatment following his arrest, and was not able to find sufficient evidence to put any police officers on any charge relating to his death (CJC, 1994). The Brisbane Aboriginal community was outraged by Yock's death and the outcome of the CJC inquiry into it. An Aboriginal leader, Mary Graham, was quoted as saying that 'the general feeling [in the Brisbane Aboriginal community] is that the police have got away with it again . . . they are never going to find the justice authorities guilty of anything in this country' (Walker, 1994b). While the CJC's finding was widely criticised by Aboriginal leaders (Walker, 1994b), the major Aboriginal antagonism remained focused on the police. It was reported that while relations between police and the Aboriginal community were 'tense at the best of times', following Yock's death they had 'broken down entirely in Brisbane' (Walker, 1994a).

To many it appeared that what happened to the three boys in the so-called Pinkenba incident in May 1994 was a major strategic victory for the police in what was increasingly being seen since Yock's death as the war between the police and the Aboriginal community (e.g. Solomon, 1993). The fact that the Aboriginal community then succeeded in having criminal charges laid against six police officers could have been seen as an Aboriginal victory in this ongoing war. Thus, the committal hearing was vested with enormous symbolic and political significance and public attention. It was not a routine case in a lower court, but a key event in the worsening societal struggle between Aboriginal people and the police force.[18] The struggle had moved from the streets to the courtroom, where the major weapon is undoubtedly language.

Conclusion

The Pinkenba case highlights the fundamental flaw in an approach to courtroom communication and misunderstanding which is based on the premise that a knowledge of cultural differences in ways of speaking promotes understanding and the delivery of justice. Scholars such as Meeuwis (1994), Shea (1994) and Sarangi (1994) have argued that a focus on cultural difference misses much that is crucial about misunderstanding in inter-cultural communication. Shea argues that the interactional sociolinguistics approach, with its emphasis on cultural differences, has ignored the way in which interpretations are negotiated and mediated. Similarly, since his (1992) work with Schultz, Erickson has insisted that it is not enough to look at cultural differences, but we must also take into account the 'context of both small-scale and large-scale political relations' (Erickson and Schultz, 1992, p. 212), and the extent to which cultural differences are allowed to become a barrier to understanding (Erickson, 1996).

In examining the role of cultural differences in intercultural communication, analysts such as Shea and Erickson have examined interactions where negotiation is possible, such as in interactions between teacher and student, between counsellor and client, or between colleagues in work or social environments. But in courtroom cross-examination we have the exemplary institutional context where negotiation between interviewer and interviewee is not possible, and further where there is no shared goal between them.[19]

It appears that the most important factor in the consideration of misunderstanding in court is that the highly restrictive rules of evidence can effectively remove the opportunity and the right for witnesses to negotiate meaning and understanding. Resourceful witnesses can pursue strategies to attempt negotiation of meaning, but they may be prevented or cut off at any stage.

In the Pinkenba cross-examination we see effectively no negotiation. These witnesses are totally powerless, on account of the fact that they are children in an adult court,[20] that they are Aboriginal people in a system which systematically oppresses Aboriginal people (McRae et al., 1997), and further that they are not experienced in the discourse structure of the courtroom.[21]

There are of course grounds for negotiation between interviewer and counsel representing interviewee, primarily through the raising of objections and ensuing legal argument. But as we have seen above, the prosecutor was extremely reluctant to pursue this avenue of negotiation and his planned post-hoc negotiation was forbidden by his superior officer.

We have seen that to understand the limited negotiations made by the boys' lawyer necessitated examination not just of the situational struggle (occurring between opposing sides in the adversarial hearing), but also of the related institutional and societal struggles. So we see that what was happening during the cross-examination of the three Aboriginal boys was not simply a situational struggle in which defence counsel were using their power as 'leading barristers' cross-examining Aboriginal child witnesses. It was also part of the institutional struggle in which progressive sectors of the legal profession (Aboriginal Legal Services and the Criminal Justice Commission) were using their institutional position and due process to counter what they saw as possible illegal and discriminatory practice by the police force requiring examination by the courts. Perhaps it was too difficult for the prosecutor seriously to challenge leading barristers defending six police officers: remember that police officers are overwhelmingly prosecutors not defendants. But further than this, the cross-examination of these boys was part of the wider societal struggle, outlined briefly above, between the Aboriginal community and the police force.

Throughout this three-part struggle (situational, institutional and societal) a key role was played by language, and specifically by the misunderstanding of Aboriginal English ways of speaking. Situationally, language was clearly the major instrument of domination and control in the cross-examination, overtly constructing the boys as liars and their allegation against the police as a lie. Institutionally and societally, the language of cross-examination, with its ways of speaking and associated interpretations, powerfully legitimised this situational achievement (which meant that the case against the police officers had to be dropped). Fairclough (1989) shows how a particular discourse type (such as cross-examination) can so dominate an institution, that 'it will cease to be seen as arbitrary, . . . and will come to be seen as *natural* and legitimate, because it is simply *the* way of conducting oneself' (1989, p. 91, original emphasis). He refers to this process as 'naturalisation'.

In both the public outcry and the subsequent judgment of the application for judicial review of the magistrate's decision, we see evidence of how this cross-examination was naturalised, despite the close to farcical nature of its extreme harassment of the child witnesses. So long as the conventional form of questions with answers was followed, it could be claimed that due process had occurred, that justice was done in testing the allegations made by the boys. In this ideological process of 'naturalisation', it was crucial that Aboriginal ways of speaking be ignored. Had they been taken into account, and the possible situated inferences of the silences and 'yes' answers of the boys been acknowledged, then the magistrate could not have come to his decision to ignore the boys' evidence; and the judge who reviewed this magistrate's decision could not have upheld it, saying that their evidence had been 'given in unequivocal terms' (*Purcell* v. *Quinlan*, 1996, p. 9).

The Pinkenba case shows how understanding is not central to the legal system; on the contrary, ensuring that witnesses are misunderstood can be crucial to the pursuit of a winning strategy in the adversarial legal system.

Finally, this review of recent developments in the role of Aboriginal ways of speaking in the legal system makes two contributions to our theorising of understanding in social life, specifically in legal contexts. First, it shows that knowledge of different ways of speaking and different contextual presuppositions is not enough to promote understanding and lead to justice. In courtroom cross-examination, we may well be dealing with institutional and societal power struggles of far greater significance than the immediate situational context. Second, following Shea (1994), we can see that it is not cultural differences in and of themselves, but the way they are taken up and manipulated without opposition which is central in the analysis of misunderstanding in legal contexts.

In the Pinkenba case, known cultural differences were used as a very effective weapon against the Aboriginal witnesses in the defence of the police officers. Defence counsel used misinterpretation of the differences in 'ways of speaking' to portray the Aboriginal boys as liars. A literal interpretation of their 'yes' answers to many damaging propositions leads to the conclusion that they are indeed liars. So, using an *understanding* of different ways of speaking combined with leading the ultimate judge of the evidence (the magistrate) to come to a *misunderstanding* of these ways of speaking gave defence counsel a powerful strategy to destroy the credibility of the witnesses. In so doing, defence counsel used language as a powerful and successful weapon in a major situational, institutional and societal power struggle between Aboriginal people and the police force.

Appendix

Transcription conventions

underlining utterance emphasis
CAPITALS   raised volume
(p)   before an utterance spoken in a low volume
=   latched utterances, i.e. no pause between the end of one
            utterance and the start of the next
            a number in parentheses indicates the length of a pause in
            seconds, e.g. (3.2)
[both the start of an interruption and the utterance which is
            interrupted

The following abbreviations are also used in the transcripts: DC = defence counsel; M = magistrate; P = prosecutor; W = witness.

Acknowledgements

I am grateful to Tony Keyes and Jeff Siegel for their valuable comments on the draft. All remaining errors are my responsibility.

Notes

1 The term 'indigenous Australians' refers to descendants of the original inhabitants, both Aboriginal people, whose ancestry comes from throughout the whole

country, and Torres Strait Islanders, from the islands between Queensland and Papua New Guinea. This chapter focuses on Aboriginal people, who number many more than Torres Strait Islanders, and who have assumed the greatest prominence in court cases involving indigenous people (CJC, 1996, p. xi).

2　This is no doubt a reflection of the fact that there was, at the time of the Royal Commission's work in the late 1980s, little research on how language and communication issues were affecting the experiences of Aboriginal people in the criminal justice system.

3　For an examination of linguistic issues affecting speakers of 'traditional' Aboriginal languages in the legal system, see Cooke (1995, 1996, 1998), or Goldflam (1995).

4　Some similarities can be noted with the use of silence in American Indian societies (Basso, 1970; Philips, 1976).

5　For an excellent linguistic treatment of the legal category of leading questions, see Berk-Seligson (1999).

6　These sources include discussions with lawyers about their interview processes and pressures, observation of other lawyer interviews, affidavits from the lawyers involved and Kina's comments and memories.

7　Expert evidence was also given by a psychiatrist on the issue of repressed memory and a social worker on the 'battered woman syndrome'.

8　*Crawford* v. *Venardos and Ors* PS 2615–2620 of 1994, Magistrate's Court Brisbane, 24 February 1995, unreported. All quotes from this case (evidence, closing submissions of counsel and magistrate's decision) come from my transcription of the official court tape recordings. I have changed all names to pseudonyms.

9　A fuller study of this case will show how this theme is a frequently repeated 'chorus' throughout the cross-examination of all three boys.

10　It is not known whether the magistrate had any knowledge about Aboriginal English ways of speaking.

11　For example, Article 14 of the International Covenant on Civil and Political Rights (to which Australia became a signatory in 1980), states: 'In the determination of any criminal charge against him, everyone shall be entitled to . . . have the free assistance of an interpreter if he cannot *understand* [italics added] or speak the language used in court' (cited in Bird, 1995, p. 6).

12　While Fairclough uses the term struggle 'in a technical sense to refer to the process whereby social groupings with different interests engage with one another' (1989, p. 34), in the Pinkenba case this engagement is well described by the ordinary English use of the word 'struggle'.

13　A Queen's Counsel (or QC, also known as 'a silk') is a senior barrister appointed to this prestigious title by the state Attorney-General, on the basis of his or her reputation and experience. Queen's Counsel charge more than other barristers, and usually only take on difficult and complex cases (Bowen, 1994, p. 808).

14　In a manner similar to the treatment of victim-witnesses in rape cases, the cross-examination of the boys treated them as accused (see Matoesian, 1993). But had they indeed been accused, they would have received more protection, as the extensive cross-examination about their criminal records would not have been allowed. As pointed out by Justice Ambrose, in his judgment on an application to the Supreme Court for judicial review of the magistrate's decision in the Pinkenba case, much of the evidence on which the boys were cross-examined 'related to matters having only the most peripheral relevance to the elements of the offences charged' (*Purcell* v. *Quinlan*, 1996, p. 2). (The criminal record of an accused cannot be mentioned, on the grounds that it may prejudice the magistrate/judge and jury. On the other hand, the criminal record of a witness is not excluded from the cross-examination of a witness, as it is considered to be relevant to questions of the witness's credibility and reliability.)

15 On the first of these three occasions, the magistrate repaired his error, pausing after the word 'defendant' and saying 'I'm sorry I mean the witness'. But on two later occasions, once with the same witness, and once with another, he addressed the witness as 'defendant' with no correction, and no apparent realisation of his error.

16 He raised a total of 11 objections in over 3 days of evidence from the 3 boys, of which the official transcript totals 160 pages.

17 This has been widely reported in the media. My most poignant experience of this resentment occurred in a rural police station on the day the Fitzgerald Report was officially presented and reported. The language used by police officers to refer to the report and its writer was full of angry expletives, being exactly the words which had formed the content of the charge brought by these same police officers in a court sitting earlier that morning, in which an Aboriginal woman was charged and convicted of the crime of using offensive language.

18 Community interest in the case is seen in the extensive media coverage of the hearing, and the fact that it was held in the largest court room available, which was filled to capacity (about 100 visitors) throughout the hearing. At the conclusion of the case, the magistrate's decision was greeted with spontaneous applause (a somewhat unusual occurrence in such a setting). This applause came from the first several rows in the visitors' gallery, which were occupied by family and friends of the police officers. These included high-school-aged boys, seemingly children of accused police officers, in school uniforms (in pointed contrast to the fact that the three Aboriginal witnesses were not at all regular in their school attendance, a point which was much emphasised in cross-examination). Relatives and friends of the three Aboriginal boys, as well as Aboriginal community leaders, occupied the back half of the gallery, together with other members of the public and legal professionals who came for parts of the hearing.

19 Note that even in Kina's case, where the most significant misunderstanding was between Kina and her own lawyers in non-courtroom interviews, it appears that there was no meaningful negotiation of different ways of speaking. My view is that this lack of negotiation was due to a number of factors, including the restrictive time pressure under which they were working, and the lawyers' ignorance of the possibility of cultural differences in ways of speaking. (Kina's trial took place in 1988 before Aboriginal ways of speaking had been presented in any accessible way to members of the legal profession.) Thus, just because negotiation is not prohibited, does not mean that it will occur.

20 Ironically, had the children been the accused, the case would have been heard in a less forbidding, and more child-oriented children's court. Because the accused in this case were adults, the child witnesses were given no special assistance or protection, except for a ban on media reporting of their names.

21 This contrasts with some other examples in the literature. For example, Drew (1992) shows strategies used by a victim witness in a rape case to dispute or challenge the cross-examining lawyers' version of events and situations.

References

Aboriginal and Torres Strait Islander Commission (ATSIC) (1997). *Five years on: Annual/five year report 1996/1997: Implementation of the Commonwealth Government responses into Aboriginal deaths in custody.* Canberra: Commonwealth of Australia.

Basso, K. (1970). To give up on words: Silence in western Apache culture. In *Southwestern Journal of Anthropology*, 26, 213–230.

Berk-Seligson, S. (1999). The impact of court interpreting on the coerciveness of leading questions. In *Forensic Linguistics*, 6 (1), 30–56.

Bird, G. (1995). International law, natural justice and language rights in Australia. In D. Eades (ed.), *Language in evidence: Issues confronting Aboriginal and multicultural Australia.* Sydney: University of New South Wales Press, 3–27.

Bowen, J. (1994). *The Macquarie easy guide to Australian law*, 2nd edn. Sydney: Macquarie Library.

Bremer, K. (1996). Causes of understanding problems. In K. Bremer, C. Roberts, M.-T. Vasseur, M. Simonot and P. Broeder (1996), *Achieving understanding: Discourse in intercultural encounters.* London: Longman, 37–64.

Coldrey, J. (1987). Aboriginals and the criminal courts. In K. Hazlehurst (ed.), *Ivory scales: Black Australia and the law.* Sydney: NSW University Press, 81–92.

Conley, J. and O'Barr, W. M. (1998). *Just words: Law, language and power.* Chicago: University of Chicago Press.

Cooke, M. (1995). Aboriginal evidence in the cross-cultural courtroom. In D. Eades (ed.), *Language in evidence: Issues confronting Aboriginal and multicultural Australia.* Sydney: University of New South Wales Press, 55–96.

Cooke, M. (1996). A different story: Narrative versus 'question and answer' in Aboriginal evidence. In *Forensic Linguistics*, 3 (2), 273–288.

Cooke, M. (1998). Anglo/Yolngu communication in the criminal justice system. PhD thesis, University of New England.

Criminal Justice Commission (CJC) (1994). *A report of an investigation into the arrest and death of Daniel Alfred Yock.* Brisbane: Criminal Justice Commission.

Criminal Justice Commission (CJC) (1996). *Aboriginal witnesses in Queensland's criminal courts.* Brisbane: Criminal Justice Commission.

Cunneen, C. (1996). Detention, torture, terror and the Australian state: Aboriginal people, criminal justice and neocolonialism. In G. Bird, G. Martin and J. Neilson (eds), *Majah: Indigenous peoples and the law.* Sydney: Federation Press, 13–37.

Drew, P. (1992). Contested evidence in courtroom cross-examination: The case of a trial for rape. In P. Drew and J. Heritage (eds), *Talk at work: Interaction in institutional settings.* Cambridge: Cambridge University Press, 470–520.

Eades, D. (1982). 'You gotta know how to talk...': Ethnography of information seeking in Southeast Queensland Aboriginal Society. In *Australian Journal of Linguistics*, 2 (1), 61–82. Reprinted in J. B. Pride (ed.) (1985), *Cross-cultural encounters: communication and miscommunication.* Melbourne: River Seine Publications, 91–109.

Eades, D. (1984). Misunderstanding Aboriginal English: The role of socio-cultural context. In G. McKay and B. Sommer (eds), *Applications of linguistics to Australian Aboriginal contexts.* Melbourne: Applied Linguistics Association of Australia, 24–33.

Eades, D. (1988). 'They don't speak an Aboriginal language, or do they?' In I. Keen (ed.), *Being black: Aboriginal cultures in settled Australia*. Canberra: Aboriginal Studies Press, 97–117.

Eades, D. (1991). Communicative strategies in Aboriginal English. In S. Romaine (ed.), *Language in Australia*. Cambridge: Cambridge University Press, 84–93.

Eades, D. (1992). *Aboriginal English and the law: Communicating with Aboriginal English speaking clients: A handbook for legal practitioners*. Brisbane: Queensland Law Society.

Eades, D. (1993). The case for Condren: Aboriginal English, pragmatics and the law. In *Journal of Pragmatics*, 20 (2), 141–162.

Eades, D. (1994). A case of communicative clash: Aboriginal English and the legal system. In J. Gibbons (ed.), *Language and the law*. London: Longman, 234–264.

Eades, D. (1995a). Cross-examination of Aboriginal children: The Pinkenba case. In *Aboriginal Law Bulletin*, 3 (75), 10–11.

Eades, D. (1995b). Aboriginal English on trial: The case for Stuart and Condren. In D. Eades (ed.), *Language in evidence: Issues confronting Aboriginal and multicultural Australia*. Sydney: University of New South Wales Press, 147–174.

Eades, D. (1996). Legal recognition of cultural differences in communication: The case of Robyn Kina. In *Language and Communication*, 16 (3), 215–227.

Eades, D. (1997). The acceptance of linguistic evidence about indigenous Australians. In *Australian Aboriginal Studies*, 1, 15–27.

Eades, D. (2000). 'I don't think it's an answer to the question': Silencing Aboriginal witnesses in court. In *Language in Society*, 29 (2), 161–196.

Elkin, A. (1947). Aboriginal evidence and justice in north Australia. In *Oceania*, 17, 173–210.

Erickson, F. (1992). Ethnographic micro-analysis of interaction. In M. D. Le-Compte, W. Millroy and J. Preissle (eds), *The handbook of qualitative research in education*. New York: Academic Press, 201–225.

Erickson, F. (1996). Ethnographic microanalysis. In S. L. McKay and N. H. Hornberger (eds), *Sociolinguistics and language teaching*. Cambridge: Cambridge University Press, 283–306.

Erickson, F. and Schultz, J. (1992). *The counselor as gatekeeper: Social interaction in interviews*. New York: Academic Press.

Fagan (1994). Liaison police blamed over Yock brawl. *The Australian*, 14 May.

Fairclough, N. (1989). *Language and power*. London: Longman.

Fitzgerald, G. (1989). *Report of a Commission of Inquiry pursuant to Orders in Council*. Brisbane: Government Printer.

Foley, M. (1984). Aborigines and the police. In P. Hanks and B. Keon-Cohen (eds), *Aborigines and the law*. Sydney: George Allen & Unwin, 160–190.

Fordham, H. (1994). Cultural difficulties in defence of Aboriginal clients. In *Proctor*, March, 17–19.

Goldflam, R. (1995). Silence in court! Problems and prospects in Aboriginal legal interpreting. In D. Eades (ed.), *Language in evidence: Issues confronting Aboriginal and multicultural Australia*. Sydney: University of New South Wales Press, 28–54.

Gumperz, J. (1982a). *Discourse strategies*. Cambridge: Cambridge University Press.

Gumperz, J. (ed.) (1982b). *Language and social identity*. Cambridge: Cambridge University Press.

Gumperz, J. and Cook-Gumperz, J. (1982). Introduction: Language and the communication of social identity. In J. Gumperz (ed.), *Language and social identity*. Cambridge: Cambridge University Press, 1–21.

Gumperz, J. (1992). Contextualisation and understanding. In A. Duranti and C. Goodwin (eds), *Rethinking context: Language as an interactive phenomenon*. Cambridge: Cambridge University Press, 229–252.

Gumperz, J. (1996). Relativity of conversational inference. In J. Gumperz and S. Levinson (eds), *Rethinking linguistic relativity*. Cambridge: Cambridge University Press, 374–406.

Harris, S. (1984). Questions as a mode of control in magistrates' courts. In *International Journal of the Sociology of Language*, 49, 5–28.

Howes, C. (1998). Police accused of brutality. *Koori Mail*, 28 January.

Jefferson, G. (1989). Preliminary notes on a possible metric which provides for a 'standard maximum' silence of approximately one second in a conversation. In D. Roger and P. Bull (eds), *Conversation: An interdisciplinary perspective*. Clevedon: Multilingual Matters, 166–196.

Kaldor, S. and Malcolm, I. (1991). Aboriginal English – an overview. In S. Romaine (ed.), *Language in Australia*. Cambridge: Cambridge University Press, 67–83.

King, M. (1993). State exercising 'reverse racism'. In *The Australian*, 1 December, 6.

Lester, Y. (1982). *Aborigines and the courts and interpreting in court*. Alice Springs: Institute for Aboriginal Development.

Liberman, K. (1981). Understanding Aborigines in Australian courts of law. In *Human Organization*, 40, 247–255.

Luchjenbroers, J. (1997). 'In your own words...': Questions and answers in a Supreme Court trial. In *Journal of Pragmatics*, 27, 477–503.

McRae, H., Nettheim, G. and Beacroft, L. (1997). *Indigenous legal issues: Commentary and materials*, 2nd edn. Sydney: Law Book Company.

Matoesian, G. (1993). *Reproducing rape: Domination through talk in the courtroom*. Chicago: University of Chicago Press.

Meeuwis, M. (1994). Leniency and testiness in intercultural communication: Remarks on ideology and context in interactional sociolinguistics. In *Pragmatics*, 4 (3), 391–408.

Meeuwis, M. and Srikant, S. (1994). Perspectives on intercultural communication: A critical reading. In *Pragmatics*, 4 (3), 309–314.

Mildren, D. (1997). Redressing the imbalance against Aboriginals in the criminal justice system. In *Criminal Law Review*, 21 (1), 7–22.

Mildren, D. (1999). Redressing the imbalance: Aboriginal people in the criminal justice system. In *Forensic Linguistics*, 6 (1), 137–160.

Ngarritjan-Kessaris, T. (1997). School meetings and indigenous parents. In S. Harris and M. Malin (eds), *Indigenous education: Historical, moral and practical tales*. Darwin: Northern Territory University Press, 81–90.

Philips, S. (1976). Some sources of cultural variability in the regulation of talk. In *Language in Society*, 5, 81–95.

Pringle, K. (1994). Case notes: R. v. Robyn Bella Kina. In *Aboriginal Law Bulletin*, 3 (67), 14–15.

Purcell and Ors v. *Quinlan and Anor* (1996). Unreported, Queensland Supreme Court, [14 February 1996]. Ambrose, J.

R v. *Kina* (1993). Unreported, Queensland Court of Appeal (CA No. 221 of 1993) [29 November 1993], President and Davies, J. A.

Roberts, C. (1996). A social perspective on understanding: Some issues of theory and method. In K. Bremer, C. Roberts, M.-T. Vasseur, M. Simonot and P. Broeder (eds), *Achieving understanding: Discourse in intercultural encounters.* London: Longman, 9–46.

Roberts, C., Davies, E. and Jupp, T. (1992). *Language and discrimination.* London: Longman.

Sarangi, S. (1994). Intercultural or not? Beyond celebration of cultural differences in miscommunication analysis. In *Pragmatics*, 4 (3), 409–428.

Shea, D. P. (1994). Perspective and production: Structuring conversational participation across cultural borders. In *Pragmatics*, 4 (3), 357–390.

Solomon, D. (1993). A case of us and them. In *The Brisbane Courier Mail*, 18 December.

Strehlow, T. G. H. (1936). Notes on native evidence and its value. In *Oceania*, 6, 323–335.

Tannen, D. (1986). *That's not what I meant!* New York: William Morrow.

Walker, J. (1994a). Arrest of the heart. In *The Australian*, 6 April.

Walker, J. (1994b). Aborigines stand firm on Yock accusation. In *The Australian*, 7 April.

10

Distrust
A determining factor in the outcomes
of gatekeeping encounters

Julie Kerekes
California State University, Los Angeles

Introduction

Research on intercultural gatekeeping encounters has shown that interlocutors may differ as to their perceptions of what is relevant in such an
interaction, the appropriate structural organisation of interactions, and intonation patterns of responses (Button, 1992; Drew and Heritage, 1992; Gumperz,
1982, 1992; Gumperz *et al.*, 1991). Such differences characterise potentially
incongruent discourse systems, which may reflect ethnic, educational or
ideological differences among interlocutors (Akinnaso and Ajirotutu, 1982;
Clyne, 1994; Erickson, 1979; Erickson and Shultz, 1982; Roberts *et al.*, 1992).
Some explanations have attributed these differences to societal inequalities
that result in discriminatory behaviour and interpretations (Sarangi, 1994;
Shea, 1994). How an interlocutor is interpreted is a crucial factor in high-
stakes gatekeeping encounters such as employment interviews, where, not
coincidentally, it is often the interviewer who belongs to the dominant cultural group and the candidate/interviewee who belongs to an ethnic/cultural
minority. Participants' preconceived ideas about their interlocutors, or about
the culture or people they believe their interlocutors represent, are influenced
by their ideological presuppositions (Foucault, 1970; Shea, 1994) and related
'Discourses' (Gee, 1996). The problem is that unsuccessful interactions such
as failed employment interviews are rarely (consciously) associated with differences in discoursal conventions.

The following investigation focuses on employment interviews in the
staffing industry, not only because of their high-stakes nature, but also
because, with the staffing industry's growing prevalence in today's market, an
increasing number of intercultural gatekeeping encounters takes place in
this arena. Approximately 2.9 million people in the United States (2 per cent

of the average daily employment) are employed by staffing companies. Client companies typically use staffing services in situations of temporary skill shortages, seasonal workloads, employee absences and special assignments or projects. The staffing industry attracts many job candidates who have recently relocated, are first-time job seekers, or are newly (re-)trained potential employees, thus comprising a high percentage of immigrants and non-native speakers of English (NNSs). At the time that data for this study were collected, the annual growth rate was 9 per cent and 90 per cent of staffing firms are currently having difficulties recruiting enough qualified job candidates.[1] It is, therefore, in their best interest as well as in the interest of potential job candidates to engage in effective gatekeeping procedures which result in accurate and successful placements.

Factors considered in an employment interview

As defined by Eder and Harris (1999, p. 2) in the *Employment Interview Handbook*, the employment interview is 'an interviewer–applicant exchange of information in which the interviewer(s) inquire(s) into the applicant's (a) work-related knowledge, skills, and abilities (KSAs); (b) motivations; (c) values; and (d) reliability, with the overall staffing goals of attracting, select-ing, and retaining a highly competent and productive workforce'. When inter-viewing for a job, it is not only important that one exhibit desired qualifications and occupational skills, nor is it enough to demonstrate skilled interviewing techniques; one must, finally, make the desired impression on the interviewer who serves as gatekeeper. An interaction which achieves this outcome requires collaboration between the interviewer and interviewee, which is, however, not automatic (Gumperz, 1996). Incongruent interpretations on the parts of interlocutors can have damaging consequences not only for the interaction, but also for the ultimate assessment an interviewer makes of an interviewee: 'In situations of differential power and interethnic stigmatization, problems that in other cases might pass as simple instances of lack of shared linguistic knowledge come to be seen as reflecting the speaker's ability, truthfulness, or trustworthiness' (Gumperz, 1992, pp. 326–327).

It is this third component identified by Gumperz – trustworthiness – whose salience proves critical to the outcome of job interviews at FastEmp,[2] the site of this study. In the following discussion, I will draw from a database of 47 job interviews and 79 interviews between the participants and me, to show how 'trustworthiness' was identified and defined by the staffing super-visors as a crucial factor in determining the eligibility of job candidates to be placed on assignments. I will then demonstrate, through an examination of transcripts from two job interviews, how, through a lack of compliance with institutional expectations, the verbal interactions of those participants *not* deemed trustworthy are misinterpreted. Using an interactionist sociolinguistic approach, I will show how distrust is established between the job interviewer and candidate in these examples. I will argue that, without trust, no matter how clearly the two interlocutors believe they are communicating with each other and no matter how eloquently the job candidate displays her or his work skills, the interaction is doomed to fail. While the job candidates are aware of their interviewer's dissatisfaction (i.e. their distrust), they are unable to access the language or strategies necessary to build up or recreate a trusting relationship with her.

The setting

FastEmp is a national employment agency with approximately 200 branches across the United States. Its South Bay branch (henceforth referred to as FastEmp), located in the heart of Silicon Valley (California), attracts a diverse range of job candidates and client companies, but has a socioeconomically homogeneous staff (Caucasian women, self-described as middle class, with two or more years of higher education). Given the preponderance of culturally diverse job candidates at this branch, the FastEmp staff are generally aware of the linguistic diversity of their job candidates as well as of FastEmp's reliance on the NNS segment of the population to fill many of their positions, especially those in the 'light industrial' sector.[3]

The data analysed in this study come from three types of interviews:

- Authentic video- and audio-taped job interviews, each of which involves one staffing supervisor interviewing one job candidate.
- Debriefing interviews between the staffing supervisors and me after each job interview, during which the staffing supervisor shared with me her impression and immediate assessment of the job candidate she had just interviewed.
- Follow-up interviews between the majority of the job candidates and me, after they had completed the application and interviewing process.

The FastEmp job interview generally begins with introductions initiated by the staffing supervisor, followed by an elicitation of information from the job candidate about her or his work preferences. This is followed by the main component of the interview, in which the candidate's work qualifications are discussed. The framework for this discussion is a chronological account of the candidate's work history. There is great variation as to which details are attended to, however, depending on the staffing supervisor's impression of the candidate thus far. While the work history component may include a detailed description of actual work done and skills learned, it may also focus solely on precise dates and locations of previous assignments. Finally, the staffing supervisor brings the interview to a close with some remarks indicating whether the job candidate can expect to be placed on assignments with FastEmp. This component of the interview also varies, depending not only on the staffing supervisor's impression of the job candidate, but also on the current availability of jobs, as well as whether or not the staffing supervisor has already checked the job candidate's references. Upon completing the interview, the staffing supervisor has made an assessment of the candidate and has a clear idea as to whether or not the candidate is hirable, with the occasional exception of candidates for whom she has not yet completed reference checks.

Components of trustworthiness

In my examination of staffing supervisors' philosophies of job candidate selection, both through observations of their choices and through discussions with them in which they described the qualities they seek in job candidates, the concept of 'trust' emerged as a salient theme in the data. The staffing supervisors at FastEmp used this term in addressing part (c) of Eder and Harris' (1999) definition of 'employment interview' – the interviewer's inquiry into the applicant's values – and part (d) – the interviewer's inquiry into the applicant's reliability. Trust has to do with whether the staffing supervisor believes she can count on the job candidate to perform well on an assignment. This encompasses several interrelated and overlapping qualities which the staffing supervisors mention repeatedly, both in generic terms (when I asked them, in general, what qualities they seek in a job candidate) and in their individual assessments of the candidates. Specifically, they refer to the following qualities: *sincerity, honesty, reliability* and *trustworthiness*. In general, the staffing supervisors focus primarily on interpersonal skills and other personality traits that they associate with a reliable, ambitious and sincere employee, as opposed to focusing on particular work-related and/or technical skills the job candidate may utilise on an assignment.

The staffing supervisors' concern with these components of trustworthiness and their conceptualisation of the term are demonstrated in the following quotes. Erin, in answer to the question of what qualities she seeks in a job candidate:

> Reliability . . . [this] is demonstrated by them keeping an appointment, being here on time, giving us a follow-up call after a couple of days of not hearing from us . . . Reliability is a big one in the temporary industry . . . yeah, it is a problem and that is what clients count on. So, reliability, friendliness, honesty, and . . . follow-through.

Amy, in answer to the same question:

> I'm looking for a sense . . . that they really want to be there . . . I really look for their, how sincere they are, how serious they are, how dedicated they seem to be.

Amy, speaking for both herself and Carol (another staffing supervisor), on how they judge the seriousness or sincerity of a job candidate:

> Eye contact, posture, um, whether they're chewing gum, spinning in their chair, looking this way and that way, y'know answering my questions with really brief answers, those types of things.

Support for the staffing supervisors' general philosophies of job candidate selection is found also in the individual assessments they offered in their follow-up interviews with me. Here, descriptors such as 'trustworthy', 'serious about working', 'open', 'honest', 'up front with . . . her intentions', 'straight with me', 'dependable', 'reliable', 'sincere' and having a 'good work ethic' were mentioned numerous times in their descriptions of successful job candidates. These aspects of 'trust' are also used by the staffing supervisors in their descriptions of failed interviews of those candidates who lack such qualities. Some comments from the staffing supervisors about failed job candidates include the following:

> Carol: 'I didn't believe he was honest . . . He seemed self-assured, which kind of scared me 'cuz he- I thought he was lying to me.'

> Amy: 'He was trying to cover up the fact that he had a lot of employment gaps until I delved in deeper. And so I didn't like that he was trying to be misleading.'

> Amy: 'She had a lot of gaps that she couldn't account for or at least had strange reasons why she wasn't working. I didn't find her very credible.'

In sum, the staffing supervisors characterise successful job candidates with terms including and related to 'honesty', 'sincerity' and 'reliability'. They also attribute inadequate job candidates' failure to a lack of the same characteristics. Their impressions are formed through both verbal and non-verbal behaviours on the parts of the job candidates. As we will see shortly, many of the instances in which distrust is established result from misunderstandings that are not overtly acknowledged or recognised by the interlocutors involved during the job interview, but that emerge in their subsequent reflections on the interaction.

Misunderstandings in the job interview

A variety of misunderstandings occur in both successful and failed job interviews. Characteristic of the misunderstandings which lead to an establishment of distrust between the staffing supervisor and job candidate, however, is the fact that these misunderstandings go unrepaired. Moreover, they stem not from surface-level misinterpretations of one another's utterances, but from deep-seated differences in the interlocutors' conceptualisations of the goals to be fulfilled and procedures to be followed in a job interview. As a third party (observing the interlocutors' interactions) and with added information I subsequently obtained from each of the interlocutors in their debriefing and follow-up interviews with me, I was privy to the fact that they misunderstood each other and, consequently, established an attitude of distrust.

What is necessary for a job candidate to appear trustworthy to a staffing supervisor? What makes a candidate *not* trustworthy? How much does a staffing supervisor's inclination to believe or disbelieve the job candidate depend on the candidate, and how much does it depend on the staffing supervisor's attitudes or preconceived perception of the candidate?

To answer these questions, we must take into consideration the institutional context of FastEmp job interviews. In institutional settings, interlocutors (in official capacities) vary the degree to which they use their institutional voice. Their epistemic stance (Ochs, 1996), whether expressing more or less certainty, may access institutional authority, or institutionally perceived authority, to varying degrees. In FastEmp job interviews, the staffing supervisors respond to the job candidates in a variety of ways, at times indexing authority through knowledge of the interviewing process or possible outcomes for the job candidate, and at other times interacting with the job candidates in less authoritative, more conversationally equal manners. Ochs (1996) describes this phenomenon as the varying degree to which interlocutors choose to 'do' their role (e.g. to 'do gender' or 'do being female' or 'do being a grandparent', etc.). In the job interview, the staffing supervisor may shift between 'stances of greater or lesser certainty to create more or less authoritarian professional identities' (Ochs, 1996, p. 424). Interpretations of the meanings of these stances (and their variations) are, however, not necessarily agreed upon by all involved interlocutors; that is, what may be viewed as indicating less certainty by or to some interlocutors may not be interpreted in the same way by those in other speech communities (Ochs, 1996). Cultural differences exist not only in expectations of appropriate stances, but also in preferences for particular stances in particular interactions or activities (Ochs, 1996, p. 428).

FastEmp staff as mediators

In the case of FastEmp job interviews, the staffing supervisors 'do' the staffing supervisor role to varying degrees, depending on their interlocutor. In spite of their more powerful and authoritative position vis-à-vis the job candidates, they must also answer to the requirements of their clients (the companies or employees of companies who place the job orders with FastEmp). On the one hand, the staffing supervisor has the power to determine the outcome of the job candidate's interview. It is her job to select candidates who will represent FastEmp well – who will fit the FastEmp image of professionalism, reliability and efficiency, regardless of how much the staffing supervisor herself likes or dislikes a particular candidate. On the other hand, the staffing supervisor must also satisfy the requirements of the client (company) to whom she is accountable. While the job candidate must answer job interview questions posed by the staffing supervisor, the staffing supervisor, unlike traditional employers who do not work through a mediator, will not have day-to-day contact with the job candidate, once he or she has been hired. So, while the job candidate is made to understand that, if hired, he or she will become a FastEmp employee and, therefore, the candidate is in fact being interviewed by his or her potential employer, it is the rules of neither the staffing supervisor nor the institution of FastEmp that the job candidate will follow throughout the day, when eventually employed.

To make matters more complicated, the staffing supervisors are not always equipped with the appropriate technical or job-specific expertise to investigate the candidate's specific job-related skills. Because the staffing supervisors are generalists at best and specialists in office work at worst, they are not prepared to probe in depth the particular types of expertise many of the candidates – especially those applying for light industrial work – may possess. They therefore choose to focus on an area in which they do feel they have expertise: trust and characteristics related to trust. Their philosophy of job candidate selection emphasises interpersonal skills, because these are the qualities they feel will be the most salient features of their employees when on assignment, and they expect the job candidates to represent FastEmp in a positive light. As stated by Erin about her assessment of job candidates:

> Really when I am sitting down in front of them, I am looking for interpersonal skills, the non-verbal communication skills, how they are sitting in their chair, their eye contact, their friendliness, all of that and then also trying to look into the clues of what position they want and . . . who has been successful in those positions, if they would also be successful in that position.

The application document: An essential part of establishing trust

While personal characteristics which are observable in the interview itself contribute to the staffing supervisor's overall impression, the job candidates provide the staffing supervisor with a wealth of information about themselves even before they have a job interview. The written application form they fill out before their interview provides the staffing supervisor with much more than the simple facts stated on the sheets of paper.[4] From this document, and before she even sees the candidate's face, the staffing supervisor forms an impression of the job candidate's qualifications. The way the candidate fills out the application – everything from the actual handwriting, to the dates of particular assignments, to the information a job candidate fails to provide – indicates to her how familiar the candidate is with the employment agency application process. It is with this information already gathered that the staffing supervisor commences the interview, in a manner according to her expectations of the candidate.

Case studies of employment verification

One characteristic of job applications that often causes staffing supervisors to investigate the trustworthiness of the job candidate is the existence of 'gaps' (the term used by FastEmp staff) in the job candidate's work history, as manifested in the 'Work History' section of their job applications. It is possible to have legitimate reasons for time lapses in one's work history. It is also possible to produce legitimate excuses – to use language in a way that persuades the staffing supervisor that the lapses are legitimate – even if they are not. But if the candidate who has gaps in her or his work history does not successfully achieve either of these manoeuvres, the default dynamic established with the staffing supervisor is one of distrust.

In the two cases I discuss below, we will see through data from both the job interviews and follow-up interviews how distrust is established through a combination of information obtained before the interview – which not only corroborates information obtained during the interview, but also very much influences the course the interview takes – and information obtained during the job interview itself. We will also see that the distrust was established because of misunderstandings which arose but were neither acknowledged nor even necessarily recognised by the interlocutors during the interactions in which they occurred (but became apparent in the participants' subsequent discussions with me).

Case 1:   Federico and Amy

Federico, an applicant for light industrial work with FastEmp, is a second generation Mexican American in his mid-twenties. His first language is Spanish, but he considers himself bilingual and is equally comfortable using English and Spanish. Federico did not finish high school, but he got his General Education Diploma (GED). He describes himself as 'working class'.

In the first part of the job interview, Amy (the staffing supervisor) and Federico clarify that he is ideally looking for a permanent position or one that would eventually become permanent ('temp to hire'). From then on, Amy focuses her attention on the work history section of Federico's application, asking him about his previous work experience and qualifications

on the basis of what she sees he has written on his application form. In the
following excerpt, Amy asks Federico about a job he held previous to the
job he had at Lambert University, which he has noted on his application and
has just finished describing to Amy. (For transcription conventions see the
Appendix at the end of this chapter.)

Extract 10.1: Federico and Amy (1)

```
 1 AMY:   Okay. And um before that=
 2 FEDE:  =was that? [(x)]
 3 AMY:              [for] like seven months you were at
 4         RineQuest International?=
 5 FEDE:  =Yeah. It was a . . warehouse.
 6 AMY:   Okay, and um what did you do between . . this
 7         [job and this job?]
 8 FEDE:  [I I had oth]er *jobs* . . in the temp agencies
 9         but I didn't put 'em 'cuz they um it was a uh=
10 AMY:   =What made you put *this* one.
11 FEDE:  'Cuz I stayed there *long*er (x).=
12 AMY:   =Okay, your other ones have been really short
13         [term?]
14 FEDE:  [Yeah] like a month, two mo:nths,=
15 AMY:   =Okay so is that what you're looking for?=
16         short term work?
17 FEDE:  N:o. I'm looking for *long* term now.
18 AMY:   Okay,=
19 FEDE:  =Yeah.
20 AMY:   Well um . . unfortunately I *can't* put you on
21         long term work right now because you haven't
22         *prov*en to me that you can *stay* on a
23         /{((laughs))*job*}\ long term. But [I] have=
24 FEDE:                                      [mm]
25 AMY:   =short term things that you know we could
26         consider for you . . until you've *prov*en your . .
27         reliability, and then we can look at other
28         opportunities,
29 FEDE:  Mkay. That's-=
30 AMY:   =I mean I'm just . . gonna be . . very honest
31         with you and and . . and what my opinion is.=
32 FEDE:  =No. Okay. Yeah 'cuz some agencies have like
33         you know you go for one two days I:I ain't
34         gonna *go* to a job like for one day or two days
35         y'know.=
36 AMY:   Ri:[ight.]
```

37 FEDE: =[If it's] like a month then . . that's all
38   right.=
39 AMY: =Y:yeah we um most of our jobs are um long term
40   temporary. We have um positions that range
41   from assembly, . . positions to working on um
42   y'know different kinds of machinery. So that's
43   that's kind of what we have available.

First, while glancing at the dates he has listed on his job application, Amy verifies that Federico has worked for seven months at RineQuest (lines 1–4). While Federico confirms this fact (line 5) and offers more information about it ('It was a . . warehouse'), notice that it was not he who calculated the length of time (seven months). It becomes apparent throughout the interview that exact lengths of time are much more significant to Amy – as these are her means of detecting gaps in his work history – than to Federico.

Amy has surmised from the dates Federico has written down that there was a long lapse of time between two jobs he has listed. This concerns her since her primary purpose is to determine Federico's reliability and stability as a potential employee. Amy therefore asks Federico (lines 6–7) what he had been doing between the two jobs he has listed (pointing with her finger to the two jobs on his application). Anticipating Amy's request, Federico interrupts her (line 8) before she finishes her question and subsequently offers two reasons for not having listed other jobs he had between the two he has supplied on his application. The first reason he states (lines 8–9) is that he had other jobs during that time through temporary agencies, thus implying that he did not think it appropriate to note jobs on his application for which he had gone through temporary services. Federico raises his voice slightly on 'jobs' (line 8) and follows up by trying to explain why he had not supplied information about those other jobs on the application (line 9). His raised volume and attempted explanation indicate a tension felt by Federico (which was confirmed in his follow-up discussion with me) and an awareness on his part that, for Amy, this gap looks problematic and requires an explanation. Amy does not allow Federico to finish explaining, however, interrupting him (line 10) to ask why he had chosen to write down the RineQuest job, as opposed to any other job in his history. The fact that he has not provided a complete list of his previous jobs indicates to Amy that he has something to hide. Federico then offers the second reason – that he had the RineQuest job longer than the others (line 11). Federico's claim is thus that he did not write down other jobs on his application both because they were through temporary agencies and because they were shorter. But offering that second reason – that the other jobs were shorter – proves to be a crucial mistake at two subsequent points in the interview.

First, we see that this answer gets Federico into trouble three turns later (lines 15–16), when Amy interprets his explanation (that his other jobs were shorter) to mean that short-term work is what he currently seeks, in spite of the fact that Federico has made explicit, on his written application as well as during the beginning of his job interview, that he seeks 'temp to hire' employment, i.e. long term. To verify her interpretation that Federico wants short-term work, Amy asks him, seemingly innocuously, whether he is indeed looking for short-term work (lines 15–16), to which Federico answers in the negative and states again that he is looking for long-term work (line 17). But Amy is now in a position to reject his request for long-term work, disqualifying him with the reason that he does not have experience doing long-term work (lines 20–23). Note that Federico never voluntarily stated that he only had short-term work experience. This was Amy's interpretation, for which Federico offered agreement when she sought verification from him (lines 12–14). In fact, in a conversationally cooperative manner, Federico even elaborated upon his affirmative answer ('Yeah'), stating that his other jobs had been one or two months in duration (line 14). Thus, by the time Federico reiterates that he is looking for long-term work, Amy can justify her unwillingness to put him on a long-term assignment with the fact that he lacks such experience.

Amy offers a certain amount of explanation, however, rather than simply rejecting Federico. She has set Federico up, to a certain degree, for his fall, and yet now she expresses remorse that she cannot place him on a long-term assignment. She lightens her message to him in three ways. First, lexically, she uses the adverb 'unfortunately' (line 20). Second, as a means of lessening the face threat, Amy offers a hesitant laugh while saying he has not proven he can stay on a job (line 22). Third, she offers him the opportunity to remedy his currently flawed employment history (lack of long-term employment) by stating that she has short-term jobs he could take, through which he could prove his reliability, after which other opportunities could be considered (lines 23–28). Her subsequent face-saving strategy is to justify her assessment that Federico is not qualified to do long-term work by saying, with a hedge, that she is 'just . . gonna be . . very honest with you and and . . and what my opinion is' (lines 30–31). While she thus attributes her assessment of Federico's employability to her personal opinion, in fact she speaks as a staff member of FastEmp. FastEmp's institutional authority over her induces her to hire with caution, as her own job could be at stake if she makes unwise hiring decisions. Tension is mounting and continues to do so as we see that Federico responds immediately (line 32), rather than allowing any time between turns and then defends his needs by stating he 'ain't gonna go to a job like for one day or two days y'know' (lines 32–35). Amy responds, now in a position to be more benevolent – as Federico is on the defensive – by reassuring him that FastEmp's temporary positions are 'long term temporary' (lines 39–43).

While, at this point, it has become clear to both Federico and Amy that he did not fill out the employment history section of his application exactly as Amy thought he should have, he has justified the time lapse between jobs he listed. A mutual understanding between Amy and Federico has not, however, been reached. Federico has attempted to repair his mistake by explaining to Amy the missing parts in his work history, but he does not realise that Amy's conclusion from this exchange is that Federico is purposely hiding something from her. Amy, in turn, assumes that Federico has purposely misled her by failing to provide a complete work history on his application, rather than assume that he had simply not understood what was expected of him when he filled out the form.

In the next excerpt, Federico gives Amy a second reason to question the gaps in his work history, as he does not remain consistent with his original statement that his other jobs – those he did not list on his application – were short. Here Federico has just finished describing various aspects of a job he had in which he used specialised equipment, upon which Amy asks him why he left that job.

Extract 10.2: Federico and Amy (2)

```
 1 AMY:   What was your reason for /leaving \that job.
 2 FEDE:  'Cuz I found a better job that's why.
 3 AMY:   What was the /better \job.
 4 FEDE:  Printing shop. [in Palo Alto]=
 5 AMY:                  [How long were you /the\re.]
 6 FEDE:  =see I don't know I don't know the . . like
 7        eight . . months or a year?
 8 AMY:   (2) It was eight months or a year?=
 9 FEDE:  =Uh eight months to a year yeah.
10 AMY:   You just told me that you put RineQuest down
11        'cuz that was your longest [job.]
12 FEDE:                             [no I] had one as a
13        . . as a warehouse too i-it was like a year too
14        but I just put those ones down. 'Cuz I I knew
15        those uh supervisors the best. I don't know if
16        you want to speak to other ones but I don't . .
17        I don't even remember their names really. I
18        don't know [(x x)]
19 AMY:              [So you-] what was the company . .
20        what was the printing company.
21 FEDE:  It was in Palo Alto I know their /add\ress six
22        sixty Henley Way I don't remember:r something
23        . . I forget the name. [It] was it was it was=
24 AMY:                          [Bu-]
25 FEDE:  =around the same time u:uh after I worked for
26        ri- RineQuest. I would have to get you the
```

```
27          information. I don't I don't rem[ember.]
28 AMY:                              [So you] were
29          you were there for a good good chunk of ninety-
30          seven but you don't
31          [remember the name of the /com/pany?]
32 FEDE:    [yeah                      yeah it] was it
33          was through Solutions. It was through
34          Solutions uh uh (1) uh (1) temp agency that's
35          why.
36 AMY:     °Solutions temp agency?°=
37 FEDE:    =Yeah.
38 AMY:     Mkay, . . and you worked there from:m
39 FEDE:    Eight months to a year (1) [I dun]no.
40 AMY:                                [okay.]
41 FEDE:    I don't remember the months was i-it was- I
42          don't remember the months.
43 AMY:     M[kay.]
44 FEDE:      [It was] around the same time that I worked at
45          uh at uh RineQuest.
46 AMY:     Mhmm . . okay
```

On each of her first three questions (lines 1, 3, 5), Amy uses a higher
pitch and slightly louder volume on the penultimate syllable, just before
ending her question on a lower pitch, making the prosodic features of these
questions more statement-like than question-like, but also entirely under-
standable as questions of a routine, sequence-like nature. She utters them
rhythmically, sounding a bit like something Carolyn Graham might use in
one of her 'jazz chants' (e.g. Graham, 1978).[5] The repetitive and rhythmical
nature of these three utterances, in combination with the intonation she
uses, indicate a mild exasperation or boredom with presenting a routine
series of questions:

What was your reason for /leaving \that job.
What was the /better \job.
How long were you /the\re.

While Federico provides a logical answer to Amy's first question (what was
his reason for leaving that job) – that he found a better job – he does not tell
her what the job was, simply reiterating his reason with 'that's why' (line 2).
Amy therefore asks him what the better job was, to which Federico also
gives a minimal answer ('Printing shop'), followed by the words, 'in Palo
Alto', which are almost indecipherable because, almost as an afterthought,
he utters these when Amy has already interrupted with her next question.
In answer to this third question – how long were you there – Federico

estimates that he worked at that job between eight months and a year (lines 6–7), because he does not know the exact dates. After two seconds pause, already indicating this answer does not satisfy her and she is therefore waiting for a better one, Amy repeats his answer (line 8) – 'It was eight months or a year?' While this serves as her way of requesting a more exact answer, Federico takes up her question literally – as a confirmation request – and simply confirms his answer, repeating again, 'Uh eight months to a year yeah' (line 9) without providing the more specific information that Amy is after. Amy now indirectly accuses him of being inconsistent in his reason for having listed the jobs he chose to list on his job application: eight months to a year is a longer period of time than the seven months he said he worked at RineQuest, which he said he had listed on the application because it had been his longest job. Federico understands that this accusation requires an explanation so he offers a new reason for having listed the particular jobs he chose to list on his application – that he 'knew those uh supervisors the *best*' (lines 14–15), thus also implying that he anticipates positive references from those supervisors. The source of Amy's and Federico's misunderstanding is the difference in their interpretations of the rules for filling out the job application. Federico tries to compensate for the gaps on his application by considering aloud whether Amy wants to speak with his other supervisors not listed, giving her that information; but, as he states, he cannot do this, because he does not 'even remember their *names* really' (lines 15–18). Amy's impatience with Federico's inadequate answers is manifested in her cutting him off as he tries to offer an explanation (line 19).

Amy now tries to get some details about the printing shop, at which Federico worked eight months to a year, but which he did not list on his job application. She asks him what the company was (lines 19–20), to which Federico offers other, related information about it – the address and approximate time that he worked there (lines 21–27) – because he cannot remember the name of the company. Continuing to show impatience and/or disbelief, Amy cuts Federico off with a rhetorical question, expressing disbelief that he could have worked at a company for nearly a year and not remember its name (lines 28–31). In addition to the content of her utterance and its structure as a yes/no question – to which a yes/no answer is not what she expects, but rather some kind of explanation for this loss of memory – prosodic markers also indicate Amy's disbelief. She raises her volume on 'don't' and the first syllable of 'company', while at the same time raising her pitch in each of the last three syllables of her utterance (the three syllables in 'company'). By this time, Federico has interrupted Amy in order to provide the explanation she seeks (lines 32–35). He does not remember the name of the company because this job was through Solutions, a temporary service. Note that this answer is consistent with part of his original reasoning for not having written down the job on his application (reason being that his other jobs were through temporary services).[6] Amy pursues one final time her initial question of the time period Federico worked at the company in question (line 38), to which Federico is yet again unable to give Amy a more accurate answer than 'eight months to a year' (line 39). He follows this with a one-second pause and an apologetic 'I dunno' (line 39), but then reiterates his inadequate answer, as if to show that he is giving Amy the best information he has. Thus, in lines 41 to 45 Federico repeats his claim of inability to recall the exact dates, as well as his best guess at estimating when he had worked at the printing company.

To sum up the results of the above interaction, Federico was asked to explain something he did wrong, without first knowing he had done something wrong (i.e. on the work history portion of his application he failed to list some of the jobs he had had). He did not carefully think through his answer, saying simply what seemed to him to make sense at the time, and causing Amy to find inconsistencies in his self-presentation. None of this might have occurred had Federico filled out the employment history section of his application 'correctly', i.e. the way Amy expected him to fill it out. Her suspicion was first aroused by what she saw on his written application – gaps in his work history. As a result, the epistemic stance (Ochs, 1996) Amy chose to employ was one of high certainty and institutional authority. Perhaps it is worth noting that nowhere on the application do the instructions state explicitly that work experience is to be listed chronologically, most recent job first, and that precise dates should be supplied. But Amy assumes that job candidates possess this institutional knowledge – they know what is expected of them, i.e. how they are to fill out the application. Someone who does not do this correctly is, therefore, suspected of trying to cover up something or of being dishonest.

Before leaving him in the conference room at the end of their interaction, Amy says to Federico, 'I'm gonna go do your references and I'll be back in a few minutes. Okay?' Amy did not, however, return to the conference room. Instead, another staffing supervisor briefly poked her head in to tell Federico the interview was over. This was Federico's cue to depart, which he did without any further contact with Amy.

Amy's assessment of Federico

In Amy's debriefing interview with me, she stated that she and Federico had understood each other very well and there had been no misunderstandings in the job interview. She did not, in other words, recognise Federico's way of filling out his job application as being a source of misunderstanding. While she stated that she would not hire him until after doing his references, and that 'if [Federico's former employees] verify the dates that he told me even in any form of a ballpark um then I'll call him back', i.e. then she would consider hiring Federico for assembly positions, she did not in fact check his references and entered his name in the database with an 'N' code for 'Not hired'. Job candidates with 'N' codes are never considered for job placements. Amy's major complaint about Federico was that he was not believable: 'I didn't believe what he was telling me about the date. He wasn't making sense. He was contradicting himself.' She does not see her assessment as having resulted from Federico's unfamiliarity with the rules of filling out the FastEmp job application and their consequent misunderstandings.

Federico's perspective on the interview

My follow-up interview with Federico differed markedly from Amy's perception that there had been no misunderstandings between Federico and her. Federico told me that, although he had understood Amy, he did not feel she had understood him:

> I understood her, I don't know if she understood me. I understood her point of view and why . . . she'd feel that way 'cuz of the differences of the jobs and, what was I doin' between the other times and uh, why was I not staying long enough at those jobs.

Federico was concerned about the way the 'timing at my job' was discussed. He explained to me, but not to Amy, that his reason for working through temporary employment agencies in the past rather than going directly to the company to seek work was so that he would be able to leave a job or 'in an emergency I could leave any time and it wouldn't affect me y'know looking for another job'.[7] In retrospect, we see, he was wrong to assume that taking short-term assignments would not have a negative effect on his future employability. Federico also explained to me the strategy he had used when he had filled out the work history spaces on his application: 'I was just pickin' the rest of the places I thought that would give me the best reference for the job I was looking for.' When I asked Federico whether he thought Amy may have expected him to write down all of his work history in chronological order, he said, 'Maybe that's what she was expecting I don't know.' Because they had not discussed their different perspectives, Federico felt that he and Amy had parted on terms of misunderstanding: 'There's some points that . . . I would have to explain to her . . . in order for her to get a better idea. But uh, I guess I would have to let her know.' In retrospect, Federico thought he should have written down 'a little more information about some of the different jobs I had'. Federico could have planned to clarify some of the misunderstandings (about his incomplete job application) upon Amy's projected return to the conference room. He did not, however, get this opportunity, because Amy did not return.

Distrust co-constructed

The question remains: What has motivated Amy's interviewing behaviour, which has resulted in a difficult and incomplete interaction for Federico? She does not trust him because he has not played by the rules of the institution she represents. He has not filled out the application correctly and his verbal behaviour does not agree with Amy's notion of how he should present his previous work experience to her. Amy's perception of Federico's inconsistency results in her distrusting him.

In the next example, we see how, even when a job candidate understands how he is to fill out the job application, answering the questions honestly can still elicit the staffing supervisor's distrust, if his answer does not please her. In this case, the problematic section of the job application is the 'desired salary' box, in which Martin, an African American male applicant for light industrial work, has printed the hourly wage of $15.00.

Case 2: Martin and Amy

Martin is a second generation monolingual speaker of English (his father immigrated to the United States from the West Indies) in his mid-thirties. Martin graduated from high school and has since taken numerous community college courses without obtaining a degree. His future career plans include moving into human resource work, in particular because he believes he possesses the skills necessary for participating in and conducting effective job interviews. He feels he is a highly competent job interviewee, stating, 'I believe I know what's needed in an interview. And the type of answers that is necessary for one to be able to have a plus on their side in getting a job.' As we see in the following interaction, however, Amy disagrees with Martin's self-assessment.

Amy begins Martin's interview in her routine manner, asking him questions about his geographical requirements while glancing at his application for light industrial work, on which he has stated as his desired salary $15 per hour.[8] In the first excerpt below, we see Amy's initial reaction to Martin's stated desired salary, followed by his response and attempt to adapt to FastEmp's expectations in order to be a more suitable job candidate.

Extract 10.3: Martin and Amy (1)

```
1 AMY:     Which ad was it that you're responding to.
2 MARTIN:  Um . . I'm responding to the ad . . um . . where
3          there's . . pretty big ad uh concerning
```

```
 4           FastEmp,
 5  AMY:     Mhm,=
 6  MARTIN:  =u:uh=
 7  AMY:     =was there a specific job description?=
 8  MARTIN:  =Yes uh it was . . u:um . . fiber optics
 9           assembly.
10  AMY:     Okay,
11  MARTIN:  Yeah.
12  AMY:     (6) Mkay. (·hhh) And I know u- know here that
13           you have technician experience,
14  MARTIN:  Mhmm.
15  AMY:     Umm the /fiber optic assem\bly . . do you have
16           fiber optic . . assembly experience
17           specifically?
18  MARTIN:  Not specifically.
19  AMY:     Okay=
20  MARTIN:  =Ri:[ight]
21  AMY:         [Mkay.] (·hhh) The position that we have
22           that we're plac/ing for? in Palo Alto, those
23           /positions \for people that don't have any
24           fiber optic assembly experience, (·hhh) are
25           starting at about seven fifty to eight
26           dollars an hour. And if someone had . . fiber
27           optic experi/ence, the most they would pay is
28           twelve dollars. And I notice that you have
29           as your minimum /fif\teen dollars.
30           {((smiles)) So} ((laughs)) . . that might
31           be kind of a . .
32  MARTIN:  Well I'm [inter]ested=
33  AMY:              u[m]
34  MARTIN:  =in um . . first getting the experience with
35           fiber optics, I'm a quick learn/er \and um . .
36           I figure that I won't have to stay . . making
37           seven fifty to eight bucks an hour too long.
38  AMY:     Mka[y,]
39  MARTIN:     [But] I need the experience
40
41  AMY:     [mkay]
42  MARTIN:  [for f]iber optics.
43  AMY:     Um . . w- one thing that . . that you should
44           know um . . you /may have \to make . . seven
45           fifty eight dollars . . for a while I mean . .
46           most of the people that we have working at
```

47		this site (·hhh) that make . . seven fifty
48		eight dollars an hour, they *may*be get a *raise*
49		. . but it's like a *quar*ter? u:um so you're
50		*real*ly I mean they *do* pay people . . eight
51		dollars an /ho\ur, . . eight fifty . . for these
52		(hhh) . . positions. So . . I mean I I I
53		*hes*itate to have you cut your salary in *half*.
54	MARTIN:	(·hhh) Well [um]
55	AMY:	[For the] for the *job*.=
56	MARTIN:	=first of all it's better to be working for
57		*some*thing than to be working for *noth*ing. Or
58		not working at all ((laughs)) not earning
59		anything so (·hhh) um I really . . must have a
60		job soon.
61	AMY:	Mhmm.=
62	MARTIN:	=Yeah.
63	AMY:	/M\kay (·hhh) well . . wh- why don't we go
64		*on*'n and talk about a few other things and
65		then we can come *back* to it.

Amy asks Martin a routine question about whether he has responded to a particular FastEmp job advertisement (lines 1–7) in order to find out what kind of work Martin seeks. Martin's answer to this question will be especially important in light of his stated desired salary, which Amy knows is significantly higher than the hourly wages FastEmp offers for most light industrial assignments (such as those for which she expects him to be eligible). Martin offers a relevant answer to Amy's question, informing her that he is responding to FastEmp's advertisement for a fiber optics assembly position (lines 8–9). Amy's suspicion is thus confirmed – that Martin is interested in, or sees himself as qualified for, a job which pays much less than his desired $15. Here, as in the previous case of Federico, we see that the ensuing misunderstanding between job candidate and staffing supervisor can be traced to what the candidate has written on his job application. In this case, the amount Martin has indicated as his desired salary does not fit Amy's expectation that he accept work which pays significantly less than $15 per hour.

Before Amy informs Martin of the mismatch between his desired salary and the pay rates for light industrial work, and in order to determine just how much lower a pay rate Martin can expect, Amy must ascertain his exact qualifications. She asks him whether he has work experience in fiber optics assembly (lines 15–17), expressing in her tentative way of asking this her suspicion, on the basis of Martin's job application, that he does not in fact have the necessary experience. Her suspicion is manifested in the following ways. Amy acknowledges Martin's technician experience (lines 12–13), but contrasts that with fiber optic assembly experience by increasing her volume and raising her pitch on the first syllable of 'fiber' (15), followed by lowering her pitch and including two pauses of hesitation, while asking him if he has experience in fiber optics 'specifically' (lines 15–17). Martin's indirect answer through repetition of Amy's exact word – 'Not specifically' (line 18) – reveals his awareness of (a) what type of answer Amy wants to hear; (b) his consequent deficiency since he does not have fiber optics experience; (c) a strategy he can use to try to save face, i.e. to hedge his answer rather than directly saying, 'No, I do not have fiber optic assembly experience.' Rather than save face, however, this indirect answer contributes to Amy's eventual perception of Martin as someone who cannot be trusted, as we shall see.

At this point (line 18) Amy has the information she needs in order to tell Martin exactly how much less than his desired $15 per hour he would make, were he to get a fiber optics assembly position such as the one in which he has expressed interest. The discrepancy between Martin's desired pay rate and the actual pay rate of such a job is clear to Amy, yet she waits to tell him directly that this is a problem. Rather, she begins by telling him about pay rates for such jobs in general (lines 21–28) and contrasts this with what she has 'notice[d]' about his minimum desired pay rate (lines 28–29). Tension over the discrepancy is manifested through Amy's smile of discomfort, followed by a laugh and two hesitation pauses in her ensuing utterance, which never gets so far as to actually tell Martin this is a problem (lines 29–31), before Martin interrupts Amy to defend himself.

By stating that he needs the work experience (lines 32, 34, 39); that he is a quick learner (line 35), such that his ability to learn things quickly will compensate for experience he lacks thus far; and that he is a confident worker (lines 36–37), in that he 'won't have to stay . . . making seven fifty to eight bucks an hour too long', Martin intends to present himself as an ambitious and appealing job candidate. Although he correctly assumes that all three of the characteristics he mentions are, generally, attractive traits that a staffing supervisor wishes to see in a job candidate (ambition, ability to learn new skills quickly and confidence), Martin's strategy of expressing them as he has done backfires. Rather than having the effect of reassuring Amy that he is, after all, willing to take a job that pays much less than he initially stated he desires, his confidence that he will not have to earn this low wage for very long confirms Amy's suspicion that he does not want a job which pays as low as she knows fiber optics assembly positions pay. In order to trust that a job candidate will stay on a job to which he is assigned, Amy must believe that he really wants the job. This is not the case with respect to Martin. Amy believes he wants a job that pays substantially more than this one, despite Martin's reiteration of his need to accrue experience in fiber optics (lines 39–42). Amy once again explains the likelihood of Martin's earning a low wage at the proposed job by referring to norms for what 'most of the people' earn, even when they get a raise, and she predicts that he

'/*may have*\ to make . . seven fifty eight dollars . . for a while.' She also makes explicit her hesitation to hire Martin due to his salary requirement (lines 52–55), thus inviting Martin to give her more compelling evidence that he truly wants the job. Martin's response – that even a low wage is better than no wage and that he 'really . . must have a job soon' (lines 56–60), rather than convince Amy that he is serious about the job, leads to a dead end. Amy proposes they continue to other topics and return to this as yet unresolved one later in the interview (lines 63–65).

In the above excerpt, Martin has strongly expressed his immediate need for a job as another reason he would be willing to take an assignment which pays approximately half of what he stated as his desired wage. The misunderstanding between Martin and Amy regarding the work he is willing to accept might be traced to their differing interpretations of the term 'desired' in the 'Desired Salary' section of the job application. It appears that an unspoken rule, of which Amy is aware but Martin is not, is that one should not ask for a wage that is not matched to the type of work advertised, despite the fact that the applicant is asked to write down the amount he *desires* to earn.

Amy subsequently directs the discussion towards a verification of Martin's employment history, in the excerpt which follows. This interaction leads her to question Martin's alleged urgency to get a job.

Extract 10.4: Martin and Amy (2)

```
 1 AMY:    Okay. Now tell me about um working at
 2         Peninsula Auto: (1) °\what is /that°
 3 MARTIN: Dismantlers.
 4 AMY:    Dismantlers okay. /First \of all um: it
 5         shows that you stopped working in there of
 6         Dec/ember of ninety/eight=
 7 MARTIN: =Y[es.]
 8 AMY:      [What] have you been doing since then.
 9 MARTIN: Uh looking for /work
10 AMY:      . . . Been four months?
11 MARTIN: Um: (1) yes well i- in between looking for
12         \work uh I'm als\o a tech/ni\cian at um: . . .
13         uh (1.5) u- going out looking uh I know
14         people who need:s uh: . . technicians from
15         time to time, (need 'cuz need) /they \need
16         work on their cars \so I've been . . doing
17         /part time \work on=
18 AMY:    =You do that on your /own \or you [(x) ]
19 MARTIN:                               [On my]
20         own. Yes.
21 AMY:    Okay, (4.5) okay.
```

Although Amy asks Martin to describe a particular job he has listed on his application (lines 1–2), Martin's single-word answer (line 3) seems to suffice or, at any rate, be less important to Amy than what he was doing when he was not on that job (lines 4–8). Amy is not satisfied with Martin's answer to her question as to what he was doing during the four-month gap between his last job and the present. While Martin gives her a straightforward answer that he was looking for work (line 9), Amy's suspicion is manifested in her response, in which she offers a rhetorical question ('Been *four* months?'), raising her volume on 'four' to indicate disbelief; that is, four months, in her opinion, is a long time to have been looking for work without finding anything, if that was his sole occupation at the time. Martin correctly interprets the illocutionary force of Amy's question as a request that he explain how this came to be (that he looked for work for four months without finding anything).

Although Martin hesitates for a full second while formulating his response (line 11), he then offers a plausible explanation – that he was not actually looking for work that whole time, because he was also working as a part-time technician sporadically during that period. His entire explanation is, however, rather disfluent, with a number of pauses, false starts and self-repairs (lines 11–17), resulting in a seemingly clumsy and unconfident response. In addition, Martin's response is suspicious because it does not agree with what appears on the employment history section of his application. Amy expects to see documented evidence of Martin's previous jobs, but the part-time technician work he claims to have done is not evident on his application. Nevertheless, Amy indicates to Martin that she accepts his explanation in two ways. First, she follows up with a request for elaboration about the nature of that work (line 18), thereby seeming to accept what he has said. Second, she responds further with an 'okay' with slight raising of pitch, followed by a second 'okay' with final lowering of pitch, indicating understanding and closure to this topic (line 21). These are the signals Amy gives Martin at that moment but, as we will see in her debriefing interview with me, she still does not believe him.

Amy's objective is to hire a job candidate who will do a good job, i.e. who will serve as a good representative of FastEmp. This entails having satisfactory job skills as well as professional characteristics such as being punctual, reliable and having integrity. So far, she has found two ways in which Martin does not meet her objective: (a) she suspects she will not be able to count on him to complete a job (reliability), because FastEmp will likely pay him significantly less than he desires for the jobs in which he is interested; (b) she believes he is covering something up and not being straightforward with her regarding what he was doing during the four-month gap between the job he has listed last on the application and the date on which their interview takes place.

In the next excerpt, Amy returns to the issue of the discrepancy between Martin's desired pay rate and what FastEmp pays for assembly positions, but approaches it from a different perspective: Martin lacks the qualifications necessary to earn more money.

Extract 10.5: Martin and Amy (3)

```
 1 AMY:     So . . and you were doing soldering, (·hhh)=
 2 MARTIN:  =Yes. /Wave solder:, \regular solder:, um:
 3          . . and . . even: microscopic solder.
 4 AMY:     Okay,=
 5 MARTIN:  =Yeah.
 6 AMY:     So /this was more of a \soldering job, (·hhh)
 7          and these were mo:re, I mean y- do you
 8          /actually have assembly experience? . . \I
 9          don't . . I think that you're a little higher
10          level \than that is what I'm gathering from
11          your=
12 MARTIN:  =Yes I [(x) I I ]=
13 AMY:            [application]
14 MARTIN:  =I I /am \higher than that but um: . . . . it's
15          uh (2) the /more experience I have \in in all
16          facets of uh: . . electromechanical assembly,
17          [um] . . uh I will make a uh final=
18 AMY:     [mhmm]
19 MARTIN:  =decision . . sometime soon of what type of
20          u:m . . engineering de/gree \I would like to
21          do: so . . I'[m . . ]=
22 AMY:               [mhmm]
23 MARTIN:  =looking at that . . closely right now.
24 AMY:     (·hhh) How long do you think you could be
25          happy, in a job . . doing (·hhh) assem\bly
26          (·hhh) very . . very fine
27          ass[embly where you're] . . where you're=
28 MARTIN:     [very fine (x) asse]m/bly
29 AMY:     =doing . . it just sitting there putting . .
30          putting stuff [toge]\ther the /fib\er=
31 MARTIN:                 [um:]
32 AMY:     =/op\tics=
33 MARTIN:  =I don't have a time limit(ed) I: I like very
34          fine and complex assemb\ly
35          [I real]ly . . um find um . . enjoy doing it=
36 AMY:     [mhmm]
```

```
37 MARTIN: =((laughs))
38 AMY:    Right,=
39 MARTIN: =Yeah [(x)]
40 AMY:    [so] a- at the pay rate that that we:
41         um . . can offer you, the range of /seven
42         \fifty to eight, maybe eight and a quarter,
43         just . . u- you know not say it's not
44         necessarily my decision the pay /rate
45         [\would be the client's]=
46 MARTIN: [((nods))]
47 AMY:    =(·hhh) um do you do you think that . . you
48         could . . stay in that type of a /job for a
49         while because the[se /are] \long term=
50 MARTIN:              [Sure.]
51 AMY:    =pos/i\tions,
52 MARTIN: Sure I can. \Yeah if it's a long term
53         posi\tion yes I can. Yea[h be]cause there=
54 AMY:                    [mhmm]
55 MARTIN: =there I figure that um: they would . .
56         eventually see my skills and \and um . . °I
57         would probably get . . a raise . . much more
58         often than . . .°
59 AMY:    But that's not something that I can
60         guarantee:.=
61 MARTIN: =I under/stand \that. Yes. \I understand
62         that. /No\thing's a guaran[tee (act]ually).
63 AMY:                      [Right.] Right.
64         Mkay.
```

In the process of establishing with Martin that he has experience in various types of soldering (lines 1–7), Amy ascertains that he does not have specific assembly experience (lines 8–12). Rather than simply tell him that he does not have the necessary qualifications, she asks whether he 'actually' has assembly experience (lines 7–8) and, before Martin responds, lessens the face-threatening nature of that question by explaining that she thinks he is above doing assembly work – that he is 'a little higher level' (lines 9–10). 'Higher level' may sound complimentary, but the fact remains that he does not qualify for assembly work (if it requires previous experience). In an effort to cooperate with Amy as well as present himself as a competent worker, Martin agrees with Amy's assessment (line 14) but defends his interest in assembly work by stating, as a reason, the fact that he would like to have more experience in 'all facets of uh: . . electromechanical assembly,' as such experience will contribute to his eventual continued education in engineering (lines 14–23).

Martin's alleged over-qualification, as identified by Amy and acknowledged by Martin, adds to Amy's suspicion that he cannot be counted on to hold down an assembly job. Her suspicion is expressed in her next utterance, in which she asks him how long he 'could be *hap*py, in a job . . doing (·hhh) as*sem*\bly (·hhh) very . . very *fine* assembly' (lines 24–27). Amy's assumption that Martin could not be happy for long doing such a job is communicated, first of all, simply by virtue of the fact that she asks him such a question, and, second, through her elaboration of the description of 'assembly' to include 'very . . very *fine* assembly where you're . . where you're doing . . it just sitting there putting . . putting stuff toge\ther the /fib\er /op\tics' (lines 26–32). In particular, Amy's use of 'just' indicates her perspective, which she expects Martin to share, that 'just sitting there' doing the assembly work is not much to keep one interested. In order to defend his interest, Martin attempts to interrupt Amy (line 31) and supports his claim that he does not 'have a time limit' (line 33) by elaborating upon Amy's description of 'very fine assembly' work in a more complimentary light. Martin repeats Amy's phrase, 'very fine', and adds to it the descriptive 'complex', followed by an expression of enthusiasm that he enjoys such work, emphasised with both his use of an intensifier ('really') and his increased volume on that word (lines 33–35). He follows this, however, with a face-saving laugh (line 37), as if to say he knows this may sound odd to her.

Not yet convinced, Amy reiterates the pay rate range (lines 40–42), distancing herself from having to take responsibility for it by stating, 'it's not necessarily *my* decision the pay /rate \would be the *cli*ent's' (lines 43–45), and then asks Martin again not simply whether he would be interested in taking such a job, but whether he would '*stay* in that type of a /job for a while because these /*are* \long term pos/i\tions' (lines 47–51). Here again, the strategy Martin uses to lend credibility to his claim that he would indeed stay on such a job backfires. He supports his claim by manifesting his confidence, stating, 'they would . . eventually see my skills and \and um . . °I would probably get . . a raise . . much more often' (lines 52–58). Martin thus implies that he would not be satisfied with the projected pay rate, but that it would soon become a moot point because he expects to be given raises and to work himself rapidly out of that pay range and into a higher one. This is not what Amy wants to hear. Rather, believing that these types of positions are highly unlikely to offer significant raises, she wants to know that Martin would be satisfied with the job (and its corresponding wage) as it is presented to him now – paying $7.50 per hour. The fact that Martin thinks he can change the job conditions (i.e. earn a greater wage than is now being offered) does nothing to instil confidence in Amy that Martin would stay with this job 'for a while'. Martin acknowledges Amy's statement that she cannot guarantee he will get the raises he expects (lines 59–62), indicating that he understands what Amy is saying, but not convincing Amy that he would still be willing to do the job at that pay rate. Further evidence that Amy is not convinced emerges in her debriefing interview with me.

Amy's assessment of Martin

In contrast to what Amy tells Martin at the end of his job interview (that she will present his application to the client who has advertised the $7.50/hour assembly position), she gives him an 'N' code – the same as she gave Federico, meaning he will not be hired for any FastEmp positions – and offers the following explanation in her debriefing interview with me:

> I don't think I can place him because I think he was too willing to agree with everything I said. He wants fifteen dollars, you know you get their honest feeling of what they want when they first fill out the application. When you start to tell them well actually this job could potentially pay $7.50 that's half of that salary. And he says yes. And that doesn't make me feel confident that he would stay on the job because he obviously wants twice as much as he would be getting. And the second he gets something for the fifteen bucks he's gone.

Furthermore, Amy's distrust of Martin is expressed through her disbelief of his explanation for why he was out of work:

> He's been out of work for four months and I don't believe what he said what he was doing on his own . . . A lot of people say oh we didn't work for five months because I had a trust fund and I wanted to travel. And it's like, well okay. That's fine. But the fact that he just tried to cover it up saying he was looking for a job raises the question in my mind as to why. He didn't find a job in four months. The market is pretty good for finding jobs so –

Ultimately, it is Martin's inability to win Amy's trust more than any particular job skills he has or does not have which is both the focus of the job interview and the deciding factor as to whether or not Martin should be hired. As we have just seen, Amy demonstrates in her criticism of Martin's excuse for being unemployed that it is possible to have a legitimate excuse for long-term employment gaps.

As we will see in Martin's follow-up interview with me, trust is a two-way street; while it is not necessary for the job candidate to trust the staffing supervisor in order to achieve a successful job interview (and it *is* necessary for the staffing supervisor to trust the job candidate), certainly the job candidate's distrust of the staffing supervisor influences his behaviour – and the staffing supervisor's resulting assessment of him – in the interview.

Martin's perspective on the interview

Martin's primary concern centres on the pay rate issue; not the actual amount he will or will not be paid by FastEmp, but the culture of employment agencies or 'job shops' which, he feels, purposely deceive their employees about *who* is making the real money in this business:

> I have worked for several job shops. And it's very unclear to a lot of technicians like myself . . . who decides what they get in terms of a pay figure. [Amy] said that she does not decide how much is paid to me. Well, if this agency is finding a job for me they must have some sort of pull, a certain amount of percentage of pull to try to get me more. . . . [I]t's the impression of technicians that the job shops are interested in making more money off of you rather than getting you the job. . . . [S]ay for instance my skills are worth $22 an hour. . . . So if they can make me take $8 an hour they're making $14. That's to me – it's a hidden, something is hidden about that. Nobody's stupid. I know what my wages are worth. My wage is worth much more than the $8.

In addition to feeling he is knowledgeable about the staffing industry (in terms of how wages are determined), Martin also feels knowledgeable about how to conduct a job interview and expresses pride in being particularly 'good' at doing job interviews. Yet his answer to my question as to what qualities he thinks Amy was looking for during the interview demonstrates a sharp lack of agreement between his and Amy's notions of desirable qualities, as well as his lack of institutional knowledge with regard to which qualities to emphasise:

> I don't think [Amy] was really specifically looking for any qualities because um, as she said my test scores were great I only failed one [made one mistake]. So I pass test scores at 100 per cent most of the time. . . . What I tried to advertise as my strengths in relation to getting the right job . . . would be that I have lots . . . of complex assembly experience. Not just assembly but complex. It's something that I really find the satisfaction doing, something that really makes my brain work. And then when I'm done with it and it's done perfect I get the satisfaction.

Martin focuses on his technical expertise and his test scores, which are of minor importance to FastEmp's staffing supervisors. In the last two sentences of his answer, Martin also demonstrates motivation and enthusiasm for doing complex assembly work, but he did not emphasise them in this way during his job interview. While Martin expresses explicit awareness of (and pride in) his job interviewing skills to me, he fails to convey to Amy that he has the interpersonal skills she seeks in job candidates, such that he would serve as a good representative of FastEmp.

Conclusion

Martin's and Federico's job interviews demonstrate the potentially detrimental effect unrecognised misunderstandings can have on the outcomes of gate-keeping encounters. For both of them, the misunderstandings begin with their job applications, on which they violate the rules for reporting their work history and stating desired income, respectively. They lack knowledge of the institutional discourse which would enable them to provide Amy with the types of answers she seeks – answers which would result in a trusting relationship with her. Their lack of familiarity with the routine discourse and processes of employment agencies such as FastEmp highlights Amy's authority and use of institutional power to effect their job interview outcomes.

The staffing supervisor's assessment of the job candidate derives from a complex web of information obtained outside and inside the interview, before, during and after the interview, as well as, on a more macro level, the staffing supervisor's – and her institution's – stereotypes of expected behaviour on the parts of particular subgroups of job candidates. In terms of Gee's (1996) notion of Discourse, the messages conveyed by the job candidates to the staffing supervisor during the interview come not only from their interview responses, but also from the content and appearance of their written job application (as well as other discourse internal and external sources).

Ultimately, the staffing supervisor's assessments of the job candidate's personal qualities cannot be based solely on the language exchanged in the interaction. One could argue that even the 'wrong' answers or explanations, such as Martin's looking for work for four months during his employment gap, can be presented in a convincingly 'right' manner, if the candidate knows how to present her/himself in such a way that complies with the staffing supervisor's expectations of professionalism, appeal and trustworthiness. Failed interviews are not simply due to a candidate's incompetence, but to the inability of both parties – the candidate and the staffing supervisor – to co-construct a climate of trust. Unfortunately, while trust is indeed addressed by the staffing supervisors as an important qualification for a successful gatekeeping encounter, it is not necessarily foremost on the minds of the job candidates, especially if they are focused more on displaying their job expertise. The mismatches of the interlocutors' notions of what must be achieved in order to effect a successful job interview can thus lead to communication breakdowns.

Appendix

Transcription conventions

[ ]	overlap
=	latching
. .	pause less than 0.5 second
. . .	pause greater than 0.5 second and less than 1 second
(1)	timed pause (in seconds)
:	elongation
–	cut-off
.	final falling tone
,	slight rise
?	final rising tone
?,	weaker rising tone
/	higher pitch in following syllable(s)
\	lower pitch in following syllable(s)
!	animated tone
italics	slightly louder volume
CAPITALS	much louder volume
o o	softer volume
(hhh)	audible aspiration (out-breath)
(·hhh)	audible inhalation (in-breath)
(text)	transcriptionist doubt; a good guess at an unclear segment
((phenomenon))	vocal or nonvocal, nonlexical phenomenon which interrupts lexical stretch
( )	unintelligible speech
(x x)	unintelligible speech with a good guess at the number of syllables (indicated by number of x's)
{((phenomenon)) text}	vocal or nonvocal, nonlexical phenomenon that co-occurs with lexical segment indicated between curly brackets.

Notes

1 Employment agency statistics discussed in this chapter were obtained from e-mail communications with representatives of the American Staffing Association, National Association of Personnel Services, US Bureau of Labor Statistics, Upjohn Institute for Employment Research, Temp 24–7, and the South Bay branch of FastEmp, the site of this study. Additional statistics were obtained from the following websites:

www.NATSS.com/staffstats/index.html,
www.temp24-7.com/LIVE/issue/current/splash_frames.html,
www.temp24-7.com/,
www.fastcompany.com/online/17/rftf.html,
www.fastcompany.com/

2 This name and all other names of people, companies, and specific locations or addresses referred to in the data are pseudonyms.

3 FastEmp offers two broad classifications of employment opportunities: 'light industrial' positions, including warehouse work, machine operation, assembly work and food handling; and 'clerical' positions, which range from basic office filing to receptionist, word processing and executive administrative responsibilities.

4 Before their interview, job candidates fill out a seven-page application in which they provide biographical data, information about their educational and work history and professional references. They complete a battery of tests including proofreading, reading comprehension, arithmetic, filing and on-the-job safety policies.

5 Graham's 'jazz chants', designed for English as a second/foreign language instruction, are 'the rhythmic expression of Standard American English as it occurs in situational contexts' (Graham, 1978, p. ix). They are widely used as a means of introducing non-native speakers of English to the rhythms and intonation patterns of spoken American English.

6 At the same time, one could argue, Federico could not have written down this job on his application even if he had wanted to do so, since he does not remember the name of the company.

7 In fact, flexibility to leave a job on short notice or avoid making long-term employment commitments is a common reason that job candidates opt for temporary assignments. Job candidates express a need for this kind of flexibility in order to take time off for child care, to look after sick family members, or to take care of other family/personal matters.

8 Most light industrial jobs at FastEmp pay between $7.50 and $12.00 per hour.

References

Akinnaso, F. N. and Ajirotutu, C. S. (1982). Performance and ethnic style in job interviews. In J. J. Gumperz (ed.), *Language and social identity*. New York: Cambridge University Press, 119–144.

Button, G. (1992). Answers as interactional products: Two sequential practices used in job interviews. In P. Drew and J. Heritage (eds), *Talk at work: Interaction in institutional settings* (Vol. 8). Cambridge: Cambridge University Press, 212–231.

Clyne, M. (1994). *Inter-cultural communication at work: Cultural values in discourse.* Cambridge: Cambridge University Press.

Drew, P. and Heritage, J. (1992). Analyzing talk at work: An introduction. In P. Drew and J. Heritage (eds), *Talk at work: Interaction in institutional settings* (Vol. 8). Cambridge: Cambridge University Press, 3–65.

Eder, R. W. and Harris, M. M. (1999). Employment interview research: Historical update and introduction. In R. W. Eder and M. M. Harris (eds), *The employment interview handbook*. Thousand Oaks: Sage, 1–27.

Erickson, F. (1979). Talking down: Some cultural sources of miscommunication in interracial interviews. In A. Wolfgang (ed.), *Research in nonverbal communication*. New York: Academic Press.

Erickson, F. and Shultz, J. (1982). *The counselor as gatekeeper: Social interaction in interviews*. New York: Academic Press.

Foucault, M. (1970). *The order of things: An archaeology of the human sciences*. New York: Random House.

Gee, J. P. (1996). *Social linguistics and literacies: Ideology in discourses*. London: Falmer Press.

Graham, C. (1978). *Jazz chants: Rhythms of American English for students of English as a second language*. New York: Oxford University Press.

Gumperz, J. J. (1982). *Discourse strategies*. Cambridge: Cambridge University Press.

Gumperz, J. J. (1992). Interviewing in intercultural situations. In P. Drew and J. Heritage (eds), *Talk at work: Interaction in institutional settings* (Vol. 8). Cambridge: Cambridge University Press, 302–327.

Gumperz, J. J. (1996). The linguistic and cultural relativity of conversational inference. In J. J. Gumperz and S. C. Levinson (eds), *Rethinking linguistic relativity*. Cambridge: Cambridge University Press, 374–406.

Gumperz, J. J., Jupp, T. C. and Roberts, C. (1991). Crosstalk at work [videorecording]. London: BBC.

Ochs, E. (1996). Linguistic resources for socializing humanity. In J. J. Gumperz and S. C. Levinson (eds), *Rethinking linguistic relativity*. New York: Cambridge University Press, 407–437.

Roberts, C., Davies, E. *et al.* (1992). *Language and discrimination: A study of communication in multi-ethnic workplaces*. London: Longman.

Sarangi, S. (1994). Intercultural or not? Beyond celebration of cultural differences in miscommunication analysis. In *Pragmatics*, 4(3), 409–427.

Shea, D. P. (1994). Perspective and production: Structuring conversational participation across cultural borders. In *Pragmatics*, 4(3), 357–389.

Index